Sunset
House
Plants

By the Editors of Sunset Books and Sunset Magazine

High in a light-bathed study *are*
Paphiopedilum *(lady's slipper, left) and*
Dracaena deremensis *(right). Interior
design: William Gaylord and Francis
Gibbons. Horticultural design: Baruch
Himmelstein.*

Lane Publishing Co. • Menlo Park, California

Ever-growing adventures await you as you turn the pages of this book. The fourth edition of *Sunset*'s overall best seller, it's packed with enough botanical wealth to answer any question, appease any curiosity, whet any indoor gardening appetite. We've fully described—and illustrated in individual color photographs—about 90 *genera,* or basic house plant groups; within these descriptions, we've detailed more than 400 varieties.

Besides all those choices of what to grow, we suggest ways to show off the leafy results. Since indoor gardening is at its best when complementing a decorating scheme, we open this book with a gallery of lushly foliaged interiors, photographed in color, to inspire your planning.

Lovely to live with, easy-going, and rewarding, the growing of house plants is one of today's most widespread hobbies. No matter what your own experience, with this book at your fingertips you'll find all the help you need for ever richer, greener pleasures with indoor gardening.

For their valuable assistance in checking our manuscript, we thank Carol Afonso; Eloise Beach Bromeliads; Bently Nursery; East Marsh Nursery; Philip Edinger; Walter A. Gammel, Sr.; Hines Nursery; Hoak's Greenhouse & Nursery, Inc.; Michael MacCaskey; Michael's Nursery and Farms, Inc.; Oakdell Nurseries; Marlene Philley; Plants by Tropico, Inc.; Audrey Teasdale; and Tropical Imports.

For their generosity in lending plants for photographs, we extend special thanks to Will Hartman of Ah Sam Flowers, Jim Daniel of Cactus Gem Nursery, Jean Schneider of Cupertino Nursery and Florist, Pamela Leaver, Marvel Sherrill of Rod McLellan, Mills the Florist, George Vaughan and Roger Valencich of Neadho Nursery, Mark Eaton of Nurserymen's Exchange, Jerry Podesta of Podesta's Plantacres, Roger Reynolds Nursery, Michael Rothenberg of Shelldance Nursery, and Zen Houseplants. And for her help in staging many of the photographs, we thank Lynne B. Morrall.

Supervising Editor
Maureen Williams Zimmerman

Research & Text
A. Cort Sinnes

Contributing Editor
Susan Warton

Design
Roger Flanagan

Illustrations
Kerry Woodward
Rik Olson
Dinah James

Photographers: Edward B. Bigelow: 2; 6; 9 bottom left; 14 bottom right; 80 bottom left. **Glenn Christiansen:** 37 left. **Beauford B. Fisher:** 69 top. **Gerald R. Fredrick:** 45 bottom. **Steve W. Marley:** 3; 4; 5 left, top right; 7 top right, bottom right; 8; 9 top left, right; 10; 11 bottom left, top right, bottom right; 12 top; 13; 14 left; 16; 33 top; 35 bottom; 36; 39; 41; 43; 44 bottom; 45 top; 48 bottom; 49; 51; 52; 53 bottom; 55; 56; 58; 59 top left, bottom right; 60 bottom; 61; 62; 63 top, center; 65; 67; 70 top; 71; 72 top, bottom right; 73; 74; 75; 78; 79; 80 top; 81; 82 top; 83 bottom; 84; 85; 87; 89; 92; 93; 95; 96. **Ells Marugg:** 11 top left; 33 bottom; 34; 35 top; 37 right; 44 top; 46; 47; 48 top; 50; 53 top; 57; 59 top right; 60 top; 63 bottom; 64; 68; 69 bottom; 72 bottom left; 76; 77; 80 bottom right; 83 top; 88; 91 top. **Don Normark:** 15. **David Stubbs:** 70 bottom. **Darrow M. Watt:** 5 bottom right; 7 left; 12 bottom; 91 bottom. **Peter O. Whiteley:** 94. **Tom Wyatt:** 1; 82 bottom.

Cover: House plant assortment includes clockwise from lower right, *Asplenium nidus* (bird's nest fern), *Kalanchoe blossfeldiana, Adiantum tenerum* (maidenhair fern), *Ficus pumila* (creeping fig), *Sansevieria trifasciata* (bowstring hemp), *Melocactus neryi* (melon cactus), and *Dracaena marginata.* Photograph by Steve W. Marley. Cover design by Lynne B. Morrall.

Editor, Sunset Books: David E. Clark

First printing September 1983

Garden corner *celebrates with greenery: a* Ficus benjamina, *a beautifully trained fuchsia (indoor-outdoor plant), and* Cymbidiums *in matching baskets.*

CONTENTS

Foliage plants *form a harmonious trio:* Ficus benjamina *at center, flanked by two* Cissus rhombifolia *(grape ivy). Design: Gayle Holmes.*

Basking blissfully *in a sunny window,* Pelargonium peltatum *(ivy geranium) gets a turn every few days for even growth. Design: Fred & Bobbie Kleinman.*

Set off on a pedestal, Epipremnum aureum *(devil's ivy) trails tendrils towards* Dieffenbachia maculata *(dumb cane). Horticultural design: Plantco.*

A HOUSEFUL OF PLANT DISPLAYS

Corner companions

Dramatic under a high ceiling, sturdy
fiddleleaf fig *(Ficus lyrata)* communes
with its coffee table companion,
a bottle palm *(Beaucarnea recurvata).*
Interior design: William Gaylord.
Horticultural design: Baruch Himmelstein.

Into any room that's bare of greenery, introduce a
frothy fern, a twining ivy, a graceful fig, or a tall,
stately palm. Better yet, introduce several. What hap-
pens? The whole room suddenly comes alive, feels
fresher, livelier, gentler. A little more warmly than
they did before, chairs and rugs invite you to relax.
Windows and tables seem to soften their angles;
even walls look unaccountably friendlier.

Many people buy house plants solely for such
wonder-working effect, without bothering much
about botanical details. Of course, to keep any plant
lustrously healthy, a gardener needs to know something of its botanical nature. Throughout this book,
you'll find all the pertinent information for popular
house plants. But our opening chapter focuses exclusively on imaginative house plant display, offering
dozens of ideas for showing off foliage and flowering plants of every size and shape. You'll also see a
variety of handsome plant containers and some
surprising perches.

For full details on how to grow most of these
plants, look up their botanical names in "A Catalog of
House Plants," pages 32–93.

A number of plants that we feature in this chapter
(cyclamen, florist's gloxinia for example) are sold by
florists as gifts to be used indoors for temporary
display. For further information on "Indoor-Outdoor & Gift Plants," see pages 94–99.

A few others that we show (viola, impatiens, and
dwarf sweet William) present ideas for ways that
outdoor plants can be brought indoors to give a
colorful but short-lived decorative effect.

Container interest

A world of container possibilities beyond the plain clay pot awaits your house plant. Just take a broad-minded look around you. As these pages show, there are many eye-catching ways to pot a plant, then show it off to fullest advantage. Also, be sure to read about containers on pages 22–24.

Herbal humor

Grassy tufts are garlic chives, planted directly into plastic-lined *pâté en croûte* pan. Bordering them are escargot shells (minus snails, of course). Light tuckings of sphagnum moss conceal soil.

Upstairs, downstairs

Antique library ladder steps in as a plant stand, supporting (top to bottom) bridal veil *(Tripogandra multiflora),* a bromeliad *(Tillandsia),* lipstick plant *(Aeschynanthus radicans),* and a second *Tillandsia.* Design: Beth Dunbar.

Suitable for cyclamen

Indoor-outdoor cyclamen has settled its shallow roots quite comfortably into a turn-of-the-century Chinese brass container, protected from moisture by a double lining of aluminum foil. Red flowers pick up color of chair's trim.

Plants & windows

Sun-loving house plants benefit from basking in a window—and you'll benefit, too, from having them there. Besides screening you from strong floods of light and conferring extra privacy, plants create leafy live window trimmings of branches and foliage—and sometimes bright flowers, too.

High impact

Decking the ledge of a lofty window with cascading green, bleeding heart vine *(Clerodendrum thomsoniae)* was trained to climb far above its floor-bound clay pot. Resting alongside, down below, are basketed African violets *(Saintpaulia ionantha*—on dresser) and a sword fern *(Nephrolepis exaltata* 'Fluffy Ruffles'). Design: Susan Mueller.

Window on the world

What better, more visible perch for a magnificent pencil tree *(Euphorbia tirucalli)* than a front window of smoked glass? Delighting onlookers both indoors and out, the tree also contrasts attractively with nearby wisteria.

Window stage

Like a troupe of performers, plants line up to stage an exciting show—in this case, a window garden. Backstage has convenient pebble-lined panel that retains moisture, reducing need for frequent watering. Airy window bathes entire troupe in exhilarating light. From left to right, on-stage stars include *Ficus benjamina* (on the floor), two small citrus plants, piggyback plant *(Tolmiea menziesii),* century plant *(Agave americana),* begonia, crown of thorns *(Euphorbia milii), Pachypodium lamieri,* Boston fern *(Nephrolepis exaltata* 'Bostoniensis'), parlor palm *(Chamaedorea elegans),* a second Boston fern, and false aralia *(Dizygotheca elegantissima).* Overhead are ivy *(Hedera helix),* yet another Boston fern, and *Coleus.* Design: Philip L. Brown.

Garden of delights

North-facing, easy-to-install greenhouse window puts a small and colorful garden just over the kitchen sink. On top shelf, left to right, sit grape ivy *(Cissus rhombifolia),* table fern *(Pteris cretica* 'Wimsettii'), and a hydrangea. Second shelf holds, from left, fancy-leafed caladium *(Caladium bicolor),* prayer plant *(Maranta leuconeura),* squirrel's foot fern *(Davallia trichomanoides),* and another fern *(Polystichum).* On third shelf are cyclamen, florist's gloxinia *(Sinningia speciosa),* maidenhair fern *(Adiantum tenerum),* and lady's slipper *(Paphiopedilum).* Bottom shelf boasts two cinerarias *(Senecio hybridus),* cape primrose *(Streptocarpus),* pocketbook flower *(Calceolaria integrifolia),* cyclamen, and *Kalanchoe blossfeldianas.* Horticultural design: Plantco.

Indoor gardens

Whether gracing balcony or bathroom, at floor level or high overhead, plants in a convivial cluster make rooms feel friendlier. Built-in planters, shown here, make it easy to plant more luxuriantly than usual. Most of these indoor gardens drain directly to the ground outdoors.

Overhead, leafy gallery

Bobbing enormous leaves that look almost like waving hands, flamboyant split-leaf philodendron (*Monstera*) basks on a sunlit balcony. Sturdier than many house plants (though it still needs moderate care to look its best), *Monstera* lends itself well to out-of-the-way locations like this one. Each pot sits in its own handsome basket, adding to the harmonious look of the upstairs garden. Design: MLA/Architects.

Wearin' o' the green

Pots of peace lily *(Spathiphyllum)* and grape ivy *(Cissus rhombifolia)* splash a stripe of luscious green along stairway top, dressing up the expanse of white that surrounds them.

Indoor window box

Looking their loveliest from the extra moisture in the air, crisp cyclamen greet you in the morning from their recessed planter, shared with ferns, behind the bathroom sink. Metal-lined planter drains directly to the outside.

Tiled garden

Lofty, lovely *Ficus benjamina* brings woodsy freshness to this high-ceilinged music room. Opening to the ground below the house, the tiled planter allows ample depth for *Ficus'* roots, along with those of (left to right) peace lily *(Spathiphyllum),* a smaller ficus, Chinese evergreen *(Aglaonema modestum),* fiddleleaf fig *(Ficus lyrata),* grape ivy *(Cissus rhombifolia),* and a second peace lily. Horticultural design: Bill Derringer.

Living room greenery

Their gentle, natural beauty invites you to wander in, sit down, relax for a while. Their ethereal bloom imparts a mood of contentment. And their foliage, sometimes as stunning as sculpture, draws your thoughts away from the busy world outside. In these and other ways, plants work wonders.

Tropical tranquility

In a quiet, monochromatic room, arching foliage brings cooling, tropical refreshment, as if softly fanning the air. Grand, stately philodendrons stand against the wall; young palms grace the mantel, and bromeliads *(Aechmeas)* adorn the table tops.
Design: Michael Taylor.

Artistry from nature

Like clouds floating in an azure sky, fragile flower spray of a moth orchid *(Phalaenopsis)* draws the eye—both to the blossoms' natural beauty and to the Oriental *objets d'art* nearby.

Beauty & the bookcase

Row upon regular row, both books and their shelves sometimes look monotonous. But here, a billowy grape ivy *(Cissus rhombifolia)* offers jaunty contrast to all those stacks and angles.

Like living sculpture

Its stark vertical trunk culminating in a burst of deep green leaves, a Spanish dagger *(Yucca gloriosa)* puts emphatic drama into a spacious, sunlit room. Design: Michael Taylor.

Springtime welcome

A host of daffodils blazes yellow before an unused fireplace; basketful of bulbs will bloom vibrantly for 2 weeks or more. Pots are hidden under packing straw.

Dinner refreshment

No artfully laid table would look complete without its vase of cut flowers. But why not stretch tradition, as shown here, by warmly welcoming guests with a living bouquet—or ushering them into the dining room through a graceful stand of trees? Plants enhance any meal, from breakfast to supper.

Trees as room dividers

A forest of *Ficus benjamina* elegantly separates living and dining areas without disturbing the airy openness of one big room. In fact, trees' lofty, leafy forms accentuate the surrounding spaciousness. Design: Gayle Holmes.

Living bouquet

Brought indoors for a dinner party, a basket brimming with exquisite cyclamen waits to welcome guests. If you place the plants outside at night (in moderate climates), the bloom should continue for 2 months or more.

Individually inviting

Cheerful violas wait to greet guests, who will later take them home. Taken from the garden outside (they must return outside after the dinner party), each was planted in a plastic-lined basket that complements the place settings.

Tea for two, violets too

How to turn a delicious little scene into a fondly remembered occasion? To the tea-time cups and cakes, add dainty African violets *(Saintpaulia ionantha)* set in a fine silver cachepot.

Kitchen companionship

Kettles and soup pots steam in many kitchens, surrounding plants with the humid atmosphere they love. But even if your kitchen's air isn't moist, bring in a plant or two—to perk up the room, to cheer and inspire the cook. Here are a few examples of such green and leafy companionship.

Pâtisserie greenery

This proud brass stand once stood in a French baker's shop, showing off fresh pastries. Today its racks are laden with botanical wares, a treat for the eyes. Shown, top to bottom, are two asparagus ferns *(Asparagus densiflorus* 'Sprengeri'), impatiens, dwarf sweet William, and piggyback plant *(Tolmiea menziesii).* Other kitchen greenery includes bridal veil *(Tripogandra multiflora)* by the counter and another asparagus fern atop the cabinet. Design: Woodward Interiors.

Cook's canopy

Growing vigorously on a lofty wire and aluminum utility shelf is kangaroo vine *(Cissus antarctica)*. Glorious foliage canopy gets its light from both overhead lamps and a skylight.

Garden aloft

Cascades of Swedish ivy *(Plectranthus australis)* spill right into the kitchen from a plant mezzanine. Also supporting philodendrons *(Philodendron selloum)*, platform includes a built-in watering system. Architect: James Oliver. Irrigation design: Michael Batori.

GREEN THUMB KNOW-HOW

Get ready *for some good, green fun. Plunge your hands right in. Just take a pot and pebbles, some soil, a pretty plant, a drink of water ... add a touch of fertilizer later on. Soon you'll have a houseful of lush and leafy plants.*

To grow with glory, to look magnificent rather than messy, to fulfill its decorative promise—for all these, any house plant, whether tolerant or fussy, needs loving care.

Remember that it's not natural for a plant to live indoors, in a confining pot. In such an artificial environment, the plant depends entirely on you for all its requirements. It looks to you to provide the light, humidity, and temperature it needs, as well as the right type of potting soil and just the right amounts of water and fertilizer. Each of these needs is fully detailed here. And for those times when you must place a plant in a location that's less than ideal, we show how to adjust conditions for the plant's benefit.

This chapter also gets you off to a good start, guiding you in choosing a healthy specimen that suits the location you plan for it. Step-by-step directions show how to plant in all types of popular containers, as well as how to repot a plant that outgrows its first home.

In addition, we give you tips on pinching, pruning, and grooming your foliaged friends to maintain their healthy good looks. And for plants, as for people, "preventive medicine" is an important part of care. You'll learn here how to recognize pest infestation or disease, and how to clear up the problem early.

To determine each plant's individual needs, combine the information in this chapter with the specific care instructions given for that plant in "A Catalog of House Plants" (pages 32–93). And may your thumbs grow greener, your indoor garden prosper...

Be choosy

When you're shopping for a house plant, carefully evaluate both the plant itself and the shop or nursery where it's sold. Be choosy; don't settle for the first plant you see. If you have any doubt at all, don't buy.

Finding a trustworthy house plant dealer is the first step. Though you may have good luck with bargain plants, it's safest to buy from a reputable nursery, plant boutique, or florist shop where you can be sure plants have received proper care.

Evaluating a plant

Here are simple guidelines for sizing up both house plant and dealer.

1) Survey the shop's entire selection. Do most plants seem healthy and happy? An attractive overall look usually means basically healthy plants that have received proper care.

2) Examine the plant itself. Does it look healthy? Is it free of leaf damage and pests? Is its color good? Does it have a pleasing shape? Does it show any new growth? If the answer is "yes" in each case, your choice is a good one.

3) See if the plant is potbound: if any roots peek through the pot's drainage hole, the plant has nearly outgrown its pot. You'd do best to choose a different plant—one that still fits comfortably in its container.

If you really like that particular plant, you can always ask whether or not the nursery or garden center will repot it for you before you take it home. There will probably be a slight charge for the service.

4) Choose a plant of the size you wish; don't buy a small version and wait for it to grow bigger (the desired size increase could take months or years). Remember, too, that a well-established, fairly mature plant usually adapts to a new environment more smoothly.

Matching plant to location

Before you choose a plant for your house, decide where you'll put it, keeping in mind that a good location for an indoor plant provides the light, temperature, and atmospheric conditions it needs to grow.

As you study possible indoor spots for your plant, ask yourself these questions: Will a house plant enhance this particular spot? How much light is available? What is the average temperature and humidity? Are there seasonal changes in light, humidity, or temperature?

Once you look into these questions, you'll have a good idea of what kind of "microclimate" your location offers. Now all you need do is select a plant to suit it. Look through "Which Plant Suits You Best?" (pages 100–109), for ideas. Then study "A Catalog of House Plants" (pages 32–93) to find more information on whether the plant that appeals to you will thrive in the type of environment you have to offer.

If you want a particular plant that doesn't quite match your chosen location, you may be able to modify the spot to make it more suitable. Perhaps you can adjust the room's temperature, or provide artificial light (see page 18) or extra humidity (see page 20).

Some of us are impulse buyers, choosing a plant for its colorful foliage or interesting flowers without thinking of its needs. If this describes your plant purchases, find out as much about the plant as possible from the shop where you purchased it and from the catalog section of this book.

It's always comforting to know that if something goes wrong with the plant, you can go back to a quality nursery for advice.

Temperature

Some like it hot, and others like it cool. Luckily, though, most house plants adjust easily to normal indoor temperatures. To play it safe, select plants that like the same house temperatures you like; unless you wish to provide a special plant room or a greenhouse that caters to hot-house temperaments, leave finicky plants to other gardeners.

Temperature ranges found in most homes divide into the following three categories: cool (55° to 65°F/13° to 18°C), average (65° to 70°F/18° to 21°C), and warm (70° to 85°F/21° to 24°C). And there are plants that thrive in each range.

Many plants like a change of temperature when the seasons change—usually a cooler spot in winter. Such individual preferences are noted in "A Catalog of House Plants," pages 32–93.

Not too hot … not too cold

Avoid putting plants through drastic temperature changes or in drafts. Air near a window may be many degrees hotter or colder than in the room's interior. During extreme weather (hot or cold, since either can be devastating), check the temperature near windows where plants are kept; move them if necessary. Also keep plants away from home heating registers, radiators, fireplaces, or the direct blast from an air conditioner.

Humidity levels relate closely to air temperatures: the warmer the air, the faster humidity in the air disappears. This is especially true when a home's central heating unit is operating; it creates a relatively hot, dry atmosphere. Many favorite indoor plants need humidity to survive. If the air in your house is dry, see page 20 for ways to boost humidity.

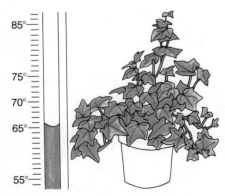

A bit cool *for people, this temperature range suits plants such as ivy* (Hedera).

Average house temperatures *are fine for many plants, such as* Dracaena.

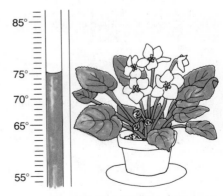

Warm spots *provide ideal environment for African violets* (Saintpaulia).

How is your natural light?

For proper growth, all plants need light—but the amount varies from one kind to another. In general, blooming and fruiting plants, and those with variegated leaves, require more light than do plants with solid green foliage. The intensity of light is important, as is the length of time each day that a plant receives light.

It's always best to place plants where they'll receive the kind of light they prefer (for light requirements of individual house plants, see "A Catalog of House Plants," pages 32–93). Sometimes, though, you may want to place a plant in a relatively dim location. The best choice here, of course, is a plant that can tolerate low light—for some suggestions, see "Plants that need little light," page 103.

If you decide to grow a house plant in less than optimum light, you have two choices. You can try to meet the plant's requirements with artificial light (see below), or you can adjust plant care: give less fertilizer than the plant would need if growing in a more suitable location, and don't repot until you see lots of roots poking out of the drain hole. By making these care adjustments, you'll simply maintain these plants. You won't encourage them to grow—they'll stay about the same size and shape indefinitely. Though plants maintained in this way will live as long as other house plants, don't expect top performance from them. To really thrive, they need more light.

Types of natural light

The following four types of indoor light are frequently mentioned throughout this book.

Direct sun refers to direct rays of sunlight coming through a window. An east-facing exposure allows morning sun and generally coolish afternoon temperatures; a west window permits afternoon sun with warmer temperatures. A south-facing exposure offers sun and warm temperatures most of the day (this is the brightest exposure). One caution: sunlight may be magnified by window glass to a temperature hot enough to burn foliage. It's best to set house plants that enjoy basking in direct sun 6 inches or so back from the windowpane.

Reflected light is indirect light, cooler than direct sun, that's reflected off walls or ceiling. This kind of light may also be quite bright, similar in quality to the light illuminating the innermost space of a sunny room. Most flowering plants need this kind of light.

Filtered light is essentially bright light, but it's softened somewhat as it shines through a sheer curtain or through trees or shrubs growing outside the window. Overhangs or translucent patio roofs may also filter light.

Low light usually refers to relatively dark parts of interiors, shadowy corners, or areas unlit by windows. Only a few plants can tolerate such situations; most will need a boost from artificial lighting.

Artificial light can give a boost

Where natural light alone isn't sufficient for plants to flourish, a boost from artificial lighting is often the solution. Plants also benefit from a combination of natural and artificial light during the winter.

Some indoor gardeners grow house plants under artificial lights alone. If these provide an intensity and quality of light about equal to natural sunlight, plants will grow quite happily, as long as they receive sufficient daily exposure.

All light, whether from sun or electric lamp, consists of waves that appear as a spectrum of colors when passed through a prism. Photosynthesis—the process by which plants manufacture their food—uses chiefly the red and blue waves found at opposite ends of the spectrum. Fluorescent bulbs provide mostly blue light, and only a little red; incandescent bulbs, on the other hand, provide mainly red light, with just a little blue. To give their plants a more balanced combination of red and blue light, indoor gardeners sometimes combine the two types of artificial light in a mix of one watt of incandescence for every three watts of fluorescence.

Always keep in mind that incandescent bulbs also give off heat—often enough to burn a plant's foliage. If you do use such a bulb, keep it at least 4 feet away from the plant. For indoor gardening, fluorescent light is generally preferable: it emits far less heat and uses less energy.

Buy a fluorescent light fixture with a white or foil reflector to direct light onto plants. When placing plants under it, remember that the strongest light shines from the center of the tube. Several fluorescent tubes placed side by side may be needed, as one tube alone will not support a plant that's dependent on artificial light alone. As a standard, all plants require 15 to 20 watts of light for every square foot of their growing surface. (You can estimate the growing surface by calculating the volume of space the plant occupies).

Special "grow lights"—tubes or bulbs developed to simulate actual sunlight—are available at many garden centers and nurseries. Such bulbs can stimulate plants to bloom, produce fruit, and set seeds. They cost a little more than regular fluorescent tubes or incandescent bulbs.

Bulb-type grow lights fit into standard light fixtures; they're especially useful for spotlighting plants.

Expect to adjust the height of any tubular bulb, be it plain fluorescent or special grow light, to allow for plant growth and varying container sizes. Start with the tubes placed 6 to 12 inches above the foliage (unless the manufacturer recommends otherwise). Since fluorescent tubes and grow light tubes won't harm plants, you can move the tube closer to the leaves if needed. If the foliage starts to bunch together unnaturally, plants are receiving too much light; if plants become leggy, they need more light.

Each day, most plants also require some period of darkness for a rest (even plants need their sleep). Most foliage plants want 10 to 12 hours of daily light; flowering plants require 16. It's important to provide a regular light/dark schedule.

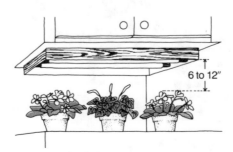

Special tubes *duplicate sunlight.*

Bulb *spotlights a large house plant.*

How to be a wise waterer

More plants fail from improper watering than from any other cause—and most often, that means too much water, not too little.

It's best to water plants in the morning, so that moisture on the foliage can evaporate by evening (cool, wet foliage can invite pest infestation). Because cold water can harm plants, many indoor gardeners fill their watering cans the night before to allow the water to reach room temperature. If your water passes through a water softener or is especially hard, tasting of minerals, use bottled distilled water on plants. Some plant lovers catch rainwater in a cistern for watering their plants.

Plant differences

Fast-growing plants and those that bloom or bear fruit heavily need more water than the slower growers. Those with a large total leaf surface, such as ferns, are thirstier than sparsely foliaged plants; those with soft, lush foliage usually require more water than plants with waxy, leathery, or succulent leaves.

No two plants use water at exactly the same rate, and many factors beyond your control (such as the time of year) further affect the amount of water any individual plant needs. But you can control a few factors—the type of container you select, for example.

The seasons

In winter, when days are short and skies are often gray, house plants generally need less water than during summer. Some plants respond to winter by retreating into a dormant state, as if hibernating. They don't require much water.

Container know-how

The type of container that holds your plant has a direct effect on how much and how often water will be needed. Plant containers are discussed in more detail on pages 22–24.

Red clay pots are porous, absorbing moisture and permitting good air circulation. Because of this absorption, plants in clay pots tend to use more water and need it more often than those in other types of containers. You'll need to check the moisture level of these plants frequently.

Plastic pots are nonporous, so the potting soil inside tends to retain moisture for longer periods than it would in a clay pot. Since the soil takes longer to dry, overwatering often becomes a real problem. Most gardeners reserve plastic pots for moisture-loving plants. (One type of plastic pot—the self-watering pot—won't cause watering problems; see page 22.)

Glazed pots, usually made of clay painted with a ceramic glaze, are also nonporous. Treat plants in glazed pots like those in plastic pots.

Pots without drainage present a problem. After a plant in such a pot is watered, moisture in the soil is retained until the plant uses it or it evaporates. Plants in drainless pots should receive less water than those in containers with drain holes: only a portion of the soil volume should become damp. As a rule of thumb, add water equal to one-fourth of the container's total volume. And let the top half of the soil dry out between waterings. Watch these plants carefully for signs of overwatering: yellow or curled leaves, fallen leaves, brown leaf edges or tips.

Does your plant need water?

Experienced indoor gardeners have devised many different ways to judge when a plant needs water. Experiment with the methods given below for testing moisture levels; adopt whatever works for you.

The touch test. It's generally agreed that this is the most accurate means of judging a plant's need for water. With your finger, feel the soil surface; if it's dry to a depth of ½ to 1 inch, add water. But if it's still moist, don't water; instead, keep checking periodically, even daily.

The water meter test. Various devices called "electronic moisture meters" or "tensiometers" are available at nurseries and garden centers; you can also order them from garden suppliers' catalogs. These instruments measure the moisture present in the soil.

All these meters operate similarly: they generate a very weak electric current whose strength depends on the relative amount of moisture in the soil. In most cases, the moister the soil, the stronger the electric current. The meter converts this current into a buzz, click, or flashing light. Some meters have a scale or dial that gives a reading of the soil's moisture level.

To use such a meter, push the probe into the soil in the plant's container and wait for the signal. Try several readings on each plant at different soil depths.

Whichever type of meter you purchase, follow the accompanying directions carefully. Also, be aware of the device's shortcomings. You may get inaccurate readings if you've used distilled water or if salt has accumulated in the potting soil. If your meter is battery operated, the battery will sometimes weaken or go dead. If a house plant looks wilted and its soil feels bone-dry, give it a drink regardless of the water meter's message.

Drooping foliage. Drooping or wilted foliage usually indicates that a house plant needs water fast! Water a wilted plant thoroughly; after several hours, the plant should regain its normal perky appearance. (Though most house plants can survive such wilting occasionally, they won't tolerate it as a regular occurrence.)

A good way to water

Assuming that your plant has a properly draining container and potting soil, here's how to water: 1) Feel the soil to a depth of 1 inch below the surface; if it's dry to the touch, add tepid water to the soil surface. 2) Continue until you see water seeping from the drainage hole. 3) Allow the plant to drain (either into a sink or drainage saucer) for at least 10 minutes. 4) Discard any water standing in the saucer (a potted plant should never sit in water). 5) When the top inch of soil again becomes dry to the touch (a few days to a few weeks, depending on pot size and type), repeat this procedure.

A watering can with either straight or slightly curved spout prevents spilling.

After following those watering steps for a time, you'll get an idea of how much water your plants really need and use.

Long spout *prevents watering mishaps.*

The occasional soak

The Boston fern is but one of many house plants that benefit from having their pots occasionally immersed to the rim in water. Do it in the warm season, about once a month. Immerse the pot to just above the rim in a container of room-temperature water; soak it until bubbles stop coming to the surface. Remove the pot and let it drain, then return it to its normal place. A good time to apply fertilizer (discussed on page 21) is immediately after such a periodic dunking.

Most plants like it humid

Most home atmospheres offer only negligible humidity. For a few plant groups, such as cactuses and succulents, dry air is just fine. But the majority of plants we try to grow indoors come originally from tropical jungles—where the air is humid. While a tropical environment would hardly be desirable for either our living room drapes or our personal comfort, we must nevertheless provide—to some extent—the humidity that our tropical house plants relish. Check "A Catalog of House Plants," pages 32–93, for the humidity needs of your individual plants.

Many factors affect humidity inside houses. During winter, heating systems reduce natural humidity. And in naturally arid regions, warm summer temperatures can do the same.

You can gauge the humidity level of your home with a hygrometer, an instrument that measures moisture in air (usually available at hardware stores or from technical supply catalogs).

The following methods boost humidity for your plants: misting, using a humidity tray, grouping compatible plants, and placing plants in naturally humid parts of the house. These measures will benefit your humidity-loving plants.

Misting

Among indoor gardeners, opinions vary on the value of misting. Daily misting is a ritual for many orchid and fern lovers; other gardeners mist only occasionally or not at all. And it's true that some fuzzy-leafed plants, such as African violets, should not be misted: water drops on such leaves may cause spotting, especially if the water is cooler than room temperature.

In general, though, misting is an inexpensive method of creating a humid atmosphere. And it offers the added advantages of lightly washing foliage and discouraging pests. But be aware that misting is no substitute for regular watering; the plant absorbs very little of the spray.

Misting should create a fine cloud of moisture that surrounds your plant and covers both sides of its leaves. (If a plant normally sits on or near furniture or other surfaces that can be damaged by water, you'll probably have to move it before misting.) So the moisture will have plenty of time to evaporate before nightfall, mist in the morning. Let water sit in the mister overnight to bring it to room temperature, or use tepid tap water.

In most nurseries or indoor plant stores, you'll find misters made of plastic or metal. Be sure the mister you choose sprays a fine mist. Leaves should look as if a light dew has settled on them; you don't want them dripping wet.

For plants that require high levels of humidity, honest-to-goodness showers given on a regular basis (once a month or more often) are beneficial (see page 27).

Humidity trays

If your plant requires high humidity, set up a humidity tray for constant water evaporation. Start with a waterproof tray, an inch or more in depth, large enough to hold one plant or several. Be sure you use only a waterproof tray—one made of metal, plastic, rubber, or glazed ceramic. A clay container absorbs and holds moisture that could damage any surface beneath. Fill the tray with pebbles, pea gravel, or small rocks; then add water, stopping when the water level is just below the top of the rocks. Place the plant's container on the rocks; since their surface is still dry, the pot never sits in water (roots that sit constantly in water may rot). This does double duty by catching any runoff from regular watering.

A slightly different style of humidity tray, for use with most orchids, is described on page 66.

Check the water level in the tray periodically, and add more water if necessary.

Some indoor gardeners create a "buffer zone" (see page 23, under "Saucers prevent runoff problems") between the humidity tray and the floor or furniture below it. Raising the tray a few inches from the surface forms an air layer to absorb any extra moisture, preventing damage from condensation.

To check the effectiveness of your humidity tray, use a hygrometer, taking a reading near the plant's foliage.

Naturally humid areas

In most homes, the use of water in the kitchen and bathroom makes these rooms more humid than other areas. Washing dishes, boiling water, and taking showers all create moisture in the air, noticeably boosting the humidity level. As long as their requirements for light and temperature can also be met, humidity-loving plants should thrive in these rooms.

Grouping compatible plants

Water evaporates from a plant's leaves during transpiration, the process by which plants cool off. This water vapor creates humidity around each transpiring plant. When you group plants (leaving enough room among them for free air circulation), the joint transpiration provides them all with somewhat more humidity.

Besides "bathing" each other in extra humidity, plants in groups often look lusher than a single specimen on its own.

A mister *surrounds a plant with fine spray that covers both sides of its leaves.*

From the humidity tray, *evaporating moisture reaches the plant.*

Grouping plants *creates a somewhat more humid atmosphere.*

Fertilizer— choosing and using

Plants growing in the ground outdoors can usually obtain nourishment; if their immediate surroundings lack needed nutrients, their roots can branch into other areas. But a house plant can use only the soil in its pot; once the nutrients in this soil are gone, the plant is stranded. That's why you need to step in and replenish these nutrients by applying fertilizer.

Complete house plant fertilizers contain three basic nutrients: nitrogen, phosphorus, and potassium (or potash). The best fertilizers also include needed trace elements. The ratio of the three main ingredients is usually shown by three numbers, such as 5-10-5 or 18-20-16, printed on the label. The first number refers to the amount of nitrogen, which stimulates leaf growth and keeps foliage a rich green. The second number indicates the proportion of phosphorus, needed for sturdy cell structure, healthy root growth, and vigorous flower and fruit production. The third number gives the amount of potassium, which fosters healthy plant development.

As long as the label indicates that the fertilizer is formulated for house plants, you can be sure of proper nutrient balance.

A few groups of plants, such as orchids and African violets (Saintpaulia), have customized fertilizers. These products are generally worth buying for superior results.

Types of fertilizers

You can buy house plant fertilizer in liquid or powdered form, or in tablets or capsules. Before application, most need to be dissolved in (or diluted with) water; some types can be scratched into the soil surface. Fertilizers marked "slow-release" allow nutrients to dissolve slowly in normal waterings over a period of time; you also place these tablets, sticks, or capsules on or beneath the soil surface (according to package directions). Experienced indoor gardeners tend to favor liquid formulations for their flexibility in dilution ratios and ease of application.

Using fertilizers

Before fertilizing a plant, check its individual needs in "A Catalog of House Plants," pages 32–93. In addition, observe these precautions: Never apply fertilizer of any form to dry potting soil; be sure to water your plant thoroughly first. And never fertilize a plant suffering from pests or disease—wait until it has completely recovered before encouraging it to grow.

Fertilize "regularly" means, for most fertilizers, once a month, using the dilution recommended on the fertilizer label. If you use a slow or timed-release fertilizer, you'll apply it on a regular basis as recommended on the label (usually every 2 to 3 months). It's helpful to keep track of dates when you apply the fertilizer.

Some indoor gardeners believe it's beneficial to apply fertilizer (but not the slow or timed-release type) more frequently than normally recommended (usually twice as often) but at a lower concentration—usually half (or less) the recommended label dose. More frequent applications provide the plant with nutrients at a more continuous rate.

A newly purchased house plant from a reliable nursery normally comes to you in well-nourished condition; it's unlikely to need fertilizer for at least 3 months. The same is true of a newly repotted plant; before you encourage it to grow with fertilizer, give it a few months to get established.

Most plants take a rest from growing during the winter months. Don't tax them at this time by applying fertilizer; wait until they show signs of new growth before coaxing them along with nutrients.

Though your plants do need fertilizer, too much presents a real danger to them— "an extra pinch to grow on" can damage or even kill a plant. You'll notice fallen, browned leaves (though these may indicate other problems too—see page 28); excess fertilizer may also show as a chalky film on the outside of a clay pot. If you find you have applied too much fertilizer, try the antidote of leaching to wash out the excess fertilizer. First water the plant until water runs out the drain hole; then let drain for a while. Repeat this watering and draining process two or three times.

Good potting soil mix is a must

Along with light and water, potting soil is a crucial ingredient for healthy plant growth. It's especially formulated to provide excellent aeration and to retain just the amount of moisture a plant needs, allowing the excess to drain away.

Commercial potting soil mixes

For most indoor gardeners, the simplest way to select house plant soil is to buy a package of prepared potting soil mix; look for these mixes at nurseries, indoor plant stores, or most garden supply stores. Potting soil comes in packages of varied sizes, so you can purchase only as much as you need at one time.

Choose a standard indoor soil mix specifically formulated for house plants. For a time, it will provide all the nutrients that a plant needs; once the plant has used these, you can replenish them with a house plant fertilizer (see above). Check that packaged potting soil has been sterilized to eliminate any pests or disease organisms that might be present.

Some lightweight soil mixes need moistening before they're ready to use. Squeeze a handful of soil in your fist; it should be damp enough to stay in a compact ball when you release it, yet it shouldn't be dripping wet. If it's dry and crumbly, add just enough water to make it cohesive.

Home-mixed soil

If purchasing a plastic bag of commercial potting soil isn't your idea of "real" gardening, you can mix your own. Combine equal amounts of coarse, washed sand (be sure it's washed; salt in unwashed sea sand may damage tender plants), garden loam or good garden topsoil, and peat moss, leaf mold, or fir bark. To each 2 quarts of this mix, add ½ cup each charcoal and perlite. All these mix-your-own ingredients are usually available at nurseries, garden supply stores, or indoor plant stores.

Every ingredient in potting soil serves a valuable purpose. Garden loam and topsoil contain clay particles that hold fertilizing nutrients so they're available as needed by plant roots. Sand and perlite hold air around roots, allowing them to breathe and protecting them from staying too damp. Leaf mold, peat moss, and fir bark perform this function, too—and they also provide nutrients. Charcoal bits keep the soil "sweet" by absorbing soil substances toxic to the plant.

Any homemade potting soil mix containing garden soil must be sterilized before use, since garden loam or topsoil may contain pests, weed seeds, or plant disease organisms.

To sterilize your soil, follow these steps: 1) Mix soil ingredients thoroughly. 2) Dampen mix slightly with water; then spread it—no more than 4 inches deep— in shallow ovenproof pans. 3) Place filled pans in a 180° oven; bake for at least 2 hours. (Baking soil gives off a nasty odor—be prepared for it. Luckily, this odor isn't lasting.) 4) Remove sterilized soil from oven and let it air, uncovered (indoors—in a garage, for example) for a few days. Store it in sturdy paper or plastic bags.

Which container for which plant?

An array of plant container choices awaits your selection. Naturally, some offer more advantages than others. Take time to find what best suits your plant, its surroundings, and your own tastes.

As you look for a pot, keep these points in mind: 1) Containers with drainage are generally a wiser choice. You can plant in a drainless container, but plant care becomes much more difficult (see page 24 for instructions). 2) Choose the container that best suits your plant's present size. Full grown but naturally small plants do not need large containers; plants that will eventually become large may need a consecutively larger container each year. 3) Purchase a drip saucer (see facing page) at the same time you buy the container—size and compatibility are easier to judge. 4) Select a container that harmonizes with your interior decor.

Clay pots

Always popular, the classic terra cotta or clay pot is inexpensive, easy to find, and available in many shapes and sizes. The earthy color (usually red, though sometimes available in shades of brown or gray) blends well with most furniture styles and doesn't overshadow the plant. Clay pots are porous; they absorb moisture and permit wholesome air circulation. They're great for beginning gardeners, since it's difficult (but not impossible) to overwater a plant in a clay pot.

If a plant has received too much fertilizer, excess salts form a white crust on the outside of the pot. Likewise, if the water given the plant has a heavy mineral concentration (hard water), the excess mineral salts leach out and form a similar white crust. Only a porous clay pot can give you such helpful warning signs.

Clay pots used to be available in one basic shape. Nowadays, clay pots—usually made in Spain, Italy, or Mexico—come in an assortment of shapes, from square to rectangular to cylindrical, often with a bas-relief design.

Some clay pots—special orchid containers, for example—have wide slits on the bottom to serve as drainage holes. In this case, use a thin layer of stones or pebbles instead of pot shards to cover the holes.

Plastic pots

Easy to clean, inexpensive to buy, and light in weight, plastic containers come in a wide variety of colors, shapes, and sizes. They're even available in clear plastic, so you can see the potting soil and root system.

There is one catch to nonporous plastic pots: they may create watering problems, since they neither absorb moisture nor permit air circulation. As a general rule, plants in plastic pots need watering less often than those in porous pots—and if you want to avoid any danger of overwatering, it's probably safest to use clay pots. Some gardeners prefer to pot only moisture-loving plants in plastic containers, since they're more tolerant of dampness.

Glazed ceramic pots

Often richly colored or vividly patterned, glazed ceramic pots offer grander ornamentation than their clay or plastic counterparts. Depending on size and decoration, this type can be costly.

Like plastic pots, glazed containers are nonporous and may create watering problems for a beginner. But if you find the perfect glazed pot, consider using it as a cachepot (see facing page).

Metal containers

Elegant but generally impractical are metal containers of copper, brass, silver or silverplate, pewter, polished steel, iron, or aluminum.

For various reasons, most metal containers are best used only as cachepots (see page 23). Many metals tarnish, requiring periodic cleaning and polishing. Since water left standing in the pot can cause corrosion, line any valuable metal container with heavy plastic or place a drainage saucer inside to catch runoff water.

Metal containers rarely have drainage holes. If you do decide to plant directly in a metal pot, be sure to provide drainage material (see page 24) to capture excess from regular waterings. If you should happen to find a metal pot with proper drainage holes, consider it equivalent to a plastic or glazed ceramic container (like them, it's nonporous). Be sure to provide a saucer below to catch water runoff.

Any roots that touch the sides or bottom of an unlined copper pot will die. However, unless the plant is potbound, this shouldn't radically affect its health; the remaining roots will continue to live.

Baskets

Basketry and foliage complement each other so gracefully, it's no wonder that baskets are popular with indoor gardeners. You'll find them in a profusion of shapes, sizes, and finishes, with prices just as varied. Though usually constructed of natural cane or straw in shades of pale gold or beige, some woven containers are painted or stained for brighter color.

Porous clay pots *come in many styles, sizes, and shapes.*

Since a basket isn't watertight, use it only as a decorative outer container. Unless you can fit a saucer inside to catch runoff, remove the pot from the basket before watering. Or waterproof the basket (see page 24); this will prevent water from leaking through and damaging the surface beneath.

Some baskets come with an inserted (and removable) metal lining; you can plant directly in these. Such liners don't have drainage holes—so if you plant in them, follow the instructions for planting in drainless containers (see page 24).

Self-watering containers

If watering house plants is a chore you're inclined to postpone, or if you travel a lot and leave your plants untended, self-watering containers may offer a handy solution. Usually constructed of plastic, these pots include a reservoir for storing water and a device that taps this stored water when the potting soil dries out. Water is drawn up into the pot by way of a sensing mechanism, sometimes a fiber wick, until the soil becomes evenly moist. When the potting soil dries out again, the cycle is repeated. Depending on the size of the reservoir, such a pot can keep the soil moist for 1½ to 2 weeks.

Imaginative containers

If your taste leans to the curious and unexpected, try housing your plants in containers originally intended for other uses. A cooky jar, Dutch wooden shoe, coffee pot, watering can, olive oil can—any item with enough space to hold a plant, potting soil, and drainage material can work as a unique container.

Obviously, these containers aren't designed to hold plants, and they won't have drainage holes. Follow the instructions for planting in drainless containers on page 24, or just use these novelty "pots" as cachepots (see facing page).

Saucers prevent runoff problems

If you give adequate water to a house plant growing in a container that has proper drainage, you're sure to have a drip problem. Within minutes, any water that the potting soil can't retain will run out the drainage holes. Unless you've provided a saucer to catch the runoff, you'll find an unwelcome puddle on floor, table top, or whatever surface is under the pot.

Many containers are sold with matching saucers. But if not, it's wise in any case to buy a drip saucer or tray at the same time you purchase a container, so you can judge fit exactly. If you're buying the saucer separately, make sure it's unobtrusive—and, of course, waterproof. Though a mismatched tray or saucer serves its practical purpose well, it can mar the house plant's visual appeal. To protect interior surfaces further, place a pad or mat under the saucer.

You can solve part of the runoff problem at watering time. Simply take plants to a sink for watering; after watering, let them drain in the sink for 10 minutes or more. Nearly all the excess water should leak into the sink; you'll still need a drip saucer, though, for the last, slower runoff.

A drip saucer or tray made of a porous material such as red clay absorbs moisture, and may damage the surface it sits on. You can waterproof its interior with silicone sealer, but be aware that water even in nonporous saucers—plastic, glazed ceramic, or waterproofed clay—can cause problems, too. Left standing in these saucers, water may condense or "sweat" on the saucer's exterior; again, this can harm the surface beneath. Whenever a plant sits on a valuable or easily stained surface, it's safest to do your watering in the sink, allowing ample drainage time before returning the plant to its place.

To minimize chances of water damage, many indoor gardeners create a "buffer zone" between drip saucer and furniture, floor, or carpet. This zone is an air space where any moisture, whether from condensation or absorption, can dissipate. Blocks of wood, metal or wooden plant holders, openwork mats, or any other means of raising the plant container and saucer off furniture or floor can create a buffer zone. If there's a carpenter in the family, it's also possible to build small, footed plant stands from scrap lumber. These mini-stands have the effect of making a plant seem more important.

Cachepots

"Cacher" means "to conceal" in French, and a cachepot conceals an already-potted house plant. Cachepots offer several advantages. If you use a valuable or easily stained container as a cachepot, you protect it from the damage that might result from direct planting. A plant displayed in such a container can be replaced quickly when out of bloom or not looking its best. Many cachepots are watertight, so you can even do without a drip saucer or tray.

Most gift plants (such as cyclamen, *Chrysanthemums*, azaleas, *Kalanchoe blossfeldiana*—see pages 94–99) are grown in standard 6-inch pots. By making a careful selection of cachepots, it's possible to have just the right size decorative container in which to slip one of these temporary beauties. As soon as the gift plant starts to fade, simply move it out and replace it.

Cachepots come in the same materials as ordinary plant containers (see facing page) and also in other decorative materials, from wicker to chrome.

Utilizing a cachepot is easy. To allow for good air circulation, the cachepot should measure at least an inch more in diameter than the plant's container. If the potted house plant sits too low in the cachepot, raise the inner pot, using bricks, another clay pot set upside down, layers of pebbles, or sphagnum moss or any similar material. This elevated base will also keep the plants from sitting in drained water.

If the runoff from normal watering could damage your cachepot, take the plant to a sink at watering time. Otherwise, line the cachepot with heavy plastic or set a drip saucer inside, under the potted plant.

Some indoor gardeners also line the space between the plant container and the cachepot to create an illusion of direct planting. Use loosely packed sphagnum moss or pebbles—these materials permit adequate air circulation around the plant's container. You can complete the disguise by covering the entire surface with a top mulch of sphagnum moss, pebbles, or bark (see photograph on page 96). Once you've done all this, you'll need to be careful not to overwater, or you'll have to take it all apart to drain out excess water.

Layer of pebbles *supports potted plant inside a decorative ceramic cachepot.*

One brick *inside a copper bucket boosts a plant to the right height.*

Stacked clay pots *lift a plant to the top of a deep, dramatic wicker basket.*

Planting in a drainless container

You can pot a plant in a container without a drainage hole, though it's a less than ideal house-plant home. The problem with such a container is that once water is poured in, it has no way out again. To keep the plant healthy, you must provide a "drainage layer," which will act as a holding tank for the excess moisture.

Place a layer of small rocks or pebbles (an inch or less in diameter) in the bottom of the container, filling about one-quarter of its total volume. (You can also use small pieces of volcanic rock or broken bits of clay pots for the drainage material.) The drainage layer retains water that has seeped through the soil until the plant can use it or until it evaporates. As long as you don't overwater, the drainage layer also protects plant roots from exposure to soggy soil and permits them to obtain oxygen.

Spread a thin layer of charcoal bits directly over the drainage layer. Besides absorbing slight amounts of water, charcoal keeps the soil "sweet" by absorbing any noxious by-products created as matter decays in the potting soil.

Begin putting in the potting soil and proceed to transplant your house plant as described on page 25. The drawing below shows the various layers used in a drainless container.

To prepare a terrarium or dish garden, follow the steps outlined above for a drainless container. Use a sterilized wide-mouthed glass container or a wide dish with a narrow lip. (The same principles apply to narrow-necked bottle gardens, but these are tricky to create, and require long-handled tools.)

In a completed terrarium, the soil surface should be about a third of the way up the sides of the container; the top soil surface in a dish garden should be close to the dish lip. Be sure the soil isn't too rich, since you don't want plants in these miniature arrangements to grow too big (don't fertilize them, either).

Plant either dish or terrarium with several of the specimens suggested for these uses throughout the Catalog section, pages 32–93. Water very gently and quite sparingly—especially in a terrarium, which creates its own "rain cycle" of evaporation and condensation.

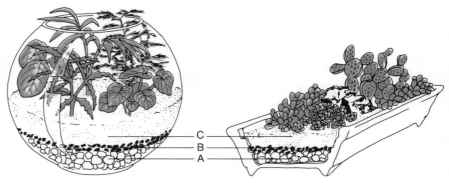

Use layers—*pebbles (A), charcoal bits (B), potting soil (C)—to plant in drainless terrarium (left) or dish garden (right).*

How to waterproof a plant's basket

Though attractive, most woven baskets used as house plant containers have the drawback of leaking like sieves. You can always line the basket with plastic or aluminum foil, but don't count on it to last long without tearing.

A more durable solution, easy to accomplish, is to coat the basket interior with newspaper strips and polyester resin; the finished lining will be quite waterproof.

You'll need a container each of clear polyester resin and hardener (sold separately), a brush, acetone to clean the brush, and newspaper strips. A quart of resin is enough for about three medium-size baskets (the size of wastepaper baskets); ask a salesperson for the appropriate amount of hardener.

Cut the newspaper into 4-inch-wide strips, each one 10 inches longer than the basket's bottom diameter (strips should come up the sides to about 5 inches). Protect your hands with gloves and work outdoors or in a well-ventilated area; strong-smelling resin fumes can be dangerous.

To prepare one medium-size basket, thoroughly mix about one-third quart of the resin with the proper amount of hardener (as directed on the can). Brush the mixture onto the basket bottom and up the sides. Press in strips of newspaper, side by side, to cover the brushed area. Brush more resin onto the paper; then apply another layer of strips at right angles to the first layer.

Continue to brush on resin and apply paper strips, arranging each layer of strips at right angles to the one beneath it, until about eight layers of paper are in place. Pour any remaining resin mixture into the bottom of the basket and let it harden. Check to be sure you have a complete seal: if there's any leakage when you pour in water, let the basket dry (takes a few hours), then mix more resin and hardener and recoat the paper-covered area.

Once the basket has been waterproofed, it's ready for a house plant. Plant directly into the basket, following directions for planting in a drainless container (see above), or use the basket as a decorative container, placing plants in clay pots or other containers inside it. A layer of rocks or a drip saucer in the bottom of the basket will keep these pots from sitting in water. A more expensive solution is to place the potted plant in a container without a hole, and put the whole thing in the basket.

Gather materials *for waterproofing.*

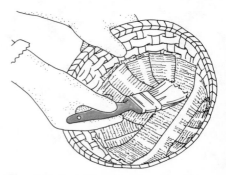

Brush polyester resin *over newspaper strips layered inside basket.*

Step-by-step planting procedure

Potting pulls it all together: your house plant, its new container, and the potting soil in which it will live.

Always plant in a clean container. Wash the container in soapy water, then rinse well to remove soap film. Old containers, especially red clay pots, may require scrubbing with a wire or stiff-bristled brush.

Soak all porous containers (such as clay pots) in water prior to planting. Dry, porous containers may draw moisture away from the newly transplanted plant. Immerse this kind of pot in water for an hour or so, then let it air-dry for a few minutes.

If you're planting in a drainless container, see the facing page for instructions.

Never put a plant in too large a pot. Its roots would have too much soil to cope with—they'd be able to extract only a little water from the overabundant soil and the soil's surplus moisture could eventually rot them. If you want to move a newly purchased plant to a different container, choose one that's the same size as the pot currently holding the plant, or only slightly larger—½ to 1 inch greater in diameter. (If the present container is wider than 10 inches, you may wish to use a somewhat larger pot—at least 2 inches wider.)

Transplanting is a messy business, so work in an easy-to-clean area. Cover the work surface with newspapers. Work quickly to minimize transplanting shock. If you're interrupted, cover the exposed root ball with a damp towel.

The basics—in six steps. With house plant, potting soil, clean container, and any other needed materials gathered together, you're ready to follow these basic steps:

1) Knock the plant out of its present container according to the instructions on page 26; be sure to keep the root ball intact (see drawing 1, below).

To free a plant from a metal nursery container, use tin snips or a can cutter (or have it cut at the nursery before you take it home). Slit the sides of the container and pull them away from the plant.

2) Place a pot shard (a curved, broken bit of an old clay pot) or stone over the container's drain hole. This prevents the soil from dribbling out of the pot whenever you water. If you use a stone, be sure it doesn't completely plug the drain hole; if you use a shard, be sure its convex curve faces upward, like a miniature bridge (see drawing 2, below). Then, using your hand or a trowel, add some potting soil.

3) Continue to add soil—enough to bring the top surface of the root ball to about ½ inch below the container rim (see drawing 3, below). Leave a little more space in larger pots.

4 & 5) Center the root ball in the container and begin filling in the sides with potting soil (see drawing 4, below). Occasionally, thump the container, gently but firmly, on your work surface to settle the soil (see drawing 5, below). Continue to add soil until the sides are level with the root ball surface. Have the point where the stem joins the root ball barely covered with soil, the stem completely exposed.

6) Smoothly "rake" the soil surface with your fingers (see drawing 6, below). Don't push down on the root ball or the plant stem; this could damage fragile hair roots.

Water the transplanted plant well.

The adjustment period. A move to a new container can be traumatic for a plant. Before moving it to its eventual location, give it a short rest to help it adjust.

Unless it's a sun-loving type, place the well-watered plant in a cool spot, away from direct sunlight, for several days. (A sun-loving plant should go immediately to its permanent, sunny location.) If it wilts, don't give more water unless the potting soil is bone-dry to at least an inch below the surface. Instead, try misting the plant to perk it up. Wait about 3 months before fertilizing (see page 21).

1) *Keep the plant's root ball intact.*

2) *Cover drain hole with a shard or stone.*

3) *Position root ball ½ inch below rim.*

4) *Fill in sides with potting soil mix.*

5) *Thump container gently to settle soil.*

6) *Smooth soil surface, then water.*

When a plant outgrows its pot

Repotting gives house plants a new lease on life—it invigorates them with fresh potting soil, increased space for roots to grow, and a foundation in better scale with expanding foliage.

Though initial transplanting (page 25) and repotting follow the same technique, the purpose differs. When you transplant a newly purchased plant, you simply shift it to the container you prefer. But repotting shifts an uncomfortably crowded plant from a potbound environment to a new and roomier one.

Symptoms of a potbound state include roots growing out of the drainage hole, foliage that looks top-heavy in proportion to the plant's pot, sluggish growth, and water that runs quickly through the potting soil, with little retention. This last symptom, less obvious than the others, requires removal of the plant from its container for a diagnosis.

To knock the plant out of its pot, hold the stem and soil surface steady with one hand and invert the pot with the other. Strike the pot rim carefully against a solid surface, such as a table top or counter; this should loosen the root ball enough for it to emerge in one clump. If the root ball refuses to budge after several thumps, run a sharp knife between the pot and root ball and invert the pot.

Examine the dislodged root ball closely. If what you see is mostly potting soil, replace the plant in its pot; it's not potbound after all. But if it shows mostly tangled roots with very little soil, it needs repotting.

Damp, brown, or mushy roots indicate a severe case of overwatering; in this case, remove all wet potting soil and repot the plant in fresh soil.

To repot your house plant, have the new pot and a supply of the correct potting soil (see page 21) ready before you start. The new container should measure ½ to 1 inch wider than the plant's present pot.

Be sure to keep the top of the old root ball near the top of the new pot, filling in around the sides with new soil. Most plants adjust poorly to having their root ball entirely buried; barely cover it with soil, and don't cover the stem at all.

After repotting, follow the directions on page 25 for giving the plant an adjustment period.

Pinch and prune for size and shape

Surroundings—the height of a ceiling, the area of a table top, the dimensions of a room—tend to dictate the size your house plants should maintain. Careful pinching and pruning is the simplest and safest way to keep many plants to the appropriate scale. Pinching encourages bushy growth; pruning reshapes a plant that's grown out of graceful proportion. Root pruning, also discussed here, can increase the indoor life of a favorite plant—though it's a somewhat drastic measure to take.

If a house plant has grown really leggy (tall and spindly, with sparse foliage), unwieldy, or misshapen, even drastic pruning probably won't do much good. It's best to simply discard such a plant.

Tools for trimming

Though the average outdoor gardener may collect a full battery of pruning tools, a house plant owner needs only a few. You don't even have to buy—and you'll never misplace—the two pruning tools most generally useful—your thumb and forefinger. These handle most pruning jobs on soft-stemmed plants. Have a sharp knife, scissors, or hand pruners for cutting tougher stems.

Pinching

Like preventive medicine, proper pinching wards off the need for more drastic pruning measures on many plants. Pinching stops growth in one direction and redirects it.

Just above a leaf or several leaves, pinch out the top growth of a stem or branch, using your thumb and forefinger. This forces the lower side buds to form new branches. The resulting growth helps create a full, well-shaped plant and keeps it from becoming leggy. Tip pinching is shown in the drawing below.

Repeat pinching as often as necessary during the plant's growing season. Be sure to pinch only stems that carry several sets of leaves; these are well established and can support new growth.

Use pinching on fast-growing, branching plants—such as Swedish ivy, wandering Jew, or *Coleus*—that readily form new growth on pinched stems. Don't pinch a plant with a single growing stem, such as a *Dracaena* or palm.

Pruning

Like pinching, top pruning restores a plant's desired shape. Removing leggy growth or branches grown awry improves the plant's appearance and, like pinching, may encourage new growth. For this job, use scissors or pruning shears if the stem is too stiff to be pinched off with thumb and forefinger.

Pinch off *growing tip just above a leaf.*

To top prune, cut stems or branches back to where you want them. Always cut stems just above a leaf bud. It's important to cut as close to the bud as possible, since that bud will become the terminal growing point on the cut stem; water and nutrients will travel no farther. Any dead or dying stem above this point becomes useless; it could even become diseased, endangering the plant.

If you decide to remove a whole branch, cut it off as close to the main stem as possible.

Root pruning

If a plant has reached the maximum size your house can accommodate, root pruning sometimes helps to slow down its expansion. This process takes courage but, if successful, permits your plant to remain in its present container. (Don't root prune plants that have fleshy roots, such as asparagus fern, *Chlorophytum*, *Dracaena,* or *Synogonium*; the procedure can harm them.)

It's best to root prune a house plant during a time of active growth, usually in the spring. Have all materials ready so the procedure can be accomplished as quickly as possible. Remove the plant from its pot. With a sharp knife, trim off portions of the root ball on all sides (never remove more than one-third of the total volume). Cut cleanly; don't saw or hack at roots.

When the root-pruned plant is replaced in its container, there should be about a 1-inch clearance on all sides. Fill in the sides with new potting soil and tamp it in; then water the plant and return it to its place. A root-pruned plant will revive more quickly if you have also top-pruned it (description is above, under "Pruning").

Propagation pointers

Propagating their own house plants is a challenge many indoor gardeners relish. New plants can be created in several ways: you can root plantlets, take stem cuttings, or divide the growing centers of large plants.

Rooting plantlets

These tiny plants appear as outgrowths or appendages above the soil on an established plant. The plantlet that forms at the base of a piggyback *(Tolmiea)* leaf (see page 91), develops on the long stems of a spider plant *(Chlorophytum,* page 45), or grows on the frond of a mother fern *(Asplenium bulbiferum,* page 56) needs only to come in contact with moist potting soil to form more extensive roots and grow into a new house plant.

The easiest method of rooting is to place the plantlet, still attached to the parent plant, in a container filled with moist potting soil. If necessary, use hair pins or a partially opened paper clip to keep the plantlet in contact with the soil. Be sure the soil stays constantly moist (like a squeezed-out sponge), but not soggy. When you notice new growth on the plantlet, sever the connection with the parent plant by cutting off the adult plant's stem close to the plantlet.

Stem cuttings

To root stem cuttings, you'll need a rooting medium. You can use perlite, vermiculite, coarse sand, a mixture of half perlite and half sand, or standard indoor potting soil with enough perlite added to make the mix lighter in texture. Whatever you choose, be sure it's sterilized (see page 21).

Cut off the top 4 inches of a stem, slicing with a sharp knife just above a leaf bud. Prepare the cutting this way: first remove lower leaves; then dip the stem into rooting hormone (available at nurseries) and insert it into the rooting medium. Keep the rooting medium moist (like a squeezed-out sponge), but not soggy. When the cutting produces new growth, you can remove it from the rooting medium (leave

enough rooting medium around the roots to cover them) and plant it in potting soil.

Divisions

With this propagation method, you create new plants by dividing the growing centers of mature plants that grow in clumps or form multiple growing centers. Each clump or crown has its own root system. An asparagus fern *(Asparagus setaceus,* page 56) or an African violet *(Saintpaulia,* pages 79–80) can be propagated this way.

All you need to do is remove the parent plant from its container, brush or wash away the potting soil around the roots, and carefully cut or pull apart the various growth centers. Then repot each separate plant.

Keep plantlet *in contact with the soil.*

Cut stem off *just above a leaf bud.*

Grooming for health

Routine grooming and inspection, whether daily or weekly, goes far to assure healthier plants. Guided by the advice given specifically for your plant in "A Catalog of House Plants" (pages 32–93), and by the pointers throughout this chapter, check that all is well. Turn the page for typical symptoms.

When you dust the furniture, don't forget the foliage on large-leafed plants nearby. Support each leaf in one hand and gently wipe it with a soft cloth. If leaves are quite dirty, wash them individually with plain water. Commercial leaf shine products are available, but be aware that they aren't for every plant; they can damage some plants by clogging their leaf pores.

Many plants (but not those with fuzzy leaves) appreciate a shower about once a month in warm weather. If you have softened water (which can harm plants) hose them gently outdoors with unsoftened water. Otherwise, give them an indoor shower.

Always remove dead leaves and branches. You can trim off brown leaf tips with scissors; try to follow the leaf's natural shape.

Wipe leaves *gently with a soft cloth.*

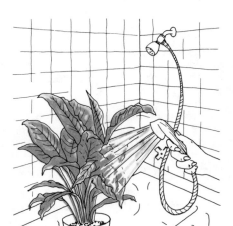

Shower plants *with tepid water.*

Trim off *brown leaf tips with scissors.*

Signs of trouble ... what to do

Most house plant problems you find will be the result of improper care. And—as with most problems —the cause is rarely a simple one. Poor indoor gardening habits, a bad growing location, or a combination of the two can cause various reactions in a plant's appearance. Treat these reactions as a call for help; left without aid, your house plant will decline rapidly, and in most cases die.

The chart below lists plant problems by the effect each problem has on a plant's appearance, offers possible causes, and suggests methods for correction. Study each plant's problem carefully; try to diagnose and treat it as quickly as possible. If you're unsure of how to correct a problem, refer to the appropriate pages in this section of the book.

Beginning on the facing page, through page 31, are plant pest and disease drawings, descriptions, and control information. Remember, if you find a sick plant in your home, isolate it from other house plants until it's cured.

Leaf tips and leaf margins turn brown	Browned tips and/or margins may result from too much or too little water; water with a high salt concentration; too much sun or heat through a window; too much fertilizer; insufficient humidity; a drafty location; or a combination of these. Study your plant's situation and try to locate the possible cause; then remedy it. If the cause isn't easily discernible, try eliminating each possibility, one at a time.
Yellowing leaves	Common causes of this problem are not enough or too much light, and too little or too much fertilizer. Yellowing leaves may also be the result of high nighttime temperatures or too much water. If you find sucking insects (probably scale or mealybugs) on the affected plant, they're another possible cause of yellowing foliage. Green color may or may not return to the damaged leaves after the problem is corrected.
Leaf drop	One factor or a combination of several can cause this. Leaves may drop as a result of overwatering or underwatering, too much sun, too much fertilizer, not enough humidity, or a drafty location. If only the lower leaves drop, your plant probably needs more light. Once leaves have fallen off because of improper care, new leaves seldom take their place. However, you can save the plant by correcting the cause of the problem.
Wilting	Plants normally wilt in reaction to too much sun or heat, too much or not enough water, or a poor growing location. Try moving the plant to a better spot and check your watering techniques. Plants that need water will perk up quickly from a drink. As long as it doesn't happen too frequently, wilting isn't detrimental to most plants.
Dry and brittle leaves	Dry, brittle leaves may indicate underwatering or insufficient humidity. Review your watering practices. Raise humidity by regular misting, or place the plant on a humidity tray (humidity trays are discussed on page 20).
Leggy growth	A lanky plant isn't getting enough light. Pinch back the leggy stems (see page 26); then remove your house plant to a location with more light.
Brown or yellow spots on leaf edges or surfaces	This symptom indicates too much water, too much direct sun, or a drafty location. Check the plant's present situation and make the needed corrections.
Failure to bloom	If a normally flowering house plant doesn't bloom, several conditions may be to blame. High nighttime temperatures during the plant's rest season and inadequate light (especially in the period of active growth) are possible causes. Try moving your plant to a spot receiving plenty of bright reflected light. During the dormant season, check the night temperature of its new location; if it's too high, find a well-lighted, cooler spot or move the plant to a cool area every evening.
Flower buds drop off	Possible causes are inadequate light or too much sun, improper watering habits, not enough fertilizer, or low room temperature (once buds appear, give your plant a few days of round-the-clock warmer temperatures). Check your plant's individual situation to pinpoint the problem.
Soft stem bases	Soft stems usually indicate rot (see facing page). Overwatering is probably the culprit. Watch your watering habits carefully.
Soggy soil	Overwatering and/or improper drainage lead to soggy soil. Knock out the root ball (see page 26) to check the drainage problem; make sure the drainage hole isn't plugged. If overwatering created the problem, try to restrain that heavy hand and water only when it's really necessary.

Recognizing and controlling pests and diseases

Indoor pests are so small—sometimes almost microscopic—that you may not even notice the little marauders until your plant takes an alarming turn for the worse. Plant diseases, on the other hand, show far more noticeable symptoms—but often attack only a few susceptible plants. A routine inspection should help you control both kinds of problems before there is much serious damage.

There are two ways to fight pests: you can simply remove them from the plant or you can use an insecticide (a less direct and not always beneficial approach).

As for disease control, it almost always requires changing the growing environment and using a fungicide or similar preparation. In some cases, however, simply changing a few care details (watering less, lowering temperature or humidity) will result in recovery. Always cut off diseased portions of the plant to reduce the chance of spread.

Pest or disease?

The following section contains information on identifying each house plant pest or disease: we describe the plant damage each problem causes and give various methods of eliminating the problem.

As a first step, use this section to identify whether the plant's problem comes from pest infestation or disease. You can easily see some pests, such as mealybugs or aphids, on the plant; others are too small to see with the naked eye, but they leave their calling cards in visible damage. Once you've identified a pest or disease problem, isolate the infected plant from other plants immediately to prevent the problem from spreading.

Use chemicals carefully

If you decide to take the direct approach to controlling pests, you can remove them by hand or wash them off under running water from a hose or faucet. Be sure to clean leaf undersides as well: many insect pests like to hide there.

The drawback to insecticides is that the cure may harm the plant as much as the pest. (This isn't necessarily true of fungicides, though.) Always follow explicitly the directions printed on the label of any chemical control. Check to make sure the insecticide or fungicide works effectively for the specific pest or disease attacking your plant; also see that it's recommended for use on house plants—and for your particular plant. When you begin to spray, be sure to keep the recommended distance between the spray canister and the plant's foliage; sprays may burn plants if applied too closely. Some delicate plants, such as ferns, are extremely sensitive to chemicals; before you use an insecticide or fungicide on these plants, check the label to be sure the product is safe for them.

Always spray plants outdoors. This ensures that any spray residue can disperse in the open air. Also, you can be sure of covering leaf surfaces, top and bottom, without having to worry about damaging nearby furnishings.

Ready-mixed spray containers of insecticide and fungicide offer the most practical option. These have been diluted to the correct extent, and are easy to apply to the affected plant.

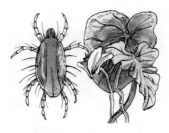

Aphids

Green, reddish, or black, aphids usually have soft, round or pear-shaped bodies. Some have wings. They tend to cluster on buds or new plant growth, where they suck plant juices; the result is poor or stunted growth, or curled, distorted leaves or flowers. Aphids secrete a substance called honeydew, which may form the base for a growth of sooty mold (see page 31).

Controls: Wash aphids off with water from a hose, or with a mixture of insecticidal soap (available at most nurseries) and water. The soap can kill aphids that hang on after hosing. Pyrethrum, rotenone, diazinon, malathion, or one of the many systemic insecticides commonly available also control aphids, but they're considerably stronger. than insecticidal soap. Read and follow label directions carefully.

Crown or stem rot

Usually brought on by poor drainage, overwatering, or both, this disease turns plants brown or makes them wilt suddenly. Often the plant's stem or trunk becomes soft and discolored near the base.

Unfortunately, most severe cases of crown or stem rot mean throwing away the plant, soil and all, and starting over. If you're really anxious to save the plant, though, you can cut out the damaged area, dust it with a fungicide, and then try to nurse the plant back to health.

Controls: If the disease isn't too advanced, try repotting the plant in a fast-draining indoor potting soil, setting it a little higher in the soil than it was before. Be sure to wash off all old soil. Corrected watering habits (see page 19) and use of a fast-draining soil mix (see page 21) will also help to prevent recurrence.

Cyclamen mites

To the naked eye, cyclamen mites look like a fine film of dust on the undersides of leaves. As their name indicates, these mites are fond of cyclamen—but they're equally likely to infest geraniums and African violets, causing stunted or deformed leaves, stems, and flower buds.

Though most types of mites cause trouble only when the air is warm and dry, cyclamen mites will attack in a highly humid environment.

Controls: Before using any control, be sure to cut off and destroy (by burning or throwing away in the trash) any obviously affected leaves. If the infestation is not severe, use a chemical control containing either dicofol (kelthane) or disulfoton (disyston). Follow label directions carefully. Severe infestations are extremely difficult to control; destroy the entire plant.

Gray mold

Easy to identify, this disease commonly preys upon such fleshy, soft-leaved plants as African violets, gloxinias, and begonias. A furry, gray mold covers parts of the leaves, stems, even flowers. Improper growing conditions are the chief cause of gray mold: check to make sure the plant's environment is not too cool or too humid. More than anything else, proper temperature, humidity, and ventilation help to keep this disease from getting out of hand.

Controls: Once a plant has been affected with gray mold, cut off all obviously diseased parts; burn them or discard in the trash. A commercial product containing benomyl (often sold as benlate) will help keep the problem from getting worse. The best control, though, is to improve growing conditions.

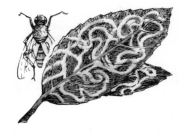

Leaf miners

These small grubs actually "mine" passages through the interior portions of leaves. Their tunnels show up as irregular white or tan squiggles on leaf surfaces. As they go their way, they suck sap, eventually destroying the leaf.

Most frequently damaged by this pest are *Chrysanthemums,* cinerarias, *Codiaeum,* and *Columnea.*

Controls: Because these pests' damage is so easy to spot, it's easy to stop the infestation early. If only a few leaves are affected, simply cut them off; then burn them or throw them away. If the infestation is more severe, spray with a systemic insecticide containing meta-systox-R or orthene. Because miners live inside leaves, you may need to spray again to be sure of control; follow label instructions.

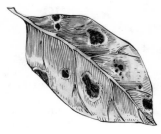

Leaf spot

Another easy-to-recognize disease, leaf spot shows up as small to large, soft, brown spots on leaves; the leaves may turn entirely brown in severe cases. *Dracaena* and *Dieffenbachia* are both highly susceptible, but other house plants, too, suffer occasional attack. Generally speaking, leaf spot results from an environment that's either too warm, too humid, or poorly ventilated.

Controls: Cut off and burn affected leaves or discard in the trash. Make certain that the affected plant has been growing in the proper environment. Spraying with a commercial product containing benomyl (often sold as benlate) will prevent the problem from becoming worse. Keep the soil and air on the dry side whenever treating leaf spot with a fungicide.

Mealybugs

Though large enough to be spotted easily, mealybugs can be hard to detect, since they normally cluster on leaf stems or in branch crotches out of the light. They have round, white, fuzzy-looking bodies. These sucking insects cause stunted or distorted growth, and eventually kill the plant. Like aphids, mealybugs secrete honeydew, which gives leaves a shiny, sticky surface and forms a base for sooty mold (see facing page).

Controls: To remove mealybugs, wash them off with water from a hose, or spray with a commercial oil spray containing refined petroleum oils (read the label carefully to be sure your plant can tolerate this). To treat delicate plants, touch the mealybugs with a cotton swab dipped in denatured alcohol (which kills them).

Powdery mildew

Probably the most common indoor plant foliage disease, mildew appears on plant leaves, stems, and flower buds as a white or gray powder. Leaves may curl or become distorted in advanced cases. Overwatering and poor air circulation are the most common causes. Begonias and other soft-leaved plants are particularly susceptible to powdery mildew.

Controls: First cut off and destroy the affected parts; then move the infected plant to a location with improved ventilation. Check your watering habits (see page 19) to be sure that you're not keeping the plant too wet. If the problem persists, spray the plant with a commercial product containing benomyl (often sold as benlate). Repeat applications as necessary. Follow label directions carefully.

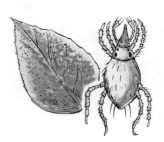

Red spider mites

A common house-plant pest, the spider mite is so small that you can detect it only in groups or by the characteristic webbing it leaves behind on plant foliage. Infected plants become stunted and may die. The mites look like tiny, moving specks of dust. Dry, warm conditions can encourage spider mite infestations.

Controls: Isolate infested plants at once; spider mites spread like wildfire. Wash plants off with water from a hose, or use a mixture of insecticidal soap (available at most nurseries) and water. For the most effective chemical control, use a product containing dicofol (kelthane). Regular misting can raise humidity and serve as an effective preventive measure. If your plant likes cool temperatures, be sure to keep it cool—this will also discourage mites.

Root rot

Chronic overwatering brings on this disease: constantly waterlogged soil invites rot-causing organisms that destroy roots. The earliest symptoms are usually yellowing leaves that wilt rapidly. Unfortunately, indoor gardeners often interpret yellow, wilted leaves as a sign that the plant is thirsty—and proceed to worsen the situation by pouring on still more water. If such drenching continues, the leaves will turn from yellow to brown and, in time, the plant will die.

When gardeners or nursery personnel talk about a plant "drowning," what they're actually referring to is root rot; the plants aren't actually drowning in the usual sense of the word. The roots, starting with the finest root hairs, start to deteriorate from the constant presence of too much moisture and not enough air. This encourages the proliferation of organisms that destroy the roots. Be sure you're using a good commercial or homemade potting soil mix (see page 21). These have a texture that drains water away quickly and allows for the excellent aeration that almost all house plants require for optimum health.

Another important precaution is to check the saucers of plants that have been recently watered. If a quantity of water has drained through to the saucer, the plant has what is commonly referred to as "wet feet"—a condition that will lead to root rot. Be sure to remove excess water in saucers after watering.

Controls: The best preventive measure is to use a fast-draining indoor potting soil; make sure the drain hole in the pot is never blocked (see page 25). And, obviously, it's important not to overwater (see guidelines on page 19). Once a plant has been affected by root rot, recovery is difficult. Following directions on page 26, remove the plant from its pot; black or brown, slimy roots are rotten. If you see that only a portion of the roots has rotted, rinse the soil from the roots, then cut off the rotten roots (to a maximum of half of the total root ball) and repot the plant in fresh potting soil. For the next few weeks, following label directions for "soil drench," water the soil with a mixture of benomyl (often sold as benlate) and keep your fingers crossed. This rather drastic cure does not always succeed.

Scale

These hard-shelled, sucking insects are brown or gray, with round or oval bodies. Some types attack leaves, others attack stems; all secrete honeydew, giving leaves a shiny, sticky surface where sooty mold (described at right) can grow. Because they closely resemble spores, scale insects may be difficult to detect on fern fronds.

Controls: Carefully scrape off insects with your fingernail or a small knife; or wash plants with a mixture of insecticidal soap (available at most nurseries) and water. Especially to treat delicate plants such as ferns, touch insects with a cotton swab dipped in denatured alcohol—deadly to scale. Commercial oil sprays containing refined petroleum oils are the standard cure—but not all house plants can tolerate them. Follow label instructions.

Thrips

So small and scurrying that you rarely see them, thrips have slender bodies of tan, brown, or black, with paler markings. If you shake an infested plant, you'll notice the insects flying or leaping in the air. Thrips feed on foliage and flowers, causing distorted growth of the plant tissue; leaves and blossoms look twisted, puckered, or stuck together. Sometimes you can see the damage from their rasping mouths as scraped edges on the stems or leaf edges of an infested plant.

Controls: Wash thrips off with water from a hose. If the infestation is serious enough, use a commercial product containing meta-systox-R or malathion. The life cycle of thrips seldom exceeds 20 days, so a good program is to spray twice, 10 days apart.

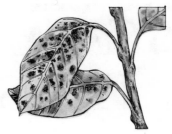

Sooty mold

Sooty mold is encouraged by insects such as aphids, mealybugs, scale, and whiteflies. These insects secrete a sticky substance known as honeydew; in heavy infestations, there's enough honeydew to serve as a breeding ground for sooty mold. As its name suggests, the mold looks like soot coating the upper surfaces of leaves.

Though more unsightly than dangerous, sooty mold should not be ignored. Eventually, it can kill the leaves it covers, and then the plant.

Controls: The first priority is to control the insects that produce the mold-inviting honeydew; identify them, then deal with them as directed in this section. Wipe mold off leaves with a soft, damp cloth. If the disease appeared only recently, leaves should survive unharmed.

Whiteflies

Both indoors and out, these are common pests. Very small, with white bodies and wings, they flutter about in a white cloud over an infested plant when they are disturbed. The young attach themselves to the undersides of leaves. Infested leaves turn a pale color; their surface is covered with a shiny, sticky layer of honeydew, which can form a base for sooty mold (see the description above).

Controls: Wash minor infestations off plants with water from a hose, or wash plant with a mixture of insecticidal soap (available at most nurseries) and water. For serious infestations, use diazinon, resmethrin, or malathion. Be aware, though, that persistence is necessary for control: you'll need to spray every 4 to 6 days for about a month.

A CATALOG OF HOUSE PLANTS

In this chapter, we invite you to explore the rich, diverse world of house plants. You'll find alphabetical listings for 92 genera (major plant groups), along with 428 varieties within these groups. We offer a full description of each plant and give specific tips on each one's individual growing needs. Accompanying color photographs show one or more favorite examples from each plant group. For a group with lots of variety, we've shown several plants for easy comparison. From the photographs, you can get an accurate idea of plant shape, relative size, and foliage and flower color.

Because common names sometimes differ from region to region, or even from one nursery to the next, plant groups are listed here according to botanical name. If you're familiar only with a plant's common name, look it up in the index (pages 110–112), which will direct you to the correct listing in this chapter.

For several widely grown favorites, we broke the botanical-name rule: bromeliads, cactuses, ferns, orchids, palms, and succulents all appear under these universally accepted common names.

You may notice that a number of popular decorative plants (chrysanthemums and poinsettias, for example) are missing from this chapter. Though these plants make charming house guests, we do not consider them true house plants. If a plant thrives indoors only temporarily, and must then return outside, we list it under "Indoor-Outdoor & Gift Plants," pages 94–99.

You'll probably use this section of the book in two ways: to identify a plant you already own (to learn its care requirements, as well as its name), and to narrow down your shopping list before you buy new plants. It makes little sense to purchase a plant that will quickly grow out of its apartment corner, or one that requires more careful tending than you have time to give it. Use the section in the back of this book—"Which Plant Suits You Best?" (pages 100–109)—to help you narrow your plant choices before reading the more detailed information in this section.

If you need background on the basics of caring for any house plant, review the information under "Green Thumb Know-how," pages 16–31. In the catalog section, we've concentrated on the specific requirements of each particular plant.

Abutilon

(uh-BYOO-ti-lahn)

Chinese bellflower, Chinese lantern, Flowering maple, Parlor maple

Several generations ago, *Abutilon* appeared alongside *Aspidistra* and Boston ferns in countless Victorian parlors. Its popularity as a house plant waned, but it has made a comeback in recent years—both as a shade-loving outdoor plant and as a handsome house plant, content to live indoors all year, provided the right conditions are met.

Abutilon fully deserves its return to popularity. With maplelike leaves and a multitude of flowers shaped like small hollyhocks, it can look absolutely stunning. In the right setting, the plant gives an almost Oriental impression.

Fast-growing *Abutilon* needs fairly constant pinching, pruning, and grooming to look its best.

Growing requirements

Abutilon requires a standard indoor potting soil, average humidity, and average room temperature (65° to 70°F/ 18° to 21°C). It should bask in at least 4 hours of direct sunlight daily; potting soil should be kept moist during the active growing season—from spring to early autumn. As winter approaches, *Abutilon* appreciates cooler temperatures (around 60°F/16°C) in a bright location. Except in autumn and winter, apply a liquid fertilizer diluted to half strength (see page 21) every 2 weeks. Withhold fertilizer during the autumn-through-winter rest period; also reduce water, allowing the soil to dry out almost completely between waterings.

Abutilon is a vigorous, fast-growing plant; to produce a bushy plant, you'll need to pinch off the tips of the growing branches frequently. Pinch heavily in autumn for better late winter and early spring bloom.

Yellowing leaves are to be expected: just remove them as they appear. Scale, red spider mites, mealybugs, and whiteflies occasionally present a problem—see pages 29–31 for methods of control.

Favorites

Abutilon hybridum comprises a group of hybrids and many named varieties. The trunks of many of these will reach 8 to 10 feet, with arching branches spreading just as far; however, frequent pinching and pruning produces much smaller and more compact plants. Besides the characteristic maplelike leaves, plants in this group put forth drooping, bell-like flowers of widely assorted colors and combinations, including yellow, white, pink, and red. The main blooming season lasts from April to June, though the white and yellow types seem to bloom almost continuously.

Abutilon megapotamicum grows vigorously from arching stems. Less upright than other types, *A. megapotamicum* is frequently treated as a trailing plant; its red and yellow flowers resemble hanging lanterns. A favorite for hanging containers, it needs frequent grooming to keep its rangy growth from looking untidy. *A.m.* 'Marianne' has superior form; *A.m.* 'Variegata' has leaves mottled with yellow.

Abutilon pictum 'Thompsonii' is similar to *Abutilon hybridum,* but the foliage is strikingly variegated with creamy yellow. The pale orange, bell-shaped flowers of *A.p.* 'Thompsonii' are veined with red.

Abutilon hybridum

Abutilon pictum 'Thompsonii'

Aeschynanthus

(es-kuh-NAN-thus)

Climbing beauty, Lipstick plant, Pipe plant, Zebra basket vine

Long drooping or trailing stems, shiny leaves, and dramatic tubular flowers characterize this broad group of plants. The main blooming season begins in summer, but flowers may appear sporadically throughout the year.

Aeschynanthus looks its best in hanging baskets or set atop a pedestal.

Growing requirements

As a group of epiphytes (see page 66), *Aeschynanthus* requires a lightweight indoor potting soil (the kind sold for African violets is good) and conditions similar to its natural jungle habitat—bright, reflected light (not direct sun), high humidity, and moist soil during the spring and summer growing season. As long as the humidity is kept high, *Aeschynanthus* will be healthy in an average-temperature room. During late autumn and winter, reduce water and, if possible, move *Aeschynanthus* to a cooler (60°F/ 16°C) location.

During the growing season, apply an acid fertilizer monthly (see page 21). Keep humidity high by frequent misting—or grow in a naturally humid room, such as the kitchen or bathroom.

Generally speaking, these are carefree plants—but don't forget to keep the soil moist, particularly during the blooming season. After flowering, prune stems back by about one-third to encourage new growth and a fuller appearance. Aphids sometimes attack new growth; see page 29 for methods of control.

Favorites

Aeschynanthus marmoratus, commonly known as the zebra basket vine, has green foliage mottled with maroon. Its yellowish green flowers are less showy than the blooms of other types, but its foliage is unusual.

Aeschynanthus micranthus, a compact plant with very thick foliage, has many small, narrow red flowers.

Aeschynanthus radicans is called lipstick plant because of the way its flowers emerge from their calyxes—like lipsticks from cases. Drooping stems and 2-inch-long tubular flowers distinguish it.

Aeschynanthus speciosus has a growth habit similar to that of other types, but bears yellow-and-orange flowers up to 4 inches long.

Aeschynanthus micranthus

Aglaonema

(ag-lay-o-NEE-muh)

**Chinese evergreen,
Painted drop tongue**

Both its toughness and its attractive foliage account for *Aglaonema's* perennial popularity. Its graceful, oblong leaves grow from a central stem; depending on the type, leaves may be solid medium green or splotched with various shades of gray and green. The flowers resemble small, greenish callas.

Somewhat slow-growing, *Aglaonema* eventually reaches a height of 2 to 3 feet. True to its tropical origin (and like most house plants), *Aglaonema* prefers good light and high humidity, but performs admirably even when both are low. When placed in a vase of plain water, cuttings taken from the mother plant will root; you can plant the cuttings or leave them in the vase for a long period.

Growing requirements

Aglaonema likes a standard indoor potting soil, warm temperatures, bright, reflected light, and frequent waterings. Though it can adapt to situations with both low light and low moisture, it responds well to increased humidity, such as that provided by a humidity tray (see page 20). Except in winter, apply a complete fertilizer regularly (see page 21).

For good health and best appearance, wipe the leaves frequently with a damp cloth.

Aglaonema will accept potbound conditions for long periods. Saplike exudation from leaf tips, especially in *Aglaonema modestum,* will spot wood finishes, so watch where you place pots.

These plants are occasionally bothered by aphids, mealybugs, red spider mites, scale, and thrips; see pages 29–31 for methods of control.

Favorites

Aglaonema commutatum, the most popular species, includes several named varieties. The glossy leaves are about 8 inches long and splashed with pale green, gray, or yellowish green markings. *A.c.* 'White Rajah' has white markings. *A.c.* 'Treubii' has bluish green leaves marked with silver splotches. It is about 10 inches tall.

Aglaonema crispum, painted drop tongue, has leaves approximately 12 inches long, patterned with variegated gray and green. *A.c.* 'Silver Queen', a popular named variety, has gray green leaves daubed with silver.

Aglaonema modestum, its solid medium green leaves (no markings) extending about 8 inches long and 3 to 4 inches wide, is the old-fashioned Chinese evergreen.

Aglaonema commutatum

Alloplectus nummularia

Alloplectus

(a-lo-PLEK-tus)

Miniature pouch flower

Like *Nematanthus* (page 65), *Alloplectus* is often sold by the name *Hypocyrta.* This relative of the African violet produces bright red or yellow flowers resembling little pouches with pinched tops. Its delicate long-stemmed leaves, olive or dull green, have a velvety texture.

Alloplectus flowers in summer or autumn; afterwards, it may enter a dormant period. During this time, the plant sheds its leaves, but new leaves quickly appear, usually in autumn.

Both upright and trailing forms of *Alloplectus* are available; trailing types look best in a hanging basket that shows off their draping form and colorful bloom.

Growing requirements

Alloplectus prefers warm temperatures (70° to 75°F/21° to 24°C) and high humidity. Boost humidity by placing the pot on a humidity tray (see page 20). Don't mist this plant—if you do, its leaves will spot. Given sufficient warmth and humidity, *Alloplectus* may produce flowers several times during the year.

Alloplectus likes bright filtered (as through a sheer curtain) or reflected light; it also responds well to a couple of hours each day of direct, but relatively cool, morning sun. Except in late autumn and winter, apply a complete fertilizer regularly (see page 21). *Alloplectus* needs the type of potting soil specially prepared for African violets. Water your plant with tepid water only, keeping the soil moist (like a squeezed-out sponge), but not soggy.

Alloplectus blooms best when slightly potbound. Occasionally, mealybugs, red spider mites, scale, and whiteflies cause trouble; see pages 29–31 for methods of control.

Favorites

Alloplectus capitatus sends up erect stems, 2 to 3 feet high. Stems have reddish hairs; olive green leaves are 6 to 8 inches long, coated on their undersides with the same reddish hairs. Yellow flowers with bright red calyxes appear in autumn.

Alloplectus nummularia, a commonly available form, has velvety, dull green leaves and—usually in summer—bright red flowers. Show it off in a hanging basket.

Aspidistra

(as-pi-DIS-truh)

Cast-iron plant

As its common name implies, cast-iron plant is strong—one of the sturdiest and most carefree of all house plants, though somewhat slow-growing.

Its tough leaves, glossy and dark green, 1 to 2½ feet long and 3 to 4 inches wide, arch elegantly; the leaves are pointed at the tips.

Cast-iron plants aren't always classed as house plants. If you don't see them among the house plants at the nursery, look among outdoor shade-loving plants.

Growing requirements

Though very tolerant of a wide range of conditions, *Aspidistra* prefers high humidity, cool temperatures, and a standard, porous potting soil. It's one of the best choices for low-light locations, but keep it away from direct sunlight. Keep it evenly moist; except in autumn and winter, apply a complete fertilizer regularly (see page 21). Allow it to dry out somewhat during the autumn and winter rest period.

Large, smooth leaves attract dust in a hurry—keep them clean with a soft, damp cloth. Don't use commercial leaf shine products. Brown or burned tips usually result from too much water or fertilizer, particularly during autumn and winter. This plant is remarkably free of pests and diseases, and quite long-lived.

Favorites

Aspidistra elatior 'Variegata' has leaves striped with cream, but loses its variegation if planted in too-rich soil.

Aspidistra minor is a dwarf form with white-spotted dark green leaves.

Aspidistra elatior (cast-iron plant)

Begonia

(buh-GO-nyuh)

Begonia is a huge and diverse group; its many members are prized for their textured, multicolored foliage and attractive flowers.

General growing requirements

Begonias will thrive in standard indoor potting soil if you add a little extra peat moss to increase the acidity. Keep the soil moist (like a squeezed-out sponge), but not soggy. When water collects in the saucer beneath the pot, pour it off promptly.

Begonias like temperatures in the 65° to 75°F/18° to 24°C range and above-average humidity; boost humidity by placing the pots on a humidity tray (see page 20). Give them bright filtered (as through a sheer curtain) or reflected light. Throughout the year, apply a complete fertilizer regularly (see page 21).

Though begonias don't suffer from pest problems, they are prone to mildew or gray mold if conditions become too damp or if air circulation is insufficient. See pages 29–31.

(Continued on next page)

Begonia hiemalis 'Toran Orange' (hiemalis begonia)

Begonia rex-cultorum (rex begonia)

Begonia masoniana (iron cross begonia)

Favorite begonias and their special needs

Of many hundreds of species and varieties, relatively few are sold widely. In the chart on the opposite page, you'll find a sampling of the most popular and widely available types of *Begonia*. These are also described below, along with a few that are less commonly available.

Such a large group of diverse plants obviously needs some type of internal categories. The American Begonia Society groups these plants according to growth habit; coincidentally, a begonia's growth habit also determines its care requirements. The following descriptions employ a version of the society's classifications.

Cane-type begonias. These plants owe their name to their stems, which grow tall and woody, with prominent bamboolike joints. The group includes begonias once classified as "angel-wing"—those with paired leaves resembling extended wings. Erect on multiple stems, these plants sometimes reach 5 feet or more. Most cane-type begonias bloom profusely, offering large clusters of white, pink, orange, or red flowers. The usual blooming season is early spring through autumn, though some types bloom virtually all year round. In early spring, before flowering, prune old canes which have no leaves down to two leaf joints to stimulate new growth.

Begonia 'Irene Nuss' (often sold as 'Irene Ness') has large, dark green leaves; drooping clusters of fragrant coral pink flowers bloom from April to December.

Begonia 'Lucerna' (often sold as *B.* 'Corallina de Lucerna' or *B.* 'Lucerne') is a tall, easy-to-grow plant producing rose red flowers in spring and summer. Its green leaves have sil-ver-spotted top surfaces; undersides are reddish. *B.* 'Lucerna' likes strong light (no direct, hot sun). After flowering, prune the plant way back.

Begonia 'Sophie Cecile' bears profuse clusters of rose pink flowers in spring and summer. Large, deeply cut, glossy green leaves are splashed with silver.

Begonia 'Orange Rubra' grows to 4 feet tall; it has silver-dotted green leaves and clusters of orange flowers.

Hiemalis begonias. Nurseries sell some of this group by the names "Rieger" or "Elatior Rieger" begonias. The flowers average about 2 inches across and appear over a long season, including winter. When a healthy, mature plant is in bloom, its green leaves and stems are all but invisible under a blanket of blossoms. In the cool winter months, give these bushy, compact plants plenty of direct light. In summer, though, they'll need indirect light; protect them from direct, hot sun. Let the top inch of the soil dry out between waterings—but each time you water, soak the soil thoroughly. (Be careful not to sprinkle leaves with water; this plant is especially prone to mildew.) If your plant gets rangy, cut its stems back to 4-inch stubs. Many named varieties are available.

Rex begonias. Bold, multicolored leaves make *Begonia rex-cultorum*, often called rex begonia, probably the most striking of all foliage begonias. Leaves grow from a rhizome (see Rhizomatous begonias for basic care). Rex begonias need high humidity (approximately 50 percent); place the pot on a humidity tray (see page 20) or mist your plant frequently.

Begonia rex-cultorum 'Helen Teupel' has bronze-red and silver-green leaves; foliage is much showier than the light pink flowers.

Begonia rex-cultorum 'Merry Christmas' has green and rose red leaves with silver highlights. This type is widely sold, but it can be finicky about water and humidity levels.

Rhizomatous begonias. Like rex begonias, these plants grow from a rhizome and are valued primarily for their beautiful foliage (though some have attractive flowers). This group includes the so-called "star" begonias, named for their leaf shape. These begonias perform well as house plants; water only when top inch of soil is dry. Because these begonias have shallow roots, it's best to plant them in wide, shallow pots. Flowering forms bloom from winter through summer, the season varying among specific types. Flowers appear in clusters on erect stems above the foliage. The plant's rhizomes will grow over the edge of the pot, so that the plant eventually becomes bell shaped. If you prefer, cut rhizomes back.

Begonia bowerae has tiny, deep green leaves with black "stitching" on the edges. Shell pink flowers bloom profusely from January through March.

Begonia 'Cleopatra' is a popular, easy-to-grow "star" begonia. Its star-shaped leaves have brown markings and chartreuse veins; undersides of leaves are reddish. Pink flowers bloom from winter through early spring.

Begonia erythrophylla, commonly called the beefsteak begonia, is a widely grown plant. It has roundish leaves, dark green on top and deep red on the underside; clustered flowers are pink. The variety *B.e.* 'Helix' has spiraled leaves; *B.e.* 'Bunchii' has lettucelike frills and ruffles on leaf edges.

Begonia 'Freddie' is an old favorite house plant. Its large leaves are coppery green on top, red beneath. Tall sprays of pink flowers appear all year round.

Begonia 'Joe Hayden' has small, satiny dark green leaves with red undersides. Red flowers bloom in winter.

Begonia masoniana, commonly called the iron cross begonia, gets its nickname from the appearance of its leaves. Large, puckered, and yellow green, they're marked with a chocolate brown pattern resembling the Maltese cross. This plant's flowers are insignificant.

Semperflorens begonias. These begonias used to be called bedding or wax begonias, and are often used outdoors. Indoors, they produce small flowers continuously from spring through early autumn, in shades of red, pink, and white. Plants are bushy, about 8 to 15 inches tall, with green, red, bronze, or variegated foliage.

Shrublike begonias. This large group of begonias is characterized by multiple stems that are soft and green, rather than bamboolike as in the cane-type group. Popular for both foliage and flowers, shrublike begonias have interesting leaves: some are heavily textured, others grow white or red "hairs," and still others develop a soft, feltlike coating. Though most grow upright and bushy (some as tall as 8 feet), others are less erect and make suitable hanging basket choices. Flowers appear in shades of pink, red, white, and peach, and can come at any time of year, depending on kind. In early spring, prune branches halfway back to produce a fuller plant.

Begonia foliosa has inch-long leaves growing thickly on twiggy branches, giving the plant an almost fernlike look. Stems, up to 3 feet long, arch or droop; flowers are small, white to red in color.

Begonia 'Medora' is an old favorite. Borne on long stems, its small green leaves have wavy edges and silver spots. Pink flowers appear from spring through autumn.

Begonia 'Richmondensis' grows to more than 2 feet in height. Its arching stems put forth shiny, crisp leaves, deep green with red undersides. Salmon pink flowers open from buds that are darker pink, almost red. A big and sturdy plant, *B.* 'Richmondensis' is a good choice for narrow spaces with limited light.

Trailing or climbing begonias. Depending on how you train these plants, their stems will trail or climb; they're best suited to hanging baskets. These begonias are rather hard to find; you'll probably need to order from a specialist.

Begonia 'Ellen Dee' has green foliage and orange flowers.

Begonia solananthera has glossy, light green leaves and fragrant flowers with red centers.

Semperflorens begonias

Elatior begonias

Rhizomatous begonias

Botanical name / Common name	Classification	Flowers	Comments
Begonia erythrophylla / Beefsteak begonia	Rhizomatous begonia	Single; pink; held above leaves on long stems. Blooms late winter to summer.	Easy-to-grow rhizomatous begonia with thick, succulent, 2 to 3-inch leaves that are dark green on top, deep red on bottom.
Begonia foliosa / Fern-leaf begonia	Shrublike begonia	Single; white to red; very small. Blooms in early summer or in autumn and winter.	Diminutive, closely set leaves give plant a fernlike look. Soft stems, to 3 feet long, arch or droop.
B.f. miniata / Hedge begonia	Shrublike begonia	Single; pink or red in drooping clusters. Blooms in early summer or in autumn and winter.	Shrubby, erect stems, arching at tips, reach 2 to 5 feet. Leaves are small, shiny, dark green. Hedge plant in native Mexico.
Begonia hiemalis 'Aphrodite' / Elatior begonia	Hiemalis begonia	Double; red, rose, or pink. Blooms in winter.	Plants sprawling.
B.h. 'Bernstein' s Gelbe' / Elatior begonia	Hiemalis begonia	Single; yellow. Blooms in winter.	Plants shrubby; profuse flowers.
B.h. 'Fireglow' / Elatior begonia	Hiemalis begonia	Single; orange. Blooms in winter.	Plants upright; profuse flowers.
B.h. 'Schwabenland' / Elatior begonia	Hiemalis begonia	Single; red, red orange, or pink. Blooms in winter.	Plants upright to about 1½ feet; glossy green leaves.
Begonia 'Lucerna' / Angel-wing begonia, Lucerna begonia	Cane-type begonia	Single; rose red in large clusters. Blooms in spring and summer.	Unusually tall and robust angel wing. Silver-spotted leaves are red underneath. Likes strong (but never hot) light. After flowering period, stake up main cane and pinch back side shoots for tall plant; for bushy plant, pinch back terminal shoots.
Begonia rex-cultorum / Rex begonia	Rex begonia	Insignificant.	Many named varieties with brilliantly colored, shieldlike leaves—maroon, lilac, rose, light or dark green, silver gray, and combinations of each.
Begonia 'Richmondensis'	Shrublike begonia	Salmon pink; buds are darker pink, almost red. Blooms in winter.	Arching stems to 2 feet or more. Leaves deep green above, red beneath. Excellent in hanging basket, indoors or out. Filtered shade is usually best, but if temperatures are cool, give strong light (for brightest leaf color).
Begonia semperflorens-cultorum / Bedding begonia, wax begonia	Semperflorens begonia	Single or double; white, red, rose, or pink. Blooms spring to early autumn.	Popular bedding and container plant. Leaves bright green to red. Many varieties: Dwarf (4 to 6 inches), intermediate (8 to 10 inches), and tall (12 to 18 inches). F_1 hybrid strains have a more uniform growth habit and are more sun resistant. Large-flowered (to 3 inches) strains named 'Butterfly', 'Cinderella', and 'Glamour'.

Bromeliads

(bro-MEL-ee-adz)

Appreciated for their diversity and rare beauty, bromeliads have gained increasing popularity with indoor gardeners. Native to the American tropics, this very large family includes the pineapple (page 109).

Most bromeliads are stemless perennial plants, growing distinctive clusters or rosettes of long, pointed leaves, sometimes handsomely marked. Flowers vary, but most are dramatically showy and colorful, borne on some type of spike. Often the bracts—modified leaves below the flower—are vividly colored. Most bromeliads take several years to bloom; after blooming, they slowly die, to be replaced by the smaller plants ("pups") that sprout from the sides of the "mother" plant's stems.

Nearly all bromeliads grown as house plants are epiphytes (see page 66).

Bromeliad enthusiasts often wire these plants to a section of tree branch, packing sphagnum moss around the roots; you can even create a bromeliad "tree" by growing several different types of bromeliad on one branch. Other indoor gardeners prefer to grow these plants in pots.

Growing requirements

Long-lived and sturdy, most bromeliads take well to indoor conditions.

Soil. If you choose to grow a potted bromeliad, be sure to use a very porous fast-draining, highly organic soil mix. Some nurseries and garden centers offer a packaged mix especially for epiphytic plants, but you can also make your own: combine three parts peat moss with one part perlite or vermiculite and one part bark chips.

Water. Some bromeliads have unique cavities or "cups" at the bases of their leaves; be sure these cups are always filled with water. Hard water causes unsightly spots on leaves, so use rain water or bottled distilled water (free of minerals). Drain off and replace the water every 4 to 6 weeks. You'll also need to water the soil; allow the top inch or so to dry out between waterings.

Temperature and humidity. Bromeliads prefer average to warm house temperatures (65° to 75°F/18° to 24°C); sensitive types will suffer damage at temperatures below 55°F/13°C. The higher the temperature, the higher the relative humidity should be. You can increase humidity by growing your bromeliads on a humidity tray (see page 20), or by frequent misting (as often as twice a day when warm).

Light. Different bromeliads need different amounts of light. In general, a bromeliad prefers light shade or filtered sunlight (as through a sheer curtain); it dislikes direct sun. These conditions are especially important for bromeliads with thin (usually green) leaves; those with hard, spiny, thick leaves and those with gray or silvery leaves can tolerate brighter light.

Fertilizer. Because bromeliads grow slowly, too much fertilizer can harm them. In spring and summer only, apply a water-soluble complete fertilizer (see page 21), diluted to half strength, once a month. Apply fertilizer to the soil only; never pour it into leaf "cups."

Pests and diseases. As a whole, bromeliads are less susceptible to pest attack than many plants. Scale presents the most common problem, but mealybugs and root mealybugs sometimes cause trouble, too. Overwatering can cause fungus diseases. See pages 29–31 for methods of control.

Trimming. To keep your plant healthy, remove all yellowing and brown leaves: cut them off, or remove by splitting them lengthwise with your finger, then gently pulling each half sideways.

Favorites

The following list describes the nine most commonly available types.

Aechmea *(eek-MEE-uh)*. These bromeliads' leaves form cups for water.

Aechmea chantinii sends up olive to brownish green leaves barred with silver. The flower cluster has yellow blooms; orange, red, or pink bracts are tipped with yellow and white.

Aechmea fasciata, the urn plant, has powdery-surfaced green leaves banded in blue. Its flower cluster is blue at first, changing to deep rose.

Aechmea fulgens discolor puts forth green leaves backed with purple. Its red flowers, tipped with blue, are followed by red berries.

Billbergia *(bil-BUR-gee-uh)*. These unusual-looking bromeliads are sometimes called vase plants. Most forms are nearly stemless, with interestingly patterned, slightly arching leaves. Showy bracts and tubular flowers appear in drooping clusters. *Billbergia* 'Muriel Waterman' has plum colored leaves banded with gray. Its small blue flowers top pink bracts.

Cryptanthus *(krip-TAN-thus)*. These are very low-growing, almost flat bromeliads; their unusual shape has earned them the name earth stars.

Cryptanthus acaulis produces green, wavy-edged leaves about 6 inches long. *C.a.* 'It' has green leaves, their edges striped with rosy pink. *C.a.* 'Pink Starlite', another named variety, resembles *C.a.* 'It'.

Cryptanthus zonatus, native to Brazil, has dark brownish red leaves that are wavy edged, banded crosswise with green, brown, or white; they form low-growing rosettes up to 1½ feet across.

Dyckia *(dy-KEE-uh)*. This group is native to tropical America.

Dyckia fosterana is the most commonly available kind; its leaf color is silvery gray or (occasionally) reddish brown. Borne in a rosette, the leaves have spike-toothed edges and thorny tips. Orange flowers bloom atop tall, slender stems.

Guzmania *(guz-MAY-nee-uh)*. These smooth-leafed bromeliads have attractive flowers.

Guzmania lingulata, the most common form, produces a rosette of smooth, metallic green leaves centered with red bracts. The inner bracts, much showier than the flowers, are orange red, tipped white or yellow.

Guzmania 'Orangeade' produces a rosette of arching medium green leaves. Its torchlike orange bract contains small yellow flowers.

Neoregelia *(nee-o-ruh-GEE-lee-uh)*. This is a large group of epiphytic bromeliads. 'Oh No' is one of numerous hybrids that show many variations

in size and color. Most have toothedged, smooth-surfaced leaves arranged in a rosette.

Neoregelia carolinae 'Tricolor' produces green and white striped leaves and blue flowers.

Neoregelia spectabilis, commonly called fingernail plant, puts forth pale green leaves with red tips. Blue flowers appear in summer.

Nidularium *(ni-dyoo-la-REE-um)*. Sometimes called bird's nest plants.

Nidularium innocentii's straplike olive green leaves, produced in the typical rosette, have spiny edges. In the center of the plant, brilliant red, bractlike leaves form a smaller rosette—like a nest. White flowers rise out of the "nest" in a dense cluster.

Nidularium scheremetiewii has light green, 10 to 12-inch leaves; short spines grow on their edges. Blue flowers appear atop short-stalked red bracts.

Tillandsia *(ti-LAND-zee-uh)*. This bromeliad group, commonly called air plants, has relatively drab leaves and highly unusual flowers.

Tillandsia ionantha is a dwarf plant. Its 2½-inch green leaves, tinged with pinkish red, conceal violet flowers.

Tillandsia lindenii's thin, smooth leaves grow in the typical rosette. Its large flower spike has crimson bracts overlapping dense, flattened clusters of small bluish purple flowers.

Vriesea *(VREE-zee-uh)*. These bromeliads have smooth strap-shaped leaves growing in a rosette. They produce feathery plumes of flowers.

Vriesea carinata, commonly called lobster's claws, has 8-inch-long yellowish green leaves, and produces red and yellow curved, clawlike flowers.

Vriesea hieroglyphica has 1½-foot green leaves with brownish green, patterned crossbands. Its flowers are yellowish tan.

Vriesea splendens produces 16-inch-long green leaves with brownish green crossbands. A red bract encases yellow flowers. *V.s.* 'Major', commonly called flaming sword, produces dark green leaves banded with deep reddish purple on their undersides, paler purple on top. Red bracts enclose yellowish white flowers.

Billbergia 'Muriel Waterman'

Neoregelia 'Oh No'

Vriesea carinata
(lobster claws)

Tillandsia ionantha

Nidularium scheremetiewii

Aechmea fasciata
(urn plant)

Cryptanthus acaulis 'It'
(earth star)

Dyckia fosterana

Guzmania 'Orangeade'

Vriesea hieroglyphica

A CATALOG OF HOUSE PLANTS **39**

Cactuses

With rare exceptions, every cactus is a succulent—but not every succulent is a cactus. Cactuses, unlike other succulents, possess structures called "areoles."

Areoles are well-defined areas on the plant's surface from which little tufts of spines, bristles, or hairs sprout; cactus flowers always bloom from the areoles, as well.

Unlike most plants, cactuses don't have branches and leaves. What looks like a cactus branch is called a "joint"; it may grow out of the central stem or directly from the ground. In some cases—Christmas cactus, for example—joints are linked together into a stem and look much like leaves.

General growing requirements

Cactuses are not difficult to grow; they have just a few simple requirements.

Soil and containers. Almost all house plant cactuses are native to the desert, and all desert cactuses must have fast-draining soil to protect them from risk of rot diseases. To prepare a typical fast-draining soil mix, combine two parts sand or fine gravel with one part peat-moss-based soil mix (available at nurseries) and one part leaf mold. For a richer soil, increase the proportion of peat-moss-based mix.

Both clay and plastic pots contain a desert cactus comfortably. But since plastic pots retain moisture longer than clay pots, cactuses in plastic containers will need less watering. Be sure the soil is dry to a depth of ½ inch before watering a cactus in a plastic pot.

Repotting. Each year, in early spring, check to see if your cactus needs repotting. Look through the pot's drain hole to examine the cactus roots; if they have begun to poke out, repot the plant in a slightly larger container.

To remove a cactus from its pot, hold the plant carefully; then turn the pot upside down and gently tap the bottom until the root ball slides out. Occasionally, you'll need to get things started by pressing through the drain hole with a pencil or your finger. If you're handling a spiny cactus, protect yourself from its thorns by using tongs, heavy gloves, or a folded towel or newspaper.

Water. Cactuses need the most water during spring and summer, their period of active growth. When you water them, give them an ample drink—but be sure to let the soil dry out almost completely between waterings. During autumn and winter, water only enough to prevent the soil from drying out completely. In winter, it's also important to water early in the morning, so any surplus moisture will evaporate before nightfall.

Temperature. During the summer, most desert cactuses will stay healthy no matter how hot it gets in your house; in an unventilated greenhouse, though, temperatures could climb too high for their comfort. In winter, most cactuses will need a rest at cooler temperatures. To keep your plant healthy, let it spend the winter in an unheated room where the temperature stays in the 40° to 45°F/5° to 7°C range (ideal winter temperature for a desert cactus is about 45°F). If a cactus is kept too warm in winter, it will keep growing—but it will probably look sickly.

Light. Since strong light is essential for both growth and flowering, keep your cactus in the sunniest window in your house; let it sit outside when temperatures are warm. If your cactus remains on the window sill all year, be sure to rotate the pot every so often for even growth.

Fertilizer. During spring and summer, the time of active growth, apply a liquid fertilizer (see page 21), diluted from one-quarter to one-half strength, monthly.

Pests and diseases. Though rarely bothered by pests, cactuses occasionally become prey to aphids, mealybugs, red spider mites, scale, thrips, and certain kinds of fungus. See pages 29–31 for methods of control.

Favorite cactuses and their special needs

Most of the following cactus favorites have just a few special growing requirements—they're not terribly demanding. We list a number of flowering types here; with a few exceptions (*Schlumbergera,* for example), you can expect to see blossoms in spring or summer.

Aporocactus (*a-POR-oh-kak-tus*). These abundantly blooming, long-stemmed plants, with the unfortunate common name of rat-tail cactus, look lovely in a hanging basket. Their stems cascade to 3 feet or more. Each stem shows eight to 12 ribs, each completely covered with tiny, reddish brown spines. A popular one is *A. flagelliformis,* with funnel-shaped hot pink flowers in spring. Plant will accept either full or filtered light (as through a sheer curtain).

Astrophytum (*as-tro-FY-tum*). Star cactus. Small and hemispherical, this cactus shows only a few prominent ribs, which are coated with a thin layer of white, woolly tufts that look like scales. This genus contains only six species, yet each has a curious and distinctly individual appearance; some species are completely spineless, but others are covered with dense, woolly "hair." All bloom abundantly, putting forth attractive yellow or red blossoms that are faintly fragrant.

Astrophytum prefers a slightly sandy soil (boost sand proportion in mix specified under "Soil and containers," at left) and less than average amounts of water. Give it full sun except during the hottest weather (100°F/38°C), when it prefers partial shade.

Astrophytum asterias is known as sea urchin cactus or sand dollar: its flattened globular body with prominent, spineless ribs resembles the ocean creatures for which it is nicknamed. Large, white, prominent areoles dot its gray green surface. Yellow flowers with contrasting scarlet throats bloom in summer.

Astrophytum capricorne. Goat's horn cactus. Twisted, almost contorted spines, curled like the horns of a goat, cover this white-flecked, globular *Astrophytum*. Yellow flowers with scarlet centers bloom in spring.

Astrophytum myriostigma. Bishop's cap. This is the easiest *Astrophytum* to grow—as well as the strangest to behold. Looking more like a five-segmented rubber ball than a plant, it has a swollen body with five prominent ribs; the entire gray green mass is coated with fine white wool. In summer, it produces a profusion of showy yellow blooms.

Borzicactus (*BOR-zee-kak-tus*). A group of columnar cactuses with distinct ribs and yellowish spines. Three-inch-long red flowers appear in summer. Very easy to grow. The most interesting type is *B. celsianus,* commonly called old-man-of-the-mountains, which produces long gray hairlike growth.

Cephalocereus (*sef-uh-lo-SEE-ree-us*). Called old man cactus, this is one of the most popular cactuses among beginning collectors. Grows slowly to be very tall. These cactuses bear many flowers—opening only at night—on their upper areoles. Plants grown indoors usually don't flower until they're 10 to 15 years old.

Use the cactus soil mix specified under "Soil and containers," at left; also check for advice on watering your *Cephalocereus* during warm weather. If its woolly "hairs" become matted, rinse *Cephalocereus* with mildly soapy water, then rinse again with clear water.

Cephalocereus chrysacanthus. Golden spines. This a shrubby plant of ribbed, bluish stems that grow to 15 feet tall. Bright yellow spines appear through thick hair; rose colored flowers are 3 inches long.

Cephalocereus fulviceps. Mexican giant. A native of southern Mexico, this giant towers up to the ceiling. Bluish joints, branching from the base, are covered with brown, woolly hair; flowers are white.

Cephalocereus palmeri. Woolly torch, billy goat, bald old man. This sturdy plant has short, blue green spines and tufts of long, white, woolly hair. It begins as a single column, then eventually branches. Fully grown plants may be 20 feet tall—or taller. Purplish brown flowers are 3 inches long.

Chamaecereus (*kam-ee-SEE-ree-us*). Peanut cactus. Even indoors, this small, foot-tall cactus produces flamboyant scarlet flowers. Though it's a dwarf form, it's characteristically cylindrical, ribbed, and spiny. Short joints branch from the base to produce a clumping, fingerlike effect. *Chamaecereus'* unusual shape and abundance of showy flowers—appearing

(Continued on page 42)

Epiphyllum 'Siegfried'
(orchid cactus)

Aporocactus flagelliformis
(rat-tail cactus)

Cephalocereus palmeri
(woolly torch)

Schlumbergera truncata
(Thanksgiving cactus)

Rhipsalidopsis rosea

Echinocactus grusonii
(golden barrel)

Rhipsalidopsis 'Shocking Pink'

even when the cactus is quite young—make it one of the most popular among indoor gardeners.

Chamaecereus sylvestri. Peanut cactus. *C. sylvestri*'s dense clusters of short, pale green joints are covered with small white spines. Funnel-shaped flowers of bright red, up to 3 inches long, bloom on stout stems.

Echinocactus *(e-ki-no-KAK-tus).* Barrel cactus. Among the easiest cactus to cultivate, *Echinocactus* is native to Mexico and the southwestern United States. When mature, it blooms intermittently throughout the year, producing flowers in a circle near the tender crown of the plant.

Plant *Echinocactus* in the standard cactus soil mix described under "Soil and containers" (page 40), and water infrequently but thoroughly. In winter, this plant prefers cool, dry conditions.

Echinocactus grandis has a globular shape; it can grow quite large, to 7 feet high and 3 feet thick. It has straight yellowish brown spines and yellow flowers, 1 to 2 inches long.

Echinocactus grusonii. Golden barrel. A favorite cultivated cactus, *E. grusonii* has sharp spines that remain a colorful dark yellow if the plant is grown in full sun. Mature plants' bright yellow flowers open from a crown of yellow wool; they need full sun to remain open for any length of time.

Echinocactus ingens. Mexican giant barrel. Easy to grow, this cactus often appears in clusters in the wild; each "barrel" may be up to 3 feet thick. Straight brown spines are set off in summer by red-centered yellow flowers.

Echinocactus polycephalus. Flattened, curved, reddish gray spines characterize this species. Three-inch-long flowers are usually bright yellow.

Echinocereus *(e-ki-no-SEE-ree-us).* Hedgehog cactus. Members of this group have free-branching clusters or mounds of upright-growing or prostrate stems. Erect stems rarely grow taller than 1 foot. In all species, highly ornamental spines densely cover the plant. Large, showy, long-lasting flowers, to 4 inches wide, appear on stems growing from the plant's base or sides. As a potted plant, *Echinoce-*

reus is enormously popular because of its easy care and overall tidy, compact appearance.

Echinocereus ehrenbergii has erect stems that branch freely from the base; they're covered with slender, glassy, white or pale yellow spines. Its flowers are purple.

Echinocereus engelmannii. Striking hot pink or magenta flowers contrast with this cactus' pale yellow spines.

Echinocereus papillosus. In this very unusual species, flowers look fluorescent, their yellow or off-white petals tinged with red.

E.p. neomexicanus, nicknamed rainbow cactus, is a small, columnar plant densely covered with soft spines. It has large yellow blooms.

E.p. rigidissimus is also called rainbow cactus; in this kind, spines form variously colored horizontal bands around the stems. Magenta flowers, up to 4 inches across, bloom in spring.

Echinocereus reichenbachii. Lace cactus. This small, clumping cactus' "lace-covered" look results from its heavy coating of spines. Pink to purple flowers, about 3 inches wide, appear in spring. *E.r. albispinus* has long, colorful spines; its areoles are shaped like narrow oblongs.

Echinocereus stoloniferus grows to 7 inches tall. It has 2-inch-thick, ribbed stems with black or red spines. Yellow flowers appear in late spring or summer.

Echinopsis *(e-ki-NOP-sis).* Easter lily cactus. Heavily spined, prominent ribs and dramatic trumpet-shaped flowers characterize *Echinopsis*. Flowers are red, pink, or white, and they're big—about 8 inches long. Most kinds of *Echinopsis* bloom nocturnally, often just for one evening, though some remain open for 2 days.

Caring for *Echinopsis* is simple: just provide a rich cactus soil mix, and slightly more fertilizer and water than recommended under "General growing requirements," page 40. Indoors, *Echinopsis* settles in happily almost anywhere, since it grows in areas that catch either full or partial sun.

Echinopsis albispinosa. This type displays gray 6-inch stems, either single or with offsets (small plantlets at the stem base). Curved, dark brown

spines turn white with maturity. Large white flowers reach 8 inches long.

Echinopsis longispina has stout, yellowish brown spines growing from deep, wavy ribs; its slender white flowers have many petals.

Echinopsis multiplex. Easter lily cactus, barrel cactus. Because of its impressive flowers, this is a good choice for indoor decoration. Sweetly scented, long-tubed, pale pink blooms sometimes reach 10 inches long.

Echinopsis tubiflora. This type produces mammoth white flowers, up to 10 inches long and 4 inches across. The plant's yellow, inch-long central spines have black tips.

Epiphyllum *(ep-uh-FIL-um).* Epiphyllum hybrids such as *E.* 'Siegfried' produce flattened, spineless, scallop-edged stems and enormous flowers in an array of brilliant colors.

Easy-to-grow *Epiphyllum* can be left alone to grow as a trailing plant, or you can stake it against a trellis or some other support. Provide bright, filtered light (as through a sheer curtain) and a standard cactus soil mix (see "Soil and containers," page 40). Let the soil dry out between waterings. Since *Epiphyllum* performs best when its roots are crowded, plant it in a small container. This cactus thrives at temperatures of about 50°F/10°C at night, 70° to 75°F/21° to 24°C during the day. In winter, let this cactus rest: keep the soil just barely moist, and—if possible—place the plant in an unheated (but not freezing) garage or porch.

Gymnocalycium *(jim-no-ka-LIS-ee-um).* Chin cactus. This cactus' nickname refers to the chinlike bulges that swell right below each areole and spine cluster.

A globular cactus, *Gymnocalycium* occasionally grows in clusters. You can easily recognize this cactus by its smooth flower buds and scaly fruit. Its long-lasting flowers, opening for several days in succession, are red, pink, white, or—rarely—yellow. Some blooms are so small that you can barely see them above the curved spines.

Give chin cactus a standard cactus soil mix and ample watering during the growing season (see "General growing requirements," page 40). Protect your plant from direct sun-

light and cool winter temperatures (unlike most cactuses, *Gymnocalycium* doesn't need a winter rest).

Gymnocalycium mihanovichii. Plaid cactus. A small, gray green globe, *G. mihanovichii* displays notched ribs and curved spines. Attractive pale yellow to chartreuse flowers bloom profusely. *G.m. friedrichii* is dark green with dark markings; there are also pure red and yellow forms, known as 'Ruby Ball' and 'Blondie'.

Gymnocalycium saglione. Giant chin cactus. Largest of the group, this *Gymnocalycium* often grows up to 1 foot across. Its long, thick, hooked spines are usually dark, but may be reddish yellow on young plants. Flowers are pink or flesh colored.

Lobivia *(lo-BIV-ee-uh).* Nicknamed hedgehog or cob cactus, these small cactuses, either globular or cylindrical, produce large, showy blooms that often appear to be as big as the plants themselves. Flower colors range from shades of red, yellow, and orange all the way to true purple. Growing on short, hairy tubes, blooms last a day or two; new ones come along regularly.

Plant *Lobivia* in a standard cactus soil mix (as described under "Soil and containers," page 40) and give slightly less water than usual. Protect this cactus from harsh, burning sun.

Lobivia famatimensis. This *Lobivia* is a small globe with shallow, notched ribs and white spines. Its flowers are typically red or yellow, sometimes white. *L.f. setosa* has white, bristly spines; its flowers are red or yellow.

Mammillaria *(MAM-uh-LAIR-ee-uh).* Pincushion cactus. This very large group of popular cactuses comes in a seemingly endless variety of shapes, sizes, and colors: solitary or clustering, spined with soft bristles or thorny hooks, crowned with a few single flowers or a circle of delicate blooms. Most are under 1 foot tall, though.

Though diverse in appearance, they have the same needs: an average or slightly sandy soil mix, infrequent but ample amounts of water, and lots of bright light.

Among the most popular *Mammillaria* are *M. guerreronis, M. elongata, M. melanocentra, M. spinosissima,* and *M. tetrancistra.*

Melocactus *(mel-o-KAK-tus)*. Exotic and fascinating, these cactuses are better known by their common name of melon cactus. They need only modest amounts of water, and a rich cactus soil mix that allows perfect drainage (see "Soil and containers," page 40). Because these plants have a shallow but spreading root structure, they do best in a wide, shallow pot. Melon cactuses need full sun.

Melocactus communis grows to 3 feet tall, with a small 2-inch-tall "cap" on top. It has yellowish spines and red or pinkish flowers.

Melocactus intortus has a 3-foot-tall body topped with a 1-foot "cap." Spines, about an inch long, are reddish brown; flowers are pink.

Melocactus neryi is the easiest to grow of this group. Including its 4-inch "cap," it reaches only 10 inches in height. Its inch-long flowers are rosy pink.

Notocactus *(NO-to-kak-tus)*. Ball cactus. Small and round, this South American cactus makes an excellent choice for a beginning gardener.

Notocactus apricus. Sun cup. This 3-inch-wide cactus produces curved, reddish, central spines surrounded by a colorful, contrasting ring of yellow spines. Yellow flowers blossom on stout 3-inch tubes.

Notocactus haselbergii. Scarlet ball. Soft white spines cover this cactus. Its month-long blooming season is in early spring; flowers are small, reddish orange, and long lasting (up to 1 week).

Notocactus leninghausii, nicknamed golden ball, is one of the heftiest ball cactuses. It produces 30 or more ribs and grows up to 3 feet tall. Mature plants bear large yellow flowers.

Opuntia *(o-PUN-tee-uh)*. Prickly pear. Widely grown as a landscape plant, *Opuntia* also basks contentedly as a house plant in a sunny window garden. Simply make sure it soaks up sufficient light to prevent branches from turning spindly and misshapen. Indoors, an *Opuntia* rarely gets large enough to produce many blooms.

Opuntia basilaris, or beaver tail, has flat, nearly spineless joints; gray or purplish pads appear where spines normally grow.

Borzicactus celsianus
(old-man-of-the-mountains)

Opuntia basilaris
(beaver tail)

Astrophytum myriostigma
(bishop's cap)

Echinocereus stoloniferus
(hedgehog cactus)

Echinopsis longispina
(Easter lily cactus)

Notocactus apricus
(sun cup)

Mammillaria melanocentra
(pincushion cactus)

Lobivia famatimensis
(cob cactus)

Gymnocalycium mihanovichii
(plaid cactus)

Chamaecereus sylvestri
(peanut cactus)

Opuntia microdasys. Bunny ears. This cactus has flat, oval joints, studded with oblong, spineless pads covered with tufts of golden bristles. It's available in many named varieties.

Rhipsalidopsis *(rip-sal-uh-DAHP-sis)*. These have flattened upper joints and shorter lower ones. Their flowers resemble *Schlumbergera* (see at right). *Rhipsalidopsis* prefers cool (55°F/13°C) temperatures and filtered light (as through a sheer curtain). Give plants an autumn rest for 6 to 8 weeks, allowing soil to almost completely dry.

Among the most popular *Rhipsalidopsis* are *R. gaertneri, R. rosea,* and *R.* 'Shocking Pink'.

Schlumbergera *(shlum-BUR-guh-ruh)*. Christmas cactus, Thanksgiving cactus. You can grow these popular epiphytic plants in pots. Native to the tropics, they're nicknamed for the holidays during which they bloom. Confusion reigns over their botanical name, however—*Schlumbergera* is often sold as *Zygocactus*.

Spineless, green, flat-jointed, and eventually arching, these cactuses can put on quite a show. On mature plants, many-petaled, tubular flowers bloom profusely in white, pink, salmon, and rosy red; some of the colors are almost fluorescent.

Schlumbergera bridgesii, commonly called Christmas cactus, may

grow up to 3 feet across in the wild. Arching, drooping stems consist of bright green, flattened joints, smooth, spineless, and scallop-edged. Rosy purplish red flowers, tubular and many petaled, appear around Christmas.

Schlumbergera truncata is also known as crab cactus or Thanksgiving cactus. Sharply toothed joints, 1 to 2 inches long, joined together in long stems; the last joint in the stem has two large "teeth" at its end. Short-tubed flowers with spreading, pointed, scarlet petals bloom from November through March. Many varieties of *S. truncata* are available, including types with white, pink, salmon, and orange blooms.

Calathea
(kal-uh-THEE-uh)

Peacock plant, Rattlesnake plant, Zebra plant

Native to tropical America, this large group of plants is known for striking foliage. Individual leaves show intricate markings in shades of green, white, pink, purple, and maroon. Undersides of some types are solid purplish red, contrasting with the patterned surfaces.

Most forms grow upright, their leaves varying in length from 8 to 18 inches. *Calathea* is closely related to *Maranta* (see page 64) and is often confused with it.

Growing requirements

Calathea performs well in a standard indoor potting soil and in a warm (70° to 75°F/21° to 24°C) room. Plenty of filtered light (as through a sheer curtain) encourages the richest leaf color; light that's too abundant or intense will damage leaves. Most importantly, *Calathea* requires high humidity. Mist frequently, and place the pot on a humidity tray (see page 20). Keep the potting soil constantly moist (like a squeezed-out sponge), but not soggy. Repot as necessary to avoid a pot-bound condition (see page 26). Except in winter, apply a liquid fertilizer diluted to half strength (see page 21) every 2 weeks.

For health and good looks, leaves should be cleaned regularly with a damp cloth; don't use commercial leaf shine products on this plant.

Calathea is occasionally bothered by aphids, mealybugs, red spider mites, and thrips; see pages 29–31 for methods of control.

Favorites

Calathea insignis, commonly known as the rattlesnake plant, has 12 to 18-inch-long yellowish green leaves striped with olive green.

Calathea makoyana, commonly known as the peacock plant, has 10 to 12-inch-long oval leaves. Leaf colors include olive green, cream, and pink displayed in interesting patterns.

Calathea ornata is a sturdy plant whose 8-inch-long leaves are rich green with undersides of purplish red. Pink stripes run between the veins of young leaves.

Calathea makoyana (peacock plant)

Calathea zebrina, commonly known as the zebra plant, is a more compact type. Leaves grow to approximately 15 inches. On their velvety green surface, bars of pale chartreuse alternate with olive green, both extending outward from the midrib; undersides are purplish red.

Callisia
(ka-lis-EE-uh)

Inch plant, Striped inch plant

A creeping plant native to Mexico, *Callisia* resembles both *Tradescantia* (page 92) and *Zebrina* (page 93), and is often confused with one or the other. Its stems stand erect when young, then start to droop as they reach their mature 2 to 3-foot length. Pointed oval leaves, appearing about an inch apart on the stems, have striking coloration: tops are olive green, striped with creamy yellow; undersides are purplish. Because of its dangling growth, *Callisia* is best displayed in a hanging basket or on a pedestal.

Growing requirements

Callisia grows best in filtered light (as through a sheer curtain), with average humidity and at temperatures from (60° to 70°F/16° to 21°C). Use a standard indoor potting soil. *Callisia* likes lots of water—during the growing season, be sure that the soil is always moist (like a squeezed-out sponge), but not soggy. Reduce watering during autumn and winter. Except in autumn and winter, apply a complete fertilizer regularly (see page 21).

Frequently pinch off growing tips to promote compact growth. *Callisia* is occasionally bothered by red spider mites; see page 30.

Favorites

Callisia elegans, the most commonly grown type, has the characteristics described at left.

Callisia fragrans is an unusual form with 10-inch-long leaves. These leaves form big rosettes that resemble loose-knit hens and chicks (see *Echeveria*, under Succulents on page 88). Long runners produce miniature plants at their tips. *C. fragrans* makes a massive hanging basket plant that is more impressive than attractive. Its branches of clustered, fragrant flowers are rarely produced indoors.

Callisia elegans (striped inch plant)

Chlorophytum

(klo-ro-FY-tum)

Airplane plant, Ribbon plant, Spider ivy, Spider plant

Chlorophytum, native to tropics around the globe, probably owes its popularity to its unique and fascinating growth habit. The mother plant, a clump of curving leaves that look like long, broad grass blades, sends out long curved stems with "baby" plants at their ends.

Tiny white flowers appear at the ends of the 2-foot-long stems before miniature plants sprout. To best protect these offspring, grow *Chlorophytum* as a hanging plant.

Growing requirements

Chlorophytum prefers bright, reflected light, standard potting soil, and average house temperatures. Though it will tolerate the low humidity of most homes, it does benefit from frequent mistings. Let the soil dry out a bit between waterings. Apply a complete fertilizer regularly (see page 21).

If you grow *Chlorophytum* in a hanging basket, rotate the basket a half-turn every week or so to produce even, well-spaced growth. Small plants at the ends of stems grow complete with roots, so you can snip them off and plant them. Scale occasionally presents a problem; see page 31.

Favorites

Chlorophytum comosum 'Mandaianum' is a compact plant, the mother plant having short (4 to 6-inch) leaves. Leaves are green with a yellow stripe down the center. *C.c.* 'Picturatum' has longer (12-inch) leaves, green with a similar yellow center stripe. *C.c.* 'Vittatum', the most common form of spider plant, has 6 to 12-inch-long leaves, green with a broad center stripe of yellow or cream.

Chlorophytum comosum 'Vittatum' (spider plant)

Cissus

(SIS-us)

Grape ivy, Kangaroo vine, Oakleaf ivy, Treebine

Cissus, related to Virginia creeper, Boston ivy, and grape, comprises a group of evergreen vines popular for their elegant looks and easy care. Most send out tendrils that latch onto any type of nearby support.

Growing requirements

On the whole an easy-to-grow plant, *Cissus* adapts readily to a broad range of indoor conditions. It prefers bright, reflected light, with average temperatures and humidity. A standard indoor potting soil suits all species of *Cissus* just fine. Allow soil to dry out a bit before watering—excessive water can hurt *Cissus.* Cut back even further on watering during the winter rest period. Except in winter, apply a complete fertilizer regularly (see page 21).

Pinch off growing tips of *Cissus* to encourage a fuller plant. Some of the more vigorous types may become leggy, with bare branches—cut these branches back halfway.

Give plants an occasional shower to keep leaves clean and lessen the chance of red spider mite infestation. *Cissus* is occasionally attacked also by mealybugs, scale, and whiteflies; see pages 29–31 for methods of control.

Favorites

Cissus antarctica, sometimes called kangaroo vine or treebine, is native to Australia and is the most popular *Cissus.* Its medium green leaves resemble those of a grapevine. It will climb if given something for its tendrils to grab. Pinch off growing tips to foster bushier plants. *C.a.* 'Minima', a dwarf form of the common kangaroo vine, has waxy green leaves and a compact growth habit.

Cissus discolor has moss green leaves that look as though they've been quilted, with red veins and silver markings. Leaves, toothed at the edges, grow to 6 inches long. This *Cissus* is considerably more difficult to grow.

Cissus rhombifolia, a South American native commonly known as grape ivy, puts forth dark green leaves in groups of three with sharp-toothed edges. Reddish hairs grow from the undersides of the leaves, giving them a bronze cast. *C. rhombifolia* toler-ates low light, grows rapidly. *C.r.* 'Ellen Danika' has leaflets deeply lobed, like an oak leaf. Known as oakleaf ivy, it is more compact, with darker green, less lustrous leaves.

Cissus striata, a miniature grape ivy, has leaves shaped like five-pointed stars, with reddish undersides. Though not as dramatic as the larger forms, it performs well in a hanging basket.

Cissus rhombifolia 'Ellen Danika' (oakleaf ivy)

Clerodendrum

(klee-ro-DEN-drum)

Clerodendron, Bleeding heart vine, Glorybower

Clerodendrum thomsoniae
(bleeding heart vine)

One of the most glamorous and exotic house plants, *Clerodendrum* is a native of West Africa. If left untrimmed, the large evergreen vine will grow to 6 feet or more. It has attractive dark green, heart-shaped leaves—but its brilliant flowers are the primary attraction. Scarlet 1-inch tubes, surrounded by large (¾-inch-long) white calyxes, are borne in flattish 5-inch-wide clusters, usually from August through October.

There are several ways to shape this plant. You can grow it as a large, upright vine trained to a trellis, let it spill from a hanging basket, or encourage a more compact, shrubby shape by frequently pinching off its growing tips. Since *Clerodendrum* grows fast and vigorously, it needs attentive pruning, pinching, and grooming to look its best; it can become rangy.

Growing requirements

Generally speaking, *Clerodendrum* requires warm temperatures, bright light, some humidity, and a standard potting soil; some additional steps are necessary to ensure flower production.

First, be sure to provide enough light (bright but filtered, as through a sheer curtain) during the growing season—spring through summer. Throughout the growing season, keep the soil mix thoroughly moist (like a squeezed-out sponge), but not soggy; create extra humidity by frequent misting or by placing pots on humidity trays (see page 20).

In winter, give the plants a rest in a very cool spot (50° to 55°F/10° to 13°C); let the soil dry almost completely between waterings. Except in late autumn and winter, apply a complete fertilizer regularly (see page 21).

Don't hesitate to give this vigorous vine a vigorous pruning—cutting back by half is not unusual. Pruning keeps it in bounds and also encourages plenty of future flowers. The best time to prune is after flowering, usually in late autumn, just before putting the plant "down" for its cool rest period during the winter.

Pinching off the growing tips throughout the growing season also keeps the plant from becoming scraggly. As soon as new growth appears (usually in early spring), move the plant from its resting place to a warmer and brighter spot.

Mealybugs and red spider mites occasionally present a problem; see pages 29–31 for methods of control.

Favorites

Of the three commonly available forms of *Clerodendrum*—*C. fragrans pleniflorum, C. thomsoniae,* and *C. trichotomum*—*C. thomsoniae* is best adapted to indoor conditions.

Clivia

(KLY-vee-uh)

Kaffir lily

This South African native of the amaryllis family becomes quite a showy house plant, especially when in bloom. *Clivia* puts forth clusters of brilliant orange and yellow funnel-shaped flowers, rising from dense clumps of dark green, strap-shaped leaves as long as 1½ feet.

Usually blooming continues from December to April, with the peak in March or April. Ornamental red berries follow the long flowering.

Growing requirements

Clivia does best in a rich, fast-draining soil mix—one of the kinds used for orchids or African violets is good. For the loveliest blooms, *Clivia* requires bright, reflected light (morning or late afternoon light is ideal) but no direct sunlight, which can scorch leaves. During the active growing season (spring and summer), keep the soil mix moist (like a squeezed-out sponge), but not soggy. Start reducing the amount of water in autumn and allow the soil mix to dry out almost completely during the plant's midwinter rest period. Average humidity in a warm room (70° to 75°F/21° to 24°C) suits *Clivia*. Except in autumn and winter, apply a complete fertilizer regularly (see page 21).

Here are a few tips to help *Clivia* produce the most magnificent blossoms: Starting in early winter, let the plant rest in a location kept at about 50°F/10°C for approximately 1½ to 2 months, letting the soil dry almost completely. Temperatures should stay around 50°F/10°C during this period. After the rest period, move *Clivia* to a bright, warm location, but wait until the flower stalk is about 6 inches long before watering and fertilizing normally. Remove the berries; let the flower stalk die before removing it. *Clivia* blooms best when potbound.

Generally pest-free, *Clivia* occasionally suffers from red spider mites and scale; see pages 29–31 for methods of control.

Favorites

Clivia miniata, with its various hybrid forms, is the only common type.

Clivia miniata (Kaffir lily)

Codiaeum

(ko-dee-EE-um)

Croton, Gold dust plant, Joseph's coat

One of the most wildly colorful groups in the house plant world, *Codiaeum* offers abundant variety of shape, pattern, and hue. Its large leathery and glossy leaves may grow long and narrow, oval, or lance-shaped, with edges either straight or notched into three deep lobes. Leaves may be green, yellow, red, purple, bronze, pink, or almost any combination of these colors.

Multistemmed and bushy, *Codiaeum* usually grows 2 to 3 feet high.

Growing requirements

To grow *Codiaeum* indoors, it's a good idea to mimic tropical conditions: bright light, warm temperatures, high humidity, and plentiful water. Mist plants frequently to raise humidity, and wipe leaves with a damp cloth to discourage pests. A standard potting soil suits *Codiaeum* fine. Except in winter, apply a complete fertilizer regularly (see page 21).

Since *Codiaeum* is naturally bushy, there's usually no need for pinching. If it grows too big, you can prune it by cutting back to half size (prune in early spring). Apply powdered charcoal on the cuts.

Aphids, leaf miners, mealybugs, red spider mites, and thrips may occasionally attack *Codiaeum*; see pages 29–31 for methods of control.

Favorites

Codiaeum variegatum pictum has glossy, oval leaves in spectacular shades of green, yellow, red, purple, pink, and bronze. *C.v.p.* 'Aucubifolium', the gold dust plant, has leaves showing yellow spots or splotches on glossy bright green. *C.v.p.* 'Spirale' has multicolored, corkscrew-twisted leaves in shades of red and dark gray green.

Codiaeum variegatum pictum (croton)

Coffea

(KAW-fee-uh)

Coffee plant

Famous for its beans, *Coffea* is a relative newcomer to the house plant scene. This native of East Africa adapts to indoor life well, and its glossy foliage makes an exceptionally handsome display. The coffee plant can be raised from unroasted coffee beans.

Its glossy leaves, dark green and oval, are distinctly ribbed; they grow to about 4 inches long and 2 inches wide. In its native tropics, the single-stemmed coffee tree shoots up beyond 12 feet tall, but indoor specimens rarely reach even half that height. Large plants are naturally bushy, with leaves so glossy they look as if they've just been polished.

Growing requirements

Coffea prefers bright, filtered sunlight (as through a sheer curtain—not direct sun), standard indoor potting soil, temperatures on the warm side (70° to 75°F/21° to 24°C), and plenty of humidity. Warm indoor temperatures are frequently accompanied by low humidity, so be sure to compensate by growing plants on a humidity tray (see page 20) or by misting several times a week. During the spring and summer growing season, keep the soil moist (like a squeezed-out sponge), but not soggy; reduce the water considerably during the autumn and winter rest period, allowing the soil to dry out almost completely between waterings. Apply a complete fertilizer (see page 21) regularly during spring and summer; withhold fertilizer applications during autumn and winter.

If you're trying to keep the plant at a particular size, pinch out the growing tips regularly during the spring and summer growing period.

Coffea will drop leaves if temperatures fall below 55°F/13°C. It's occasionally attacked by scale; see page 31 for methods of control.

Favorites

Only one species, *Coffea arabica*, grows well indoors. This is the same plant that produces high-quality coffee beans in commercial production. The dwarf coffee plant, *C.a.* 'Nana', is sometimes available; it's said to flower and fruit much earlier.

Coffea arabica (coffee plant)

Coleus hybridus (painted nettle)

Coleus

(KO-lee-us)

Flame nettle, Painted leaf plant, Painted nettle

Brilliantly colorful foliage and ease of care explain why *Coleus* is a favorite with indoor gardeners. Velvety leaves, often ruffled or scalloped, display a rich variety of color: shades of green, chartreuse, yellow, salmon, peach, orange, red, magenta, purple, and brown, in veined and dappled patterns.

Growing requirements

Most important for a healthy *Coleus* is a balance of light; too much shade or sun causes leaf colors to fade and may give the plant a leggy or stunted shape. *Coleus* prefers temperatures in the 60° to 70°F range (16° to 21°C), standard potting soil, and ample water. It thrives on a humidity tray (see page 20) or with misting when the air is dry. Apply a complete fertilizer (see page 21) regularly all year long.

Most standard (nondwarf) types may grow sparse and leggy if you don't pinch off the growing tips frequently.

Mealybugs and whiteflies are the pests most commonly bothering *Coleus*. For light infestations, control by rinsing leaves with lukewarm water. In more severe cases, use one of the controls listed on pages 29–31.

Favorites

Smaller leaves and hanging stems distinguish *Coleus pumilus* from the various *Coleus* hybrids, known botanically as *Coleus hybridus*. Giant Exhibition and Oriental Splendor are both large-leafed strains; Carefree is a dwarf, self-branching type with deeply lobed, ruffled 1 to 1½-inch leaves. Salicifolius has long, narrow leaves crowded on its stems, making the plant look like a foot-high feather duster.

Columnea

(ko-lum-NEE-uh)

Norse fire plant

Columnea 'Aladdin's Lamp'

Closely resembling *Aeschynanthus* (page 33), this very large group of plants originated in tropical America. Plants in the group produce a variety of leaf shapes, with either glossy or hairy leaf surfaces. Branches either arch horizontally or distinctly "weep"; either type of *Columnea* looks attractive in a hanging basket.

Columnea's tubular flowers, in shades of brilliant red, orange, or yellow (or combinations of these), are its main attraction. The primary blooming period lasts for several months; flowers range from ½ inch to over 3 inches long. Under the right conditions, *Columnea* will bloom on and off almost the year around.

Growing requirements

Though you wouldn't guess it from appearances, *Columnea* is related to African violets and requires similar care. But *Columnea* prefers slightly cooler temperatures (65° to 75°F/18° to 24°C) and isn't as touchy about water.

Provide *Columnea* with bright, reflected light; plant it in packaged African violet potting soil. Keep the soil moist (like a squeezed-out sponge), but not soggy. Be especially sure to use tepid water when watering the soil. Except in winter, apply a complete fertilizer regularly (see page 21).

Keep humidity high by placing the pot on a humidity tray (see page 20), or grow in a naturally humid room such as the kitchen or bathroom. For some reason, *Columnea* doesn't take kindly to misting, which may cause brown spots on the leaves. (Some reports indicate that misting strictly with tepid water may eliminate spotting.)

To encourage flowering, cut back older branches by ⅓ to ½ in spring. Long branches can be cut back to any length desired after flowering.

Aphids, leaf miners, mealybugs, or cyclamen mites sometimes bother *Columnea*; see pages 29–31 for methods of control.

Favorites

Columnea 'Aladdin's Lamp', one of the many *Columnea* hybrids, has trailing branches with glossy, 2½-inch-long leaves. Orange red flowers measure 3 inches long.

Columnea 'Stavanger', commonly called the Norse fire plant, is a popular *Columnea*. Trailing stems may wander for several feet if the plant is grown in a hanging basket. All along the stems are neat pairs of rounded shiny leaves, ½ inch wide; in the blooming season, 3 to 4-inch-long red flowers appear.

Columnea microphylla's long (to more than 5 feet), drooping branches carry tiny coppery leaves. Bright red flowers, about 3 inches long, have yellow throats.

Cordyline
(kor-di-LY-nee)

Good luck plant, Hawaiian ti, Ti plant, Tree-of-kings

Looking almost like palms, with swordlike leaves and woody trunks, these relatives of agave and yucca make dramatic, supersize house plants.

Growing requirements

Though it will tolerate lower light conditions, *Cordyline* prefers at least 4 hours per day of bright, filtered sunlight (as through a sheer curtain). Average room temperatures are fine; increase humidity by setting the pot on a humidity tray (see page 20). It's best not to mist leaves.

Use a standard indoor potting soil, keeping it moist during the growing season from spring through autumn. In winter, let the top half of the soil dry out between waterings. Except in winter, apply a complete fertilizer regularly (see page 21).

Cordyline is occasionally bothered by aphids, mealybugs, scale, or thrips; see pages 29–31.

Favorites

Cordyline stricta's swordlike leaves are about 2 feet long, dark green faintly etched with purple. Indoors, it occasionally produces lavender flowers. After flowering, cut the tallest canes to the ground to keep the plant compact; new canes will soon appear. If you push long canes into soil after cutting, they'll root quickly.

Cordyline terminalis, commonly known as the ti plant, is usually started from "logs" (small sections of mature branches) imported from Hawaii. Lay short lengths in standard indoor potting soil, covering about half their diameter. Keep logs moist during the rooting period. When shoots grow out and root (in 3 to 4 weeks), cut them off and pot them. Some varieties have solid green leaves; others display a variegated pattern or edging of pink with red or yellow with green.

Cordyline terminalis (ti plant)

Crossandra
(kro-SAN-druh)

Firecracker flower

An attractive native of India, this evergreen plant is a relatively new arrival to the house plant scene. Its overnight popularity is hardly surprising. *Crossandra* glistens with lovely, glossy, gardenialike leaves of deep green. In spring and summer, it offers short, full spikes of scarlet orange or coral orange flowers, centered with bright yellow "eyes." Blossoms appear in clusters of two or three; each flower may reach 2 inches or more across. In favorable growing conditions, each flower spike continues to produce blooms for 1½ to 2 weeks. The foliage looks stunning all year. You can grow *Crossandra* from seed; expect the first blooms 6 to 9 months after the plant sprouts.

If you start this plant in a 4 or 5-inch pot, you'll never need to repot it; its height rarely exceeds 1½ feet. It's naturally shrubby, needing no pinching.

Growing requirements

To keep *Crossandra* really healthy, give it the same light and humidity conditions as you'd give an African violet (see pages 79–80): strong filtered light (as through a sheer curtain), and high humidity. To boost humidity, mist *Crossandra* frequently or place the pot on a humidity tray (see page 20). Your plant will appreciate warm temperatures (never below 65°F/18°C). Use a standard indoor potting soil, and keep it moist (like a squeezed-out sponge), but not soggy; the roots should never dry out completely. Except in winter, apply a complete fertilizer regularly (see page 21).

As the flowers fade, remove them; cut off spikes after they've bloomed.

Though you can avoid most pest problems by keeping *Crossandra* in a warm, humid location, you may still have trouble from mealybugs, red spider mites, scale, and whiteflies. See pages 29–31 for methods of control.

Favorites

Crossandra infundibuliformis is the only form commonly available.

Crossandra infundibuliformis (firecracker flower)

Ctenanthe compressa (bamburanta)

Ctenanthe
(ste-NAN-thuh)

Bamburanta, Giant bamburanta, Never-never plant

Grown mostly for its unusual foliage, *Ctenanthe* is a close relative of *Maranta* (see page 64). The plant may start as several short stalks, each producing a long stem, or as one long upright stalk with stems branching from it. Leaves show markings in various shades of green; in some forms, green leaves have yellow markings and reddish undersides. Inconspicuous white flowers form in spikes.

Growing requirements

Ctenanthe likes bright, filtered light (as through a sheer curtain), average house temperatures (65° to 70°F/18° to 21°C), a standard indoor potting soil, and high humidity. Increase the humidity by frequent misting or by placing the pot on a humidity tray (see page 20). Keep the potting soil moist (like a squeezed-out sponge), but not soggy. In winter, allow the soil to dry out almost completely between waterings. Except in winter, apply a complete fertilizer regularly (see page 21). Pests rarely bother *Ctenanthe*.

Favorites

Ctenanthe 'Burle Marx' grows to 15 inches. Tops of leaves are gray green feathered with dark green; leaf undersides and leaf stems are maroon.

Ctenanthe compressa grows to 2 to 3 feet high. Leathery leaves are oblong, asymmetrical, about 15 inches long. Leaves are green and waxy on top, gray green beneath.

Ctenanthe oppenheimiana is a larger, branching plant that grows 3 to 5 feet high. The narrow, leathery leaves are dark green, banded with silver above, purple beneath. They grow upward from down-covered stalks. *C.o.* 'Tricolor', never-never plant, has leaves with showy patches of cream on green; undersides are dark red.

Dieffenbachia maculata (dumb cane)

Dieffenbachia
(deef-en-BAHK-ee-uh)

Dumb cane, Tuftroot

Offering generous size, fascinating foliage, and good tolerance of indoor conditions, *Dieffenbachia* has long enjoyed favor as a house plant.

Leaves are variegated in greens and cream colors. Young plants generally grow on single stems, but older plants may develop multiple stems. Flowers that look like odd, narrow calla lilies form on mature plants.

Acrid sap from the leaves, if eaten, burns the mouth and throat and may actually paralyze the vocal cords.

Growing requirements

Dieffenbachia likes filtered light (as through a sheer curtain) or a northern exposure. It's happy with standard indoor potting soil, average household temperatures, and average humidity. Water it when the potting soil feels dry to the touch. Except in autumn and winter, apply a complete fertilizer regularly (see page 21). Turn plants occasionally for even growth.

Dieffenbachia will not survive constant overwatering. And sudden changes from low to high light levels usually inflict sunburn on foliage.

If the plant becomes leggy, cut it back to 6 inches from the soil line.

Clean leaves regularly with a damp cloth. Dieffenbachia is usually quite pest-free.

Favorites

Dieffenbachia amoena grows to 6 feet or taller. Its broad dark green leaves, 18 inches long, are striped with narrow, slanting streaks of white.

Dieffenbachia exotica is a more compact form with 10-inch leaves. Leaves have dull green edges, much creamy white variegation, and a creamy white midrib.

Dieffenbachia maculata towers to 6 feet or more. Its leaves are wide green ovals 10 inches or more in length, flecked with greenish-white dots or patches. *D.m.* 'Rudolph Roehrs' grows to 6 feet, with 10-inch leaves of pale chartreuse dappled with ivory and edged with green. *D.m.* 'Superba' offers thicker foliage than other forms. Leaves are heavily spattered with creamy white dots and patches.

Dizygotheca

(diz-uh-go-THEE-kuh)

False aralia, Threadleaf

Lacy-leafed and faintly bronze-toned, *Dizygotheca* makes a rather refined and elegant impression. Its single stem can stretch 5 to 6 feet tall, with foliage spreading from 18 to 24 inches. Leaves divide like fans into long, very narrow leaflets with notched edges—4 to 9 inches long and barely ½ inch wide. Shiny dark green on top and reddish beneath, they give *Dizygotheca*'s foliage an overall bronze tone.

As plants mature, leaves grow bigger, with coarsely notched leaflets up to 12 inches long and 3 inches wide. As a house plant, *Dizygotheca* rarely flowers.

Growing requirements

This plant likes bright, filtered light (not direct sunlight), and requires a potting soil that drains quickly and retains moisture well. *Dizygotheca* prefers high humidity and average household temperatures. Let the top half of the soil dry out between waterings. (Both waterlogged and overly dry soil will cause leaves to drop.) Except in winter, apply a complete fertilizer regularly (see page 21).

For a fuller effect, try planting several plants in one pot—they don't mind being potbound.

Improper watering—dry or waterlogged soil—causes leaf drop.

Dizygotheca is occasionally attacked by aphids, mealybugs, red spider mites, scale, or thrips; see pages 29–31 for methods of control.

Favorites

Dizygotheca elegantissima is the most commonly available form; it has the characteristics described at left. You may find this plant sold under its earlier botanical name, *Aralia elegantissima*.

Dizygotheca elegantissima (false aralia)

Dracaena

(drah-SEE-nuh)

Cornplant, Dragon tree, Gold dust plant, Gold spot dracaena

Palmlike *Dracaena* comes in a variety of types that, given enough time, may reach as high as the ceiling. Popular in homes with contemporary interiors, large specimens look particularly dramatic.

Some grow in the shape of graceful fountains, their 3 to 4-inch-wide ribbonlike leaves occasionally striped with chartreuse or white. Other varieties put forth very stiff, swordlike leaves, ½ to 1 inch wide.

Easy-to-grow *Dracaena* tolerates low light, low humidity, and infrequent watering—though it grows faster and looks healthier with more attentive care. For a fuller effect, many people plant three or more plants together.

(Continued on next page)

Botanical name / Common name	Size	Comments
Dracaena deremensis	15 feet	Stiff leaves 2 feet long, 2 inches wide.
D.d. 'Bausei'	15 feet	Leaves green with white center stripe.
D.d. 'Janet Craig'	15 feet	Leaves broad and dark green.
D.d. 'Janet Craig Compacta'	6–8 feet	Popular for dwarf size.
D.d. 'Longii'	15 feet	Leaves characterized by broad white center stripe.
D.d. 'Warneckii'	15 feet	Leaves wide, rich green, striped white and gray.
D. draco / Dragon tree	20 feet high, 20 feet wide	Stout trunk holds upward-reaching or spreading branches topped by clusters of heavy 2-foot-long, sword-shaped leaves.
D. fragrans / Cornplant	20 feet	Heavy, ribbonlike, blue green leaves, typically 18 inches long and 2 inches wide, becoming twice as large when mature. Tolerates darker conditions than other *Dracaenas*.
D.f. 'Lindenii'	20 feet	Wide, creamy-yellow leaf margins.
D.f. 'Massangeana'	20 feet	Broad yellow green stripe down center of leaf.
D.f. 'Victoria'	20 feet	Leaves striped with creamy white.
D. marginata	12 feet	Slender, erect, smooth gray stems. Leaves to 2 feet long, ½ inch wide, deep glossy green with narrow margin of purple red.
D.m. 'Candy Cane'	10 feet	Leaf margins deeper red, lengthwise stripes of yellow and chartreuse.
D.m. 'Tricolor'	10 feet	Similar to 'Candy Cane'.
D. surculosa / Gold dust plant Gold spot dracaena	4 feet	Dark green leaves 5 inches long, 2 inches wide with varying degrees of white spotting.
D.s. 'Florida Beauty'	4 feet	So heavily spotted, some leaves look more white than green.
D.s. 'Kelleri'	4 feet	More and larger spots than species, but fewer than 'Florida Beauty'.

Dracaena deremensis 'Warneckii'

Dracaena fragrans

Dracaena deremensis 'Janet Craig'

Dracaena marginata

Dracaena fragrans 'Massangeana'

...*Dracaena*

Growing requirements

Dracaena prefers bright, indirect light; it tolerates dimmer light, but growth slows as a result. The plant grows well with standard indoor potting soil and average house temperatures and humidity. Keep soil moist (like a squeezed-out sponge), but not soggy; fertilize regularly during spring and summer with complete fertilizer (see page 21).

During autumn and winter, water less frequently and stop fertilizing.

All *Dracaenas,* particularly the wider-leafed forms, have smooth leaves that tend to attract dust. To keep *Dracaena* in good health and looking its best, regularly wipe leaves off with a damp cloth, or move your plant to a location where it can be given a gentle shower (see page 27). It's best not to

use commercial leaf shine products on this plant.

If for any reason your *Dracaena* develops brown tips at the ends of its leaves, you can simply cut the brown areas off with a pair of scissors. (Be sure that the trimmed leaves still have a natural shape—see drawing on page 27.) Check your growing conditions and care schedule carefully to make

sure the problem does not repeat itself. With good care, *Dracaenas* will live for decades.

Watch to make sure water doesn't collect in saucer or cachepot; roots may rot from too much moisture.

Dracaena will tolerate a pot-bound condition for long periods. It's rarely bothered by pests or diseases, but occasionally suffers attacks from aphids, mealybugs, red spider mites, scale, or thrips (see pages 29–31).

Favorites

Dracaena deremensis offers several named varieties. Most commonly sold is *D. deremensis* 'Warneckii', which is erect and slow growing but eventually reaches 15 feet tall. Its 2-foot-long leaves are 2 inches wide, rich green, and striped white and gray. Other named varieties include *D.d.* 'Bausei', green with white center stripe; *D.d.* 'Longii', with broader white center stripe; and *D.d* 'Janet Craig', with broad dark green leaves. Compact versions of 'Janet Craig' and 'Warneckii' are also available.

Dracaena draco, commonly referred to as dragon tree, has a stout trunk with upward-reaching, spreading branches topped with clusters of heavy, 2-foot-long, sword-shaped leaves. Its unusual silhouette makes it a good conversation piece.

Dracaena fragrans has an upright blonde trunk from which sprout heavy, ribbonlike, blue green leaves, 2 inches wide and 1½ to 3 feet long. It tolerates darker indoor situations than other kinds of *Dracaena.* Variety 'Massangeana' is noted for broad yellowish green stripes down the center of each leaf. Other striped varieties of *D. fragrans* are 'Lindenii' and 'Victoria'.

Dracaena marginata has smooth gray stems, slender and erect, eventually growing to 20 feet. Stems end in crowns of narrow, leathery leaves ½ inch wide and up to 2 feet long. Leaves are deep glossy green, edged in purplish red. This kind is very easy to grow; named varieties include *D.m.* 'Tricolor' and *D.m.* 'Candy Cane', both of which have narrow stripes of gold, green, and red.

Dracaena surculosa, commonly referred to as gold dust plant, is small and slow growing, its dark green leaves irregularly spotted with yellow or white.

Epipremnum

(ep-uh-PREEM-num)

Devil's ivy, Golden hunter's robe, Pothos

These easy-to-grow evergreens are similar in appearance to their relative, *Philodendron* (see pages 75–76)—and, like *Philodendron,* they're climbers. Stems put forth leathery heart-shaped leaves, 2 to 4 inches long, of bright green splashed with yellow.

You can train *Epipremnum* to climb long distances, or plant it in a hanging basket to dangle.

When grown in a greenhouse and given plenty of room, *Epipremnum* becomes a very large vine with deeply cut, 2 to 2½-foot-long leaves. But don't expect showy flowers.

Growing requirements

Epipremnum requires only a standard indoor potting soil; bright, filtered light (as through a sheer curtain); and typical household temperature and humidity. Allow potting soil to dry out slightly between waterings. During winter, let the top 1 to 2 inches of the soil dry out. Except in winter, apply a complete fertilizer regularly (see page 21).

Keep leaves clean by regularly wiping with a damp cloth, but don't use commercial leaf shine products. Pinch off growing tips to prevent leggy growth. If stems become bare, cut them back halfway. Pests rarely bother *Epipremnum.*

Favorites

Epipremnum aureum is the most commonly available form.

Epipremnum aureum (pothos)

Fatshedera

(fats-HED-uh-ruh)

Botanical wonder, Ivy tree

A most unusual hybrid between *Fatsia japonica* and *Hedera helix,* this attractive and carefree house plant looks like oversize ivy. Showing traits from both parents, *Fatshedera* puts forth glossy leaves that are 6 to 8 inches wide, with 3 to 5-inch pointed lobes. Unlike ivy, it assumes a shrubby shape, with long trailing or climbing stems.

Growing requirements

Fatshedera likes bright, filtered light (as through a sheer curtain), high humidity, and temperatures in the 60° to 65°F range (16° to 18°C). An easy plant to grow, it also accepts less than ideal conditions—higher temperatures, lower humidity, and less light. A standard indoor potting soil is all *Fatshedera* requires. It tolerates pot-bound conditions quite well.

Fatshedera responds well to a winter rest period, when it's advisable to reduce the amount of water given and withhold fertilizer applications. During the growing season, apply a complete fertilizer regularly (see page 21). If indoor winter temperatures consistently exceed 70°F/21°C, mist daily.

Water well—so that water drains out of the drain hole—during the spring and summer growth period, but allow the top 2 inches of soil to dry out between waterings.

Fatshedera tends to grow in a straight line, but it can be shaped if you work at it. Pinch off growing tips to force more side branches; guide and tie the stems on a trellis before they become brittle. Because this is a fast-growing plant, the branches should be trained and tied as often as 2 to 3 times a year. If the plant becomes too large or misshapen, it can be cut to within a few inches of the ground in early spring; it will resprout quickly. As *Fatshedera* becomes older, it tends to become leafless at the base. Some gardeners compensate for this by planting young plants at the base.

Fatshedera is occasionally bothered by aphids, red spider mites, scale, and thrips. The disease gray mold may attack *Fatshedera* if you grow it in a particularly cool, dark location. See pages 29–31 for methods of pest and disease control.

Favorites

Fatshedera lizei, with the characteristics described previously, is the most common type. A variegated variety with white-bordered leaves is sold under the name *F. l.* 'Variegata'.

Fatshedera lizei (ivy tree)

Ferns

Vast and ancient, this group of plants has become enormously popular with many indoor gardeners: a beautiful, healthy fern adds a little woodland romance and mystery to its surroundings. Taken as a whole, ferns offer an obvious attraction in their lovely and fascinating foliage; in fact, the whole show is foliage alone, since these plants produce no flowers at all. Fern leaves, called fronds, are usually finely cut.

General growing requirements

Ferns don't just look delicate—they really do have a delicate constitution. Too much of anything—water, light, fertilizer—will result in problems. But if you follow the guidelines below with care, your fern should flourish.

Soil. In general, most ferns grow well in standard indoor potting soil. Because nearly all ferns have shallow roots, you can use a shallow pot.

Water. Ferns are fairly fussy about their requirements. As a rule, keep the soil evenly moist (like a squeezed-out sponge), but don't let it get soggy. During winter, when temperatures drop to a cooler range and there are fewer daylight hours, let the soil surface dry out between waterings. If you keep a saucer under your potted fern, don't let the runoff water stand in it for more than a few hours.

Humidity and temperature. Ferns benefit from extra humidity in addition to ample water. To achieve this, you can place the fern's pot on a humidity tray (see page 20) or mist the plant daily. It's best to mist in the morning—foliage that stays damp overnight invites fungus disease attacks. When misting ferns, keep the mister 1½ to 2 feet away from the plant; you don't want to spray the foliage directly, but rather to let moisture from the surrounding air settle onto the plant. Always use tepid water, both for humidifying and for watering a fern.

Average to warm house temperatures (from 65° to 75°F/18° to 24°C) suit the majority of ferns just fine. If your home is at the higher end of the temperature range, be sure you also keep air humidity high; warmer air is usually also drier, which can quickly spell trouble for ferns. Temperatures much below 55°F/13°C send ferns into a dormant state, during which time you should reduce water, allowing the top inch of the soil to dry between applications.

Light. While it's true that the vast majority of ferns sold as house plants cannot tolerate hot, direct sun, neither will they accept dark, shady locations, as some owners believe. In the wild, these plants make up the forest undergrowth beneath mature trees, receiving a combination of shade and dappled sunlight. You can most closely match these natural conditions by placing your fern where it will receive filtered light—for example, sunlight that's screened through a sheer curtain or largely blocked by the foliage of trees, shrubs, or other plants outside. Or put your fern in a north or east-facing window, which usually offers just the right light conditions.

Fertilizer. Once a month, apply a liquid fertilizer (see page 21) diluted to half strength. Ferns have extremely tender roots, which can be damaged by a full-strength dose of fertilizer. Never apply fertilizer to a plant whose soil is dry. As long as the house temperature stays above 55°F/13°C, most ferns don't have a distinct winter rest or dormancy period, so they need fertilizer all year.

Pests and diseases. Scale and mealybugs occasionally attack ferns— but be cautious with control measures. Since most chemical products will damage a fern's foliage, many fern fanciers prefer to avoid insecticides, instead controlling both scale and mealybugs with denatured alcohol—which won't hurt the plant. (See pages 30 and 31 for ways to use alcohol against these pests.) If you do decide to treat your fern with insecticide, check the label carefully to be sure the product is guaranteed safe for use with ferns; then follow the directions explicitly, paying particular attention to dilution instructions.

Aphids are another occasional trouble-maker; to get rid of them, simply give the fern a shower, being sure that the water knocks off all the insects.

Summering outdoors. Many people like to put their ferns outdoors in summer; some owners report that their ferns grow exuberantly during their stay outdoors, enlarging to generous fullness in just a short time. Certainly the lush, lacy foliage adds elegance to a porch or patio—but be sure the outdoor conditions are as easy on the plant as those indoors. Too much sun or wind will burn foliage quickly, and birds may find ferns an appealing site for their nests. Protect plants from voracious slugs and snails.

Favorite ferns and their special needs

The following list describes 13 of the currently popular and commonly available fern groups.

Adiantum (a-dee-AN-tum), commonly called maidenhair fern, is among the most delicate and beautiful of all ferns, just about irresistible when healthy and well grown. Most are native to the tropics, though a few come from the western United States.

Extremely thin and wiry, the stems of maidenhair ferns are usually dark brown or black. Bright, apple green foliage is very thin textured and delicate; fronds are finely cut and most leaflets are fan shaped. Keep plants in a semishaded location, and never allow the soil to dry out completely.

Adiantum peruvianum, the silver dollar maidenhair, is native to Peru. The plant grows to 1½ feet tall and produces leaflets larger than *A. raddianum,* to 2 inches wide. This fern is most often grown in greenhouses.

Adiantum raddianum, a Brazilian native, grows fronds from 15 to 18 inches long, fluffy and dense with leaflets in multiples of three. These ferns, more than most other types, benefit from summering outdoors in a well-sheltered location. Many named varieties are available, all differing in texture and compactness of habit. Varieties commonly sold are *A.r.* 'Fritz-Luthii', *A.r.* 'Gracillimum' (the most finely cut of them all), and *A.r.* 'Pacific Maid'.

Adiantum tenerum (also sold as *A. wrightii*) is native to the New World tropics. Its long, broad fronds arch gracefully and are finely split into many deeply cut segments, ½ to ¾ inch wide.

Asparagus (uh-SPAR-uh-gus). Of about 150 kinds of *Asparagus*—not counting the edible one—many have become popular house plants. None of them is really a fern, but the best known of the ornamental types is called asparagus fern (*A. setaceus*). Ornamental asparagus is valued mostly for its unusual lacy foliage, growing in bright green needlelike leaflets; some types also offer small, fragrant flowers and colorful berries. Favorites for hanging baskets, these "ferns" are sometimes placed where they can trail over a second-story balcony.

Asparagus asparagoides, commonly called the smilax asparagus, is a many-branched vine with stems to 20 feet or more. (Unlike some types of *Asparagus, A. asparagoides* has thornless stems.) Glossy, grass green leaves, to 1 inch long, are sharp pointed and rather stiff. Small, fragrant white flowers bloom in spring, followed later by blue berries. It's a good idea to train this climbing plant on a trellis; left on its own, it can become a tangled mass. The variety *A.a.* 'Myrtifolius', commonly called baby smilax, grows in a more graceful, less sprawling form, with smaller leaves.

Asparagus densiflorus 'Myers', commonly sold as Myers asparagus, sends up several to many stiff, upright stems, to 2 feet or higher. These stems are densely covered with deep green needlelike leaves, giving the plant a fluffy look. *A.d.* 'Sprengeri', commonly sold as Sprenger asparagus, produces 3 to 6-foot-long arching or drooping stems. Shiny, bright green leaves, like inch-long needles, appear in bundles. Bright red berries add color in late summer or autumn. Sprenger asparagus is popular for hanging baskets, both indoors and out; it can also be trained upright on a trellis. It tolerates low levels of humidity indoors, but needs bright filtered light (as through a sheer curtain). The type sold as *A.d.* 'Sprengeri Compacta' or *A. sarmentosus* 'Compacta' is denser, with shorter stems.

Asparagus falcatus, also called sickle-thorn asparagus, takes its common name from curved thorns along its stems. These thorns help the plant climb to great heights—sometimes 10 feet or more. It gets there quickly, too, so pinch back the growing tips

Davallia trichomanoides
(squirrel's foot fern)

Asparagus densiflorus 'Sprengeri'
(Sprenger asparagus)

Asplenium nidus
(bird's nest fern)

Adiantum raddianum
(maidenhair fern)

Adiantum tenerum
(maidenhair fern)

Selaginella
kraussiana
(moss fern)

Pellaea rotundifolia
(button fern)

Cyrtomium falcatum
(holly fern)

Polystichum tsus-simense

Pteris cretica 'Albolineata'

keep the plant under control. Two to 3-inch-long leaves are borne in clusters of three or four, at the ends of the branches. Tiny white flowers, in loose, fragrant clusters, appear in spring and summer. Brown berries follow as summer turns to autumn.

Asparagus setaceus, commonly known as fern asparagus or asparagus fern, is actually a branching, woody vine whose wiry, spiny stems can climb as far as 10 to 20 feet. Its tiny threadlike leaves grow in dark green, feathery sprays that resemble fern fronds. Tiny white flowers are followed by purplish black berries. *A.s.* 'Nanus' is a dwarf form.

Asplenium *(ah-SPLEE-nee-um).* This group of ferns offers considerable diversity.

Asplenium bulbiferum, commonly called mother fern, comes from New Zealand. Its graceful, light green fronds are very finely cut, sometimes reaching 4 feet in length. Unlike most ferns, *A. bulbiferum* produces plantlets along its fronds that can be removed and planted—hence the plant's common name.

Asplenium daucifolium, quite similar in appearance to *A. bulbiferum*, has smaller fronds—growing only to 2 feet—and they're divided even more finely. Like *A. bulbiferum*, this fern produces plantlets from its ''mother'' fronds.

Asplenium nidus, commonly called bird's nest fern, produces showy, apple green fronds to 4 feet long and 8 inches wide. Its strikingly smooth, shiny fronds grow upright in a cluster; they're completely undivided or cut. This plant benefits from summering outdoors.

Cyrtomium *(seer-TO-mee-um).* This rather coarse-textured fern can also be grown outdoors in areas where winters are mild, with temperatures never falling below 25°F/ − 4°C.

Cyrtomium falcatum, the only widely available form, gets its common name—holly fern—from its hollylike foliage. Leaflets are large, dark green, glossy, and leathery to the touch; on some forms, leaflets are fringed. A handsome plant, *C. falcatum* grows 2 to 3 feet tall, sometimes taller. One of the tougher ferns, it readily adapts to indoor conditions.

56

Nephrolepis exaltata 'Bostoniensis' (Boston fern)

Polypodium aureum (hare's foot fern)

Dicksonia antarctica (Tasmanian tree fern)

Asplenium bulbiferum (mother fern)

Davallia (dub-VAL-ee-uh). This fern puts out unusual rhizomes that crawl along the top of the soil and even outside the plant's container. Because the rhizomes have a furry texture, *Davallia* is commonly called rabbit's foot or squirrel's foot fern.

Davallia trichomanoides has very finely divided fronds, up to a foot long and 6 inches wide, rising from the reddish brown, furry rhizomes that creep over the soil surface. This fern is best grown in a hanging basket, especially the wire type lined with sphagnum moss. Mature specimens with long rhizomes send out fronds that cover the basket, making it look like a large fern "ball." *D. trichomanoides* needs somewhat less water than most other ferns.

Dicksonia (dik-SO-nee-uh). This good-looking, large-scale fern is rugged and slow growing. The most popular type is *Dicksonia antarctica,* commonly called the Tasmanian tree fern. Indoors, it's usually seen in a juvenile state—2 to 4 feet tall and about as wide. Outdoors, though, it can reach 15 feet tall, with 3 to 6-foot-long arching fronds extending out from a brown, fuzzy central trunk. Each frond produces many light green, finely cut leaflets.

Nephrolepis (nee-FRAH-luh-pus). Members of this group are among the easiest to grow of all ferns. They adapt quite successfully to indoor conditions.

Nephrolepis cordifolia, the southern sword fern, forms tufts of bright green, narrow, upright fronds, growing 2 to 3 feet tall and 2½ inches wide. The fronds are split into closely spaced, finely toothed leaflets. *N. cordifolia*'s roots often have small roundish tubers. If grown in a roomy planter rather than in a pot, this fern will spread over larger areas by means of thin, fuzzy runners.

Nephrolepis exaltata, commonly called the sword fern, looks very much like *N. cordifolia,* but grows taller (to 5 feet high), with fronds to 6 inches wide.

N.e. 'Bostoniensis', commonly called Boston fern, grows in a spreading and arching manner; its graceful fronds droop with age. The classic parlor fern of grandmother's day, Boston fern grows best in a north-facing window in a cool room (60° to 65°F/16° to 18°C). Several named varieties offer more finely cut leaflets and more feathery forms. Among the best known are *N.e.* 'Fluffy Ruffles', *N.e.* 'Rooseveltii', and *N.e.* 'Whitmanii'.

Pellaea (pe-LEE-uh). Collectively, these ferns are known as cliff-brake. Though these plants don't have a dramatic silhouette, they do produce charmingly detailed foliage.

Pellaea rotundifolia, commonly called the roundleaf or button fern, is relatively small, its fronds growing to a foot in length. Nearly round, ¾-inch-wide leaflets are evenly spaced all along the fronds. *P. rotundifolia* is a good choice for mixed plantings; it makes a nice contrast to finer-textured ferns. Or show it off on its own.

Pellaea viridis, sometimes called green cliff-brake, grows fronds up to 2 feet long, with grass green oval or lance-shaped leaflets. In a planter, *P. viridis* spreads like a ground cover, but it assumes a bushy shape in a more confined container.

Platycerium (pla-ti-SEE-ree-um). Known as staghorn fern, this plant is native to tropical regions. In its natural environment, *Platycerium* is an epiphyte: it attaches to the side of a tree, sustaining itself on the leaf mold and moisture that gathers around its roots. Gardeners grow staghorn fern on a slab of bark, on the stem of a tree fern, or occasionally in a hanging basket or on a tree. *Platycerium* is a striking plant, often used as a decorative accent on patios or lanais, or indoors. Keep this fern on the dry side, watering only when the plant's bark or moss base feels dry.

Platycerium has two kinds of fronds—sterile and fertile. The first are flat; they're pale green when young, later tan or brown. These form a support for the plant, accumulating organic matter to help feed it. The fertile fronds appear in forked configurations resembling deer antlers, inspiring the fern's common name.

Platycerium bifurcatum (often sold as *P. alcicorne*) is a native of Australia and New Guinea. Its fertile fronds, gray green and up to about 3 feet long, grow in clusters. From their bases grow runners that produce small offsets; these can be planted.

Platycerium grande is native to Australia. Its fertile and sterile fronds are both forked; the former look something like moose antlers, broad and divided. These fronds grow to 6 feet long. Don't overwater this one.

Polypodium (pahl-i-PO-dee-um). This widespread group of ferns includes widely varying types.

Polypodium aureum, a big plant commonly called hare's foot fern, is beautifully suited to a hanging basket. Thick brown creeping rhizomes, like flattened pencils, produce coarse bluish green fronds, 3 to 5 feet long. A native of tropical America, this fern needs semishaded conditions and plenty of water; keep the soil continuously moist—don't let it dry out between waterings. *P.a.* 'Mandaianum', sometimes called lettuce fern, puts forth fronds with frilled and wavy edges. Both forms look very showy on display.

Polypodium subauriculatum 'Knightiae', commonly called Knight's polypody, produces gracefully drooping fronds with frilled edges, growing to 3 or more feet long and up to a foot wide. When well grown, this fern makes a spectacular hanging basket specimen, looking something like a glorified Boston fern.

Polystichum (pahl-i-STY-kum). Among the easiest to grow of all ferns, *Polystichum* is often grown outdoors where conditions permit.

Polystichum munitum, the sword fern, is the most common form. It has leathery, shiny, dark green fronds, 2 to 4 feet long (older plants may have 75 to 100 fronds). Compared to some of the Boston ferns, this is a rather coarse plant, but still lush and fernlike. *P. munitum* grows best in rich soil with plenty of leaf mold added to it; give it ample water the year around.

Polystichum tsus-simense has shorter (about 12 inches long), more finely cut fronds than *P. munitum*. Its soil and water requirements are the same.

Pteris (TEE-ris). Sometimes called brake or table ferns, this group includes mostly small ferns of subtropical or tropical origin, best suited to dish gardens or small pots.

Pteris cretica grows fronds to 1½ feet in length and has long, narrow leaflets, comparatively few in number.

Platycerium bifurcatum (staghorn fern)

Numerous varieties exist, some with forked or crested fronds, some variegated with yellow. *P.c.* 'Wimsettii', when mature, has pale green fronds with forked tips and grows so dense and frilly that it doesn't look like a fern. *P.c.* 'Albolineata' is not frilled; it has an attractive band of greenish white in the center of each leaflet.

Pteris quadriaurita 'Argyraea', commonly called silver fern, is a native of India. Its fronds, growing 2 to 4 feet tall, are rather coarsely divided and heavily marked with white. This is a showy plant.

Pteris tremula, a fast-growing type, is commonly known as Australian brake. It produces extremely graceful 2 to 4-foot fronds on slender, upright stalks.

Selaginella (sel-uh-ji-NEL-uh). Neither a true moss nor a true fern, *Selaginella* has characteristics of both. It does look mosslike, but it's taller and fluffier than real moss—and so is often taken for a fern. Its common names, moss fern and spike moss, reflect some of the confusion. Since it has a creeping growth habit, it's a good ground cover in terrariums and dish gardens. It will even trail if planted in a small hanging basket.

Selaginella kraussiana, a fast-growing dwarf form, puts forth bright green leaves. Individual stems grow to about a foot tall. *S.k.* 'Aurea' has a similar look but its leaves are golden green.

Selaginella uncinata, commonly called peacock fern, produces leaves of iridescent, metallic blue green.

Ficus
(FY-kus)

Fig, Rubber plant, Weeping Chinese banyan

The wide-ranging *Ficus* group includes all types of plants—shrubs, trees, even vines. Best known to house plant lovers is *Ficus benjamina*, the weeping fig or weeping Chinese banyan. Since entering the house plant market a number of years ago, this particularly popular *Ficus* has brought exceptional beauty to interior decorating.

Because of their rather leathery leaves, which hold up well in the low humidity of typical interiors, most members of the *Ficus* group make reliable house plants, easy to grow as long as you attend to their moderate needs.

General growing requirements

As a rule, *Ficus* likes bright, reflected light and average room temperatures. Except in autumn and winter, apply a complete fertilizer regularly (see page 21).

Provide a standard indoor potting soil, keeping it moist (like a squeezed-out sponge), but not soggy. Mist during warm summer months, and in winter if the indoor air is warm and dry. In winter, let the soil dry out slightly between waterings; overwatering (or allowing water to collect in a saucer or cachepot) commonly leads to leaf drop. (Unwitting owners may increase water, thinking loss of leaves is a symptom of drought.)

Ficus is generally pest-free, but some types occasionally attract aphids, mealybugs, red spider mites, scale, or thrips. See pages 29–31 for methods of control.

Favorites and their special needs

Described below are a number of the most popular plants in the group.

Ficus benjamina has upright trunks that spread into a many-branched crown, delicate and rather open. If not cut back, *F. benjamina* may grow to ceiling height. Shiny, dark green, leathery leaves are 2 to 5 inches long; new growth is pale green. The older the plant, the more "weeping" branches it will have. These plants are particularly attractive in groups.

F. benjamina thrives in standard indoor potting soil; keep it moist (like a squeezed-out sponge), but not soggy. Apply small amounts of fertilizer (see page 21) frequently, and provide abundant indirect light. This plant dislikes overwatering, low light, drafts, home heating sources, and sudden changes in environment. If you have a *Ficus benjamina* growing happily, don't move it—that could cause it to drop leaves (though it would probably grow new ones). Recently purchased plants, too, often drop leaves as a re-

Ficus benjamina (weeping Chinese banyan)

Botanical name / Common name	Size	Comments
F. benjamina / Weeping Chinese Banyan	30 feet	Among the most popular and reliable house plants. Prefers abundant indirect light, but adapts (gradually) to weak or strong light. Dislikes overwatering, extended periods of low light, drafts, home heating sources, and change of location. Shock from moving may cause leaf drop, but new leaves usually appear soon.
F.b. 'Exotica'	30 feet	Like *F. benjamina*, but leaves wavy-edged with long, twisted tips.
F.carica / Edible fig	6–30 feet	Trees have gray bark and rough, bright green, large leaves; attractive silhouette.
F. deltoidea / Mistletoe fig	8–10 feet	Leaves thick, dark green, roundish, 2 inches wide. Interesting open, twisting branch pattern. Grow in part shade or strong filtered light.
F. elastica / Rubber plant	10–40 feet	Familiar, foolproof indoor plant. Leaves thick, glossy, leathery, dark green, 8–12 inches long and 4–6 inches wide. Let soil dry somewhat between waterings.
F.e. 'Decora'	10–40 feet	Leaves wider, glossier than *F. elastica*'s; tinted bronze when young.
F.e. 'Rubra'	10–20 feet	New leaves reddish; mature leaves have red edges, green center.
F.e. 'Variegata'	10–20 feet	Leaves long, narrow, variegated yellow and green. Attractive way to brighten dark corners.
F. lyrata / Fiddleleaf fig	6–20 feet	Large fiddle-shaped leaves (15 inches long and 10 inches wide), dark green and prominently veined. Very popular and good-looking, but somewhat more demanding than other types of *Ficus*.
F. microcarpa nitida	6–30 feet	Branches upright and covered with shiny, pointed leaves. Thin or shear any time to desired shape. Use systemic insecticide (see page 31) to control thrips.

Ficus elastica (rubber plant)

Large plant at left is *Ficus carica* (edible fig); large plant at right is *Ficus lyrata* (fiddleleaf fig).

Ficus deltoidea (mistletoe fig)

sult of moving shock. Don't rush to cure them with heavy watering—this only worsens things. Just give it time.

Ficus carica, the edible fig, is rarely recommended as a house plant —but as you can see in the photo above, there's no reason not to give it a try. The edible fig eventually reaches a height of 6 to 30 feet. Its rough, bright green, three to five-lobed leaves are 4 to 9 inches long and nearly as wide. Its trunk and stems are smooth, with gray bark (trunks become gnarled on mature plants). Give *F. carica* a warm location. Allow the top few inches of the soil to dry out between waterings.

Ficus deltoidea, commonly referred to as mistletoe fig, grows very slowly but eventually reaches a height of 8 to 10 feet. *F. deltoidea* is an attractive plant with an interesting open, twisted branch pattern; its dark green 2-inch-long leaves are roundish and thick, sparsely stippled with tan specks on the upper surface and black specks below. Small greenish yellow fruits,

borne all year long, make the tree's branches look like holiday mistletoe. *F. deltoidea* needs more water than other types of *Ficus*.

Ficus elastica, commonly known as the rubber plant, is one of the most foolproof of all indoor plants. It tolerates less light than most plants of its size. Let the soil get fairly dry.

Thick, glossy, and leathery, its dark green leaves are 8 to 12 inches long, 4 to 6 inches wide. New leaves unfold from rosy pink sheaths that soon wither and drop. Where conditions permit, the rubber plant can reach ceiling height.

F.e. 'Decora' is considered superior to the species because it has broader, glossier leaves—new leaves have a bronze hue. *F.e.* 'Rubra' puts forth reddish new leaves; as they mature, leaf edges stay red, but the centers turn green. *F.e.* 'Variegata' has long, narrow leaves, variegated yellow and green.

Ficus lyrata, the handsome fiddleleaf fig, has huge dark green, fid-

dle-shaped leaves. Prominently veined and glossy, the leaves grow to 15 inches long and 10 inches wide. Prune the top to make the plant bushy.

F. lyrata tolerates low light; it doesn't require a large pot, but be sure to stabilize a large plant in a small pot so it won't tip over. For health and best appearance, keep the leaves clean— wipe them with a damp cloth, or give your plant an outdoor shower.

Ficus microcarpa nitida is similar in appearance to *F. benjamina*, but it has straighter branches and fewer, more leathery leaves. It's a good indoor specimen, though it needs frequent pruning (see page 26) to maintain an attractive shape.

Ficus pumila is a creeping vine; young plants have tiny, heart-shaped leaves. This *Ficus* usually fares poorly if kept indoors for any length of time.

A CATALOG OF HOUSE PLANTS **59**

Fittonia verschaffeltii argyroneura (mosaic plant)

Fittonia

(fi-TOE-nee-uh)

Mosaic plant, Nerve plant

A popular choice for terrariums, *Fittonia* is a South American native. This low-growing, creeping plant has dark green oval leaves, 2 to 4 inches long and conspicuously veined in red or white.

Growing requirements

Fittonia prefers bright, reflected light, high humidity, and warm temperatures (70° to 75°F/21° to 24°C). Use a standard indoor potting soil and give the plant plenty of water—never let the soil dry out completely. Except in winter, apply a complete fertilizer regularly (see page 21). Because *Fittonia* prefers warm temperatures, high humidity, and constant moisture, many indoor gardeners have an easier time growing it in a terrarium or bottle garden, which creates an environment ideal for this plant. To grow successfully outside a terrarium, *Fittonia* needs special attention.

Pinch off growing tips in spring to promote bushiness. *Fittonia* is occasionally bothered by mealybugs, red spider mites, and scale; see pages 29–31 for methods of control.

Favorites

Fittonia gigantea is a relatively new form and different from others in two ways: it is quite bushy, and it will reach 18 to 24 inches tall under the right conditions. Its leaves, approximately 4 inches long, are dark green with magenta veins.

Fittonia verschaffeltii has dark green leaves veined with red or bright pink. *F.v. argyroneura* is similar, but the veins on its leaves are white.

Gynura aurantiaca 'Purple Passion' (purple velvet plant)

Gynura

(jy-NOO-ruh)

**Purple passion vine,
Purple velvet plant**

An East Indian native, *Gynura* catches the eye immediately with its vivid and exotic foliage. The lance-shaped leaves grow to 6 inches long and 2½ inches wide, with toothed edges. Velvety violet hairs cover both leaves and stems. In shrubby fashion, this plant may reach 2 to 3 feet in height. Small yellow or orange flowers form in spring or summer, but since their scent is unpleasant, it's best to pinch them off before they bloom.

Growing requirements

Gynura needs bright, filtered light (as through a sheer curtain) or direct sunlight as long as the room temperature is below 75°F/21°C. With too little light, this naturally leggy plant will become even lankier and will lack its characteristic purplish color.

A standard indoor potting soil suits *Gynura* fine. Apply a complete fertilizer (see page 21) regularly from spring through early autumn, but don't overdo it—plant will become lanky.

Gynura will also suffer from too much water. Allow the top 1 inch or so of potting soil to dry out between waterings. Temperatures in the 60° to 70°F range (16° to 21°C) are fine, but be sure to keep the humidity high by placing the plant on a humidity tray (see page 20). Don't mist *Gynura*, and try not to wet its foliage.

Gynura's growing tips should be pinched off regularly to produce a bushy plant. It's occasionally bothered by aphids, mealybugs, red spider mites, or whiteflies; see pages 29–31.

Favorites

Two forms of *Gynura aurantiaca* are commonly sold: *G.a.* 'Purple Passion' and *G.a.* 'Sarmentosa'. 'Purple Passion' fits the description at left. 'Sarmentosa' has narrower, deep-lobed leaves; it climbs or trails.

Hedera

(HED-uh-ruh)

Ivy

Popular for many generations, these evergreen, fast-growing vines include only one ivy that thrives indoors: *Hedera helix*. But dozens of named *H. helix* varieties exist, offering an ample choice of leaf shapes and colors. Other *Hedera* species, such as *H. canariensis* (Algerian ivy) and *H. colchica* (Persian ivy) can be grown inside, but their rampant growth presents problems for most indoor gardeners.

Plants look graceful when draped or trailing over sides of pots, or when trained to climb up almost any kind of support. Almost all types produce aerial roots along their stems. These act as anchors to any rough surface such as bricks or masonry; they'll take root if they come into contact with soil.

Growing requirements

Ivy prefers bright, reflected or filtered (as through a sheer curtain) light. Though it will tolerate some direct (but weak) winter sun, it must stay out of direct sun during the warm months. All types of ivy grow well in a standard indoor potting soil. During spring and summer, keep the soil moist (like a squeezed-out sponge), but not soggy. During cooler autumn and winter months, allow the top inch or so of the soil to dry out between waterings. The year around, apply a complete fertilizer regularly (see page 21).

Ivy appreciates extra humidity—especially when summer temperatures climb, or during winter if the room is heated. Mist your plant daily or place the pot on a humidity tray (see page 20).

The most important point to remember when growing ivy indoors is that it needs constantly cool temperatures—in the 60° to 65°F/16° to 18°C range. Higher temperatures sometimes encourage pests and diseases; simply by keeping your plant cool, you can avoid all types of problems. If your house gets fairly warm, ivy probably won't grow well for you.

Though ivy is a vigorous plant when properly cared for, it can become prey

Hedera helix 'Manda's Crested'

Hedera helix 'Emerald Gem'

Hedera helix 'Gold Dust'

Hedera helix 'Glacier'

Hedera helix 'Needlepoint'

to insect pests if it starts to falter. Common pests include red spider mites, thrips, aphids, and scale. Numerous fungus diseases will also attack ivy if growing conditions are poor. See pages 29–31 for methods of control.

If your ivy begins to do poorly, try summering it outdoors, where most varieties will soon revive and be ready to return indoors in the autumn.

Favorites

Only one type, *Hedera helix,* is commonly grown indoors.

H.h. '**Baltica**' has dark green leaves half the size of *H. helix*'s; they're split into five deeply cut lobes.

H.h. '**Conglomerata**' is a slow-growing dwarf variety with crinkly, stiff, dark green leaves about 1 inch across.

H.h. '**Glacier**' is a variegated type; its leathery, triangular leaves are 1 inch across, grayish green bordered with white. It needs more light than the other varieties.

H.h. '**Hahn's Self-branching**', a dense, branching variety, has pale green leaves that are angularly lobed, 1 to 1½ inches across.

H.h. '**Hibernica**', commonly called Irish ivy, is the largest of all varieties of *Hedera helix*. It's characterized by dense growth and round, deep green leaves with veining of paler green.

Leaves are up to 5 inches across.

H.h. '**Minima**' has medium green leaves ½ to 1 inch across, each with three to five pointed lobes.

H.h. '**Needlepoint**' has sharply pointed, dark green leaves, three-lobed and ¾ inch across.

H.h. '**Sweetheart**' puts forth heart-shaped, dark green leaves, 1 to 1½ inches across, with no visible lobes.

Other named varieties, of various forms and colorations, include 'California Gold', 'Cristata', 'Emerald Gem', 'Emerald Jewel', 'Fluffy Ruffles', 'Gold Dust', 'Gold Heart', 'Heart', 'Jubilee', 'Little Diamond', 'Manda', 'Ripple', 'Shamrock', and 'Star'.

Hemigraphis
(hem-i-GRAF-is)

**Purple waffle plant, Red ivy,
Red-flame ivy, Waffle plant**

Fascinating foliage draws attention to this creeping plant. Leaves on arching or trailing stems are oblong or heart-shaped, about 3 inches long and 2 inches wide. Deeply puckered or "waffled," their curiously metallic color is gray green or purplish green on top, dark red underneath. *Hemigraphis* is a blooming plant, but its flowers hardly show at all.

Growing requirements

Hemigraphis likes filtered light (as through a sheer curtain), average room temperatures, and average humidity. Use a standard indoor potting soil, kept moist (like a squeezed-out sponge), but not soggy. Except in winter, apply a complete fertilizer regularly (see page 21).

Pinch off the growing tips of *Hemigraphis* to promote a bushy shape. If the plant becomes spindly, it may help to prune it back by half. *Hemigraphis* is rarely bothered by pests.

Favorites

Hemigraphis alternata has ivylike, heart-shaped 3-inch leaves, gray green above with wine red undersides.

Hemigraphis 'Exotica' puts forth elongated oval leaves that are heavily puckered, giving its foliage a "waffled" look. Leaves are purplish green above, magenta underneath.

Hoya carnosa
(wax plant)

Hoya carnosa 'Krinkle Kurl'
(Hindu rope plant)

Hoya
(HOY-uh)

Hindu rope plant, Wax plant

Shrubby or climbing, *Hoya* sometimes needs a small trellis or taut string for support. A rather old-fashioned house plant, it has long been a favorite for training around the frame of a sunny kitchen window; it's also attractive in a hanging basket.

Most types of *Hoya* have waxy, thick leaves, though leaf shape and color vary. Star-shaped white flowers (sometimes with colored centers), also waxy, appear in tight clusters in summer; in some types, they're fragrant.

Growing requirements

Many owners grow *Hoya* in windows receiving the strong, reflected (not direct) sunlight that this plant needs. It prefers a standard indoor potting soil; let the soil dry out a bit between waterings. *Hoya* grows best at constant temperatures around 70°F/21°C. It needs slightly higher than average levels of humidity, so mist your plant daily.

The plant becomes semidormant in winter, when it requires less light, less water (let the soil dry out almost completely between waterings), and lower temperatures. Except in winter, apply a complete fertilizer (see page 21) every 2 months.

Hoya blooms best when potbound. Branches that have borne blossoms shouldn't be cut back to soil level, since new flower clusters appear from the stumps of old branches. Mealybugs, red spider mites, and scale can cause trouble; see pages 29–31.

Favorites

Hoya australis has round, dark green leaves, pointed at the ends. A fast-growing vine, it produces white flowers in dense umbrella-shaped clusters.

Hoya bella's slender, upright branches droop with age. The plant eventually develops a shrubby shape—about 1 foot tall, with branches trailing to about 3 feet—that looks best in a hanging basket. It offers unscented, purple-centered flowers.

Hoya carnosa (wax plant), usually grown on a trellis, has 2 to 4-inch-long oval leaves (young leaves are red). Its fragrant, creamy white flowers bloom in big, round, tight clusters; a perfect five-pointed pink star winks in the center of each flower. *H.c.* 'Variegata' has leaves edged with pinkish white; this edge color may change according to the plant's age and the availability of light. This variety isn't as vigorous as the green-foliaged type. *H.c.* 'Exotica' shows yellow and pink leaf variegation. *H.c.* 'Krinkle Kurl' (Hindu rope plant) produces crinkly leaves, closely spaced on short stems; it's often sold as *H.c.* 'Compacta'.

Hypoestes
(hy-po-ES-tes)

Baby's tears, Flamingo plant, Freckle face, Polka dot plant

Its common names make it obvious that *Hypoestes* has rather unusual foliage. Irregular pink spots or polka dots brighten the green tops of its 2 to 3-inch oval leaves. The plant grows as high as 1 to 2 feet. Spikes of lavender flowers sometimes appear, but it's best to remove these inconspicuous blossoms to keep the rest of the plant vigorous.

Children are fascinated with this pink polka-dotted plant.

Growing requirements

Hypoestes likes filtered light (as through a sheer curtain), moderate humidity, and temperatures in the 65° to 70°F range (18° to 21°C)—never let the temperature drop below 60°F/18°C. Use a mixture of equal parts standard indoor potting soil and peat moss; keep soil moist (like a squeezed-out sponge), but not soggy. Except in winter, apply a complete fertilizer regularly (see page 21).

Pinch off growing tips regularly to produce a full plant. *Hypoestes* is oc-casionally attacked by mealybugs, red spider mites, scale, and whiteflies; see pages 29–31 for methods of control.

As *Hypoestes* matures, the plant can become woody and straggly. Frequent pinching when the plant is young will help postpone the problem. Replace plants with new ones grown from seed or propagated with stem cuttings (see page 27).

Favorites

Hypoestes phyllostachya, the most commonly available type, fits the description at left. This plant is a native of Malagasy. One named form, *H. phyllostachya* 'Splash', has larger pink spots.

Hypoestes phyllostachya (polka dot plant)

Iresine
(i-ree-SY-nee)

Beefsteak plant, Bloodleaf plant, Chicken gizzard plant

People prize this native of Brazil primarily for its intensely colorful foliage. Its oval or round leaves, 1 to 2 inches long, are purplish red with a glowing pink midrib and veins—or sometimes green or bronzed with yellowish veins. Leaves are usually notched at the end.

Mature plants will sometimes produce flowers indoors, but the foliage is *Iresine*'s main claim to fame. When backlit by bright light, these plants will practically glow with fluorescent color.

Growing requirements

Bright, reflected light promotes the best leaf color. *Iresine* likes average house temperatures and humidity, and a standard indoor potting soil; keep it moist (like a squeezed-out sponge), but not soggy. Except in winter, apply a complete fertilizer regularly (see page 21 for directions).

Left to grow its own way, *Iresine* can become somewhat straggly. Start pinching out growing tips when the plant is young to produce the best-looking specimen. Pinch off growing tips frequently to encourage a bushy shape (see page 26 for further directions on guiding growth).

Iresine is occasionally bothered by mealybugs, red spider mites, and whiteflies; see pages 29–31 for methods of control.

Favorites

Iresine herbstii, the most commonly available type, fits the description given previously.

Iresine lindenii, a native of Ecuador, is similar, but its red leaves are pointed at the ends, not notched.

Iresine herbstii (bloodleaf plant)

Kohleria
(ko-LEER-ee-uh)

Tree gloxinia

Fuzzy and floral, these attractive natives of tropical America grow from rhizomes (fleshy underground stems). Stems grow from 1 to 4 feet long, depending on the form; you can train them upright, or let them trail from a hanging basket.

Fuzzy leaves create a plain green or patterned background for attractive tubular flowers in shades of pink, red, orange, or white. Flowers have flat, 5-lobed faces; on some, markings such as dots contrast with the predominant color. Like the foliage, flowers are fuzzy.

Growing requirements

Kohleria likes average house temperatures, filtered light (as through a sheer curtain), high humidity, and an African-violet-type potting soil. Keep soil moist (like a squeezed-out sponge), but not soggy. Increase humidity around a plant by placing the pot on a humidity tray (see page 20).

All year, apply a liquid fertilizer diluted to half strength (see page 21) every 2 weeks. After the plant blooms, remove all old growth to ensure continued bloom and health.

Kohleria is usually free of pests and diseases.

Favorites

Kohleria amabilis performs well in hanging baskets. Its dark green leaves have a purplish green pattern; darker pink streaks the bright pink flowers of this plant.

Kohleria bogotensis offers dark green foliage marked in pale green or white, with undersides of maroon. Bright red flowers have yellow dots.

Kohleria eriantha has green leaves with red margins, and orange red flowers with yellow markings on their lower 3 lobes.

Kohleria lindeniana has a compact growth habit. Its green leaves are veined with silver and bronze; its white flowers have violet markings.

Kohleria 'Rongo' has leaves that are veined and marked with dark green above, red veins beneath. Magenta marks the face of the rosy white blooms and colors the tube.

Kohleria 'Rongo' (tree gloxinia)

Lysimachia nummularia (creeping Jennie)

Lysimachia

(ly-si-MAK-ee-uh)

Creeping Jennie, Moneywort

A creeping evergreen, appreciated for its grace in hanging containers, *Lysimachia* produces round, pale green leaves on 2-foot-long runners that will root if in contact with the soil. Its small (1½ to 2-inch) roundish leaves give the plant a fine-textured appearance.

In summer, 1-inch yellow flowers add touches of color at leaf joints.

In addition to its use as a hanging plant, *Lysimachia* can be grown as a ground cover (plants spaced 12 to 18 inches apart) in a large indoor planter. When grown horizontally, it eventually forms an attractive, light green mat. It can also be used in an atrium, protected from frost yet exposed to rains and indirect sun. In this environment it will grow vigorously, covering large areas.

Lysimachia will also grow well in small dish gardens. It is particularly attractive when combined with other foliage plants of contrasting texture and color. Position the plant near the edge of the dish and allow it to drape or trail.

Many gardeners move these attractive plants outdoors for the summer onto a shaded, protected patio.

Growing requirements

Lysimachia likes bright, reflected light (not direct sun), average house temperatures, and moderate humidity. Use a standard indoor potting soil and keep it moist (like a squeezed-out sponge) but not soggy. Except in winter, apply a complete fertilizer regularly (see page 21 for directions).

For a more compact plant, frequently pinch off growing stems. *Lysimachia* is rarely bothered by pests.

Favorites

Only one type, *Lysimachia nummularia*, is commonly available; it has the characteristics given previously.

Maranta leuconeura erythroneura (prayer plant)

Maranta

(mah-RAN-tuh)

Arrowroot, Prayer plant, Rabbit tracks

Dramatically beautiful foliage distinguishes this low-growing, bushy native of tropical America. The surfaces of its large green leaves (up to 8 inches long and 4 inches wide) display intricate patterns of color. Colors include dark green, olive green, dark brown, and bright pinkish red.

At night, leaves fold together, resembling praying hands (actually, it's the plant's technique for conserving moisture). If your *Maranta*'s leaves regularly fold at night and open again the next day, rest assured that it has sufficient light for healthy growth. If its leaves stay closed most of the time, move the plant into brighter light.

Occasionally this plant blooms indoors, but its flowers aren't showy.

Growing requirements

Maranta prefers filtered light (as through a sheer curtain); direct sun scorches leaves. To look its best, it also needs high humidity and temperatures in the 65° to 75°F range (18° to 24°C). A standard indoor potting soil suits *Maranta;* keep it moist (like squeezed-out sponge), but not soggy. During the winter, allow the soil to dry out somewhat between waterings. Except in winter, apply a complete fertilizer regularly (see page 21).

If your tap water is hard, use rain water or bottled mineral-free water.

Snip off old or straggly leaves regularly. Aphids, mealybugs, red spider mites, and thrips sometimes infest *Maranta;* see pages 29–31 for methods of control.

Favorites

Maranta leuconeura erythroneura has olive green leaves with jagged silver centers and striking red veins. *M. kerchoviana*'s light green leaves are spotted down both sides of the midrib with dark brownish green; leaf undersides are grayish green with red spots. *M.l. leuconeura,* often sold as *M.* 'Massangeana', has large, prominently veined leaves with pink spots and purple undersides.

Monstera

(MAHN-ster-uh)

Splitleaf philodendron, Swiss cheese plant

Monstera is a large tropical vine, often confused with its relatives of the *Philodendron* clan. *Monstera's* gigantic heart-shaped, leathery leaves—up to 18 inches across—are dark green, perforated, and deeply cut.

The plant itself also grows as tall as 15 feet and up to 8 feet across.

If you want *Monstera* to grow vertically, you'll have to give it help; a moss-covered pole, available at nurseries, should provide enough support. (Don't use a plain wooden pole.) Long, cordlike roots dangle from stems as the plant matures.

A young plant won't display split or perforated leaves, but the older it grows, the more finely cut and perforated its leaves will become. Large plants may produce flowers resembling calla lilies, with thick, creamy yellow 10-inch spikes surrounded by white boatlike bracts. With enough heat, light, and humidity, the spike develops into an edible fruit—delicious when fully ripe.

Growing requirements

Monstera prefers bright light but will tolerate extreme shifts from direct sun to dim light. Give the plant warm temperatures and high humidity; use a standard indoor potting soil, kept moist (like a squeezed-out sponge), but not soggy. Except in winter, fertilize regularly (see page 21).

Wipe or wash leaves about once a month with tepid water. Leaves that remain small or fail to split are suffering from inadequate light or humidity. If a tall, mature plant becomes bare at the base, replant it in a larger container, adding younger, smaller plants around the base. Occasionally bothered by aphids, red spider mites, and mealybugs; see pages 29–31.

Favorites

Monstera deliciosa, the most commonly available type, fits the description given previously.

Monstera friedrichsthalii puts forth smaller, more delicate leaves with wavy edges that are less deeply cut than those of *M. deliciosa.* Its common name, Swiss cheese plant, comes from the oval holes appearing on either side of the leaf midrib.

Monstera deliciosa (splitleaf philodendron)

Nematanthus

(nee-muh-TAN-thus)

Candy corn, Goldfish plant

Nematanthus is relatively easy to grow. (Like another house plant, *Alloplectus,* it's sometimes sold as *Hypocyrta.*) Its foot-long, arching or trailing branches are closely set with leaves. Orange, red, or yellow flowers, about an inch long, look puffy, with pinched "goldfish mouths."

Growing requirements

Nematanthus needs an African violet-type potting soil. Keep the soil moist (like a squeezed-out sponge), but not soggy. Water with tepid water only. This plant prefers warm temperatures (in the 70° to 75°F/21° to 24°C range) and high humidity. Boost humidity by frequent misting or by placing the pot on a humidity tray (see page 20). Given sufficient warmth and humidity, the plant may produce flowers all year long. *Nematanthus* also likes bright filtered (as through a sheer curtain) or reflected light, and responds well when it receives a couple of hours of direct, cool morning sun each day. Except in autumn and winter, apply a complete fertilizer regularly (see page 21).

Nematanthus blooms best when somewhat potbound. Occasionally, mealybugs, red spider mites, scale, and whiteflies appear; see pages 29–31.

Favorites

Here we list some of the most popular types of *Nematanthus.*

Nematanthus gregarius has flowers colored bright orange and yellow orange. It's a compact plant with small, thick, glossy dark green leaves.

Nematanthus nervosus, with red orange blossoms, has dark green leaves on arching stems.

Nematanthus perianthomegus has yellow flowers with brownish purple stripes.

Nematanthus gregarius (goldfish plant)

Orchids

At one time, most people shied away from orchids, believing you needed a greenhouse to grow them satisfactorily. But as more and more people are discovering, you can grow orchids successfully without taking a lot of trouble to create special environments.

The 25,000 or so species that make up the orchid family vary so markedly in appearance that you'd never guess they were related. Blossoms can be tiny or flamboyantly big and showy. The spectrum of flower color includes everything but true black; predominant shades are lavender, pink, brown, red, yellow, and white. Often two or more colors, sometimes in vivid contrast, appear in a single flower. The enchanting beauty of some orchids is enhanced by an exquisite fragrance.

It's simplest to classify orchids by the way they grow in nature. One type, "epiphytic," grows on trees; the other, "terrestrial," grows in the ground. Variations in these two patterns do occur.

Epiphytic orchids rely on trees only for their physical perch—they are not parasites, as was once commonly believed. They take their nutrients from whatever the rain may wash in their direction, as well as from organic debris that collects around the roots.

Many epiphytic orchids have thickened stems called "pseudobulbs." These are storage sites for food and water.

Terrestrial orchids grow in the ground, often in wooded areas, but sometimes in open meadows as well. They prefer a moist, porous soil, rich in humus. Terrestrial orchids require constant moisture and regular applications of fertilizer.

General growing requirements

Be sure to know the basic growth habit of each orchid you buy, for orchids' needs differ accordingly. For example, terrestrial types need water all year round, but most epiphytes must stay dry during part of the year.

For more specific information on all phases of growing orchids, consult the *Sunset* book *How to Grow Orchids.*

Soil. Orchids have been grown in such "soils" as coconut shreddings, osmunda fiber (which contains plentiful nutrients), charcoal, and even gravel. For epiphytic orchids, fir bark is today's most popular potting material. Readily available, it's also easy to handle and reasonably priced. Choose fine grade fir bark for small pots (3 inches or less), medium grade for pots 4 inches or more in diameter.

Terrestrial orchids, such as *Cymbidiums,* some *Epidendrums,* and some *Paphiopedilums,* grow best in a potting soil made entirely of organic matter. It's safest to use one of the ready-made mixes sold by orchid growers and most nurseries.

Containers. Ventilation at the base of the pot is vital to an orchid's well-being, and excess water must not accumulate at the roots. Slotted clay pots, specifically designed for orchids, take care of both the ventilation and drainage problems; they're available at most large nurseries and garden centers. If you use a standard clay pot, enlarge the drainage hole by gently chipping away its edges.

Miniatures and smaller species of epiphytic orchid don't need a container at all. Often grown successfully on rafts or slabs of osmunda or tree fern fiber, they'll also roost on pieces of bark or logs. Some people suspend these slabs from ceiling hooks or affix them to a wall. (Larger epiphytes do need pots, though.)

Water. Unfortunately, there's no simple rule of thumb on how often to water orchids. The amount of water depends on such factors as pot size (a small pot requires more frequent watering); season of the year (generally, less water is needed in winter); and average temperature of the room (warmer rooms call for more water).

There's one convenient safeguard, though: When in doubt, don't water. Most orchids, both epiphytic and terrestrial, have their own water reservoirs, so that a few days without extra moisture won't harm them. When you do water your plant, always use tepid water—barely warm.

Temperature. Besides falling into two general growth habit groups, orchids also fall into three general categories based on preferred winter nighttime temperatures.

Cool-growing orchids prefer temperatures between 50° and 55°F/10° to 13°C, rising to 60° to 70°F/16° to 21°C during the day; this group includes *Cymbidium, Odontoglossum,* and some *Paphiopedilums.* Intermediate temperatures—55° to 60°F/13° to 16°C at night, and 65° to 75°F/18° to 24°C during the day—are best for *Cattleya,* some *Oncidiums,* and hybrid *Paphiopedilums.* For warm-growing orchids such as *Vanda, Phalaenopsis,* and tropical *Paphiopedilums,* night temperatures shouldn't fall below 60° to 65°F/16° to 18°C; day temperatures should be in the 70° to 80°F/21° to 27°C range.

Fortunately, both cool and warm environments can usually be arranged under the same roof. Place cool-growing plants closer to a window, where temperatures will be lower in winter; locations farther from the window pane will probably suit orchids that require more warmth.

Humidity. Orchids don't demand that you turn your home into a steaming jungle for their comfort. Most respond happily when the relative humidity in the air measures between 30 to 40 percent, a healthy amount for people.

One favorite method for boosting the humidity around orchids is to make the following special humidity tray: Fill a 2 to 4-inch-deep waterproof metal or plastic tray with gravel, stopping about an inch from the rim; then add enough water to cover the gravel to just below the surface (surface of gravel should remain dry). Stretch hardware cloth (screening wire) across the top of the tray, leaving about an inch of space between gravel and wire. Set pots on hardware cloth; replenish water as needed.

During spring and summer, mist orchids daily—even those on a humidity tray—to compensate for a drop in humidity. (This may not be necessary where summers are naturally humid.) Mist less frequently during the cooler autumn and winter months.

Essential to raising healthy, flowering orchids is a "fresh" atmosphere: give your plants near-continuous air circulation, but keep them out of hot and cold drafts.

Light. While many orchids thrive in a sunny window, need for light varies widely. For example, if you place a sun-loving orchid in a shady location, it won't bloom and will begin to decline. Place a shade-loving orchid in a sunny spot, and its leaves will probably scorch. Sometimes moving a plant only an inch or two—into more sun, or less, than it formerly received—makes all the difference.

Fertilizer. Most orchids can tolerate a mild fertilizer, such as a 10-10-5 formulation (see page 21). Fertilizers especially formulated for orchids are easiest to use. Here are two general guidelines to help you establish a fertilizing schedule for your plant: 1) Since orchids grown in fir bark require extra nitrogen, they'll need to be fertilized more often than plants grown in osmunda fiber. During the plant's growing season, you may want to apply a very weak solution of fertilizer at every other watering. 2) Orchids, like most plants, need very little fertilizer (or none at all) when they're not actively producing new growth and when light intensity is low, as it is in winter.

Pests. Though not especially pest-prone, orchids do suffer occasional attacks from weevils, cattleya flies, sowbugs, springtails, and slugs or snails. Mottled or disfigured foliage usually signals the presence of sucking pests—scale, thrips, mealybugs, or red spider mites. You can brush off light infestations of many insects by hand, or wash them away with a solution of soap and water. You'll need to use insecticide only for thrips and red spider mites and for heavy populations of scale and mealybugs.

See pages 29–31 for additional methods of pest control.

Diseases. Both fungal and bacterial diseases flourish when humidity is high. Though some get started at low temperatures, most don't appear until both temperature and humidity climb simultaneously. To discourage disease organisms, water an orchid as early in the day as you can.

If an orchid should become diseased, immediately isolate it from other, healthy orchids. Cut off all diseased parts of the plant, sterilizing the tool after each cut so it won't spread the

Phalaenopsis
(moth orchid)

Cymbidium,
miniature size

Miltonia Rouge 'California Plum'
(pansy orchid)

Odontoglossum

Cymbidium,
standard size

Phalaenopsis
(moth orchid)

Paphiopedilum Milmoore
(lady's slipper)

Oncidium

Vanda

Cattleya

Coelogyne burfordiense

...*Orchids*

infection to other parts of the plant. Treat the cut surface with a fungicide such as benomyl (sometimes sold as benlate, captan, or folpet).

Favorite orchids and their special needs

The following orchid favorites range from fairly easy to grow, to fussy.

Cattleya *(KAT-lee-uh)*. An epiphytic group, these orchids come from tropical America. The most popular and widely known of all orchids, *Cattleya* includes the familiar corsage blossom. All *Cattleyas* have pseudobulbs; these bear leathery leaves and one to four or more flowers on a single stem. Plants range in height from a few inches to more than 2 feet tall. Flowers appear in shades of lavender, purple, white, yellow, orange, red, green, and bronze.

Many *Cattleya* species, varieties, and hybrids exist. The newest hybrid forms include miniature *Cattleyas* and the bifoliates, standard-sized plants with leaves in pairs. Sometimes called multifloras, they produce large clusters of 3 to 5-inch flowers and—best of all—many bloom more than once a year.

Cattleya should be grown in osmunda fiber or fir bark and given a sunny location in either a western or southern exposure. Temperatures should stay at 55° to 60°F/13° to 16°C at night, 65° to 75°F/18° to 24°C during the day. Although *Cattleya* likes moisture, let it dry out thoroughly between waterings. Water more often in summer than in winter. Follow fertilizer guidelines on page 66; also use a humidity tray as on that page.

Coelogyne *(suh-LAH-juh-nee)*. Native to the eastern hemisphere, this group of epiphytic orchids produces dark green, spoon-shaped leaves and small flowers in shades of brown, cream, beige, or green.

Coelogyne prefers cool temperatures (50° to 55°F/10° to 13°C at night, 60° to 70°/16° to 21°C during the day) and shaded, low-light locations. Give it abundant water during the growing season (early spring through early summer), but don't let excess water collect in new growth where flower buds form, since it may cause them to rot.

Coelogyne burfordiense is a hybrid that produces pale yellowish green flowers with blackish brown spots on the bottom lip. Flower clusters appear on arching stems.

Coelogyne cristata, probably the most popular form, has pale green foliage crowned with big, showy 3 to 4-inch white flowers with yellow throats. *C. cristata* blooms from winter through spring; each stem carries three to eight pendulous blossoms.

Cymbidium *(sim-BID-ee-um)*. These popular terrestrial orchids come from high-altitude regions in Southeast Asia having heavy rainfall and cool nights.

Their long, narrow, grasslike leaves form a sheath around stout oval pseudobulbs. Long-lasting flowers blossom on erect or arching spikes, usually from February to early May. You may discover a few new early or late-blooming hybrids.

Cymbidium flowers most gloriously if given as much indirect light as possible; be sure it's bright filtered (as through a sheer curtain) or reflected light. Keep the orchid out of direct sunlight, since its foliage may burn in these conditions. Healthy foliage looks yellow green; if it's dark green, increase the light.

Most commonly available *Cymbidiums* are cool-growing orchids. Through summer and early autumn, they need night temperatures from 45° to 55°F/7° to 13°C.

Plant these orchids in packaged *Cymbidium* orchid potting soil; from March through October, keep the soil constantly moist (like a squeezed-out sponge), but not soggy. Apply fertilizer every 2 weeks from January through July, then monthly from August through December, following guidelines on page 66. Keep *Cymbidium* potbound for the best blooms.

Most *Cymbidium* growers list only hybrids in their catalogs—large-flowered varieties that offer white, pink, yellow, green, or bronze flowers. On the throat of most, yellow and dark red markings highlight the lip of the bloom. These large-flowered forms bear a dozen or more 4½ to 5-inch blossoms on each of their numerous stems. Miniature forms, about one-quarter the size of the standard types, are prized for their daintiness, flower color, and abundant bloom.

Epidendrum *(ep-uh-DEN-drum)*. Looking for an easy-to-grow orchid? This native of tropical America is just the ticket. Either epiphytic or terrestrial, *Epidendrum* offers considerable choice in both plant and flower form. Some have pseudobulbs and require a rest after flowering; others—the cane-stemmed types, such as *E. ibaguense*—need moisture all year round. Follow the general care given for *Cattleya*, at left.

Epidendrum atropurpureum grows to 16 inches from a pseudobulb. Its chocolate and pale green flowers, four to 20 on each stem, have lips of white and rosy purple. *E. atropurpureum* blooms in spring and early summer; after blooming, rest the plant by giving it cooler temperatures and less water.

Epidendrum ibaguense, native to Colombia, shoots up to 2 or even 4 feet high with canelike, leafy stems (it has no pseudobulb). Orange yellow flowers bloom in dense clusters at various times during the year. Numerous hybrids offer flowers of yellow, orange, pink, red, lavender, and white.

Epidendrum mariae reaches about 8 inches when in bloom. The 3-inch green flowers have broad white lips. Best grown on a slab of bark in bright light. Several named varieties exist; *E.m.* 'Doris' is a favorite.

Epidendrum nemorale grows to 16 inches from a pseudobulb, bearing 4-inch rose and purple flowers in spring and summer.

Epidendrum stamfordianum, growing to 2½ feet from a pseudobulb, produces tiny red and yellow flowers in spring.

Lycaste *(ly-KAS-tuh)*. These Central American orchids take either epiphytic or terrestrial form. Most are epiphytic types with large pseudobulbs that put forth one to three pleated-looking leaves. Long-lasting flowers are usually green, but some turn out in shades of pink, white, yellow, or brown.

Lycaste likes bright reflected light (no direct sun), cool temperatures (50° to 55°F/10° to 13°C at night, 60° to 70°F/16° to 21°C during the day), and high humidity; grow it on a humidity tray like that described on page 66. Plant *Lycaste* in fast-draining orchid soil mix and keep the soil constantly moist, except for the 2-week period after flowering. During that time, reduce watering to a minimum (keep soil barely moist) until new growth appears.

Lycaste aromatica grows to 16 inches high; it produces bright yellow, fragrant flowers in winter.

Lycaste cochleata is an impressive plant when in bloom. Flowers are 3 to 4 inches across, with yellowish green petals and yellowish gold columnar throats.

Lycaste deppei reaches a height of over 2 feet. At various times during the year, it bears greenish white flowers dotted with brown.

Lycaste virginalis grows to 2½ feet. Its flowers—white spotted with rose, or pink spotted with red—bloom during winter.

Miltonia *(mil-TO-nee-uh).* These beautiful epiphytes, also called pansy orchids, grow wild in tropical and subtropical regions of the Americas. Graceful, pale green, bladelike leaves, borne from short pseudobulbs, form a clump of foliage 10 to 12 inches tall and just as wide. Flat, velvety flowers, borne singly or in clusters, resemble pansies. Colors include whites, yellows, reds, and blends of these hues; flowers are sometimes spotted or patterned. Some *Miltonia* blossoms have a spicy-sweet fragrance.

All *Miltonias* require fairly cool nights to flower; *Cattleya*'s preferred temperatures of 55° to 60°F/13° to 16°C are satisfactory. It's best to keep daytime temperatures below 80°F/27°C. Colombian and Panamanian species and their hybrids prefer bright filtered or dappled sun, but no direct sunlight. Brazilian species and hybrids, on the other hand, are sun-lovers; give them a western or southern exposure, as you would a *Cattleya*.

For best results, grow *Miltonia* on a humidity tray, as described on page 66. Following the guidelines on the same page, give *Miltonia* monthly applications of fertilizer during the growing season, but none at all in winter. While flower spikes are forming, keep the soil moist (like a squeezed-out sponge), but not soggy; water less frequently during the winter, letting the soil dry out somewhat between waterings.

Odontoglossum *(o-DAHN-to-glah-sum).* Here's yet another epiphyte native to tropical America. Sheathing its flat, oval pseudobulbs are small, leathery leaves; two more leaves push up from the top. *Odontoglossum*'s ruffled flowers are generally white, yellow, brown, or pink. This orchid likes it cool in winter (45° to 55°F/7° to 13°C at night, 60° to 65°F/16° to 18°C during the day), and as cool as possible during the summer—preferably 60° to 70°F/16° to 21°C, but never warmer than 80°F/27°C. Give *Odontoglossum* bright light, but protect it from direct sun. This plant needs lots of moisture throughout the year; give it plenty of water, and boost the humidity by daily misting and by placing the pot on a humidity tray (see page 66). *Odontoglossum* blooms best when crowded or potbound.

Oncidium *(ahn-SID-ee-um).* Comprising a group of epiphytic orchids from tropical America, *Oncidium* has various forms. It typically produces compressed pseudobulbs with leathery leaves, although foliage appears pencil-like in some types. Some *Oncidiums* have small, numerous flowers; others display single blooms.

In general, care for *Oncidium* as you would for *Cattleya* (page 68). *Oncidium* appreciates high humidity and average temperatures (55° to 60°F/13° to 16°C at night, rising to 65° to 75°F/18° to 24°C in the day). Give it at least 4 hours of filtered (as through a sheer curtain) or reflected light per day, but protect it from direct sun. For most of the year, keep the soil constantly moist (like a squeezed-out sponge), but not soggy—but reduce water for several weeks following the completion of new growth, letting the soil dry out somewhat.

Paphiopedilum *(paf-ee-o-PED-uh-lum).* Native to the Asian tropics, this group of terrestrial orchids is commonly called lady's slipper. All types have gracefully arching foliage; leaf color differs according to the plant's blooming season. *Paphiopedilums* with plain green foliage usually bloom in winter; those with mottled leaves bloom in summer. Flowers of some types are so shiny they look lacquered. Colors include white, yellow and green, marked with beige, mahogany, maroon, green, or white.

Mottled-leaf forms need 60° to 65°F/ 16° to 18°C nighttime temperatures, rising to 70° to 80°F/21° to 27°C during the day; forms with solid green leaves require temperatures of 55° to 60°F/13° to 16°C at night, 65° to 75°F/ 18° to 24°C during the day.

Since *Paphiopedilum* has no real rest period, keep the soil moist (like a squeezed-out sponge) at all times, but not soggy. Each year, repot after bloom is over, using a pot that's one size larger; *Paphiopedilum* thrives when crowded. This plant prefers bright light (but no direct sun), average humidity (use a humidity tray as described on page 66), and good air circulation.

Paphiopedilum is sensitive to fertilizers. If your plant is growing in fir bark, apply a liquid fertilizer (see page 21), diluted to half strength, monthly during spring and summer; don't fertilize at all during autumn and winter. Plants grown in osmunda fiber never need fertilizer.

Phalaenopsis *(fay-luh-NAHP-sis).* Nicknamed moth orchids, this group of epiphytes is native to tropical Asia. *Phalaenopsis*' thick, broad and leathery leaves emerge directly from the soil (the plant has no pseudobulbs); white, pink, yellow, or multicolored flowers, looking like large moths, inspire its common name. Some small hybrids are available.

Phalaenopsis likes filtered light (as through a sheer curtain); keep it out of direct sun. It prefers warm temperatures (75° to 80°F/24° to 27°C, never lower than 60°F/16°C), and high humidity. All year, keep the soil moist (like a squeezed-out sponge), but not soggy. Use a humidity tray (page 66).

Vanda *(VAN-duh).* Native to the Philippines, Malaysia, and the Himalayas, these especially lovely orchids produce more leaves than most, arranged opposite one another. Beautiful open-faced flowers bloom in clusters atop long stems.

Vanda likes warm temperatures (70° to 80°F/21° to 27°C in the day, never below 60°F/16°C at night), good air circulation, and high humidity; grow your plant on a humidity tray, as described on page 66, and mist it frequently. *Vanda* also needs plenty of bright filtered (as through a sheer curtain) or reflected light, especially from November through February (to help set its flower buds). Water lightly during these winter months. During the rest of the year, *Vanda* appreciates plenty of water, but requires excellent drainage—use the orchid soil mix on page 66. During the growing season, apply a liquid fertilizer diluted to one-quarter strength, once a month.

Vanda coerulea, native to India, blooms from late summer to early autumn. Its 3 to 4-inch flowers come in shades of pale to dark blue.

Vanda sanderana grows to 3 feet high; in autumn, it bears flat 3 to 4-inch flowers in combinations of white, rose, brown, greenish yellow, or red.

Vanda teres, a Burmese native, is grown commercially in Hawaii, where it's used extensively to make leis. Flowers appear in shades of rose with tinges of white and yellow, and bloom from May to September. To bloom properly, *V. teres* needs a winter rest and lots of bright reflected light.

Epidendrum mariae 'Doris'

Lycaste cochleata

Oxalis bowiei (wood sorrel)

Oxalis

(AWK-suh-lis)

Clover, Shamrock, Wood sorrel

Native to South and Central America as well as to South Africa, *Oxalis* comprises a very large group of plants. Most thrive happily as house plants, though several are garden weeds.

Many grow from bulbs or rhizomes; all have cloverlike leaves divided into 3 or 4 leaflets. Depending on the type, *Oxalis* offers flowers of pink, white, and various shades of rose, lavender, and yellow. Leaves and flowers close at night and on cloudy days.

Growing requirements

Oxalis needs bright sunlight, either filtered or direct, but fairly cool temperatures (60° to 65°F/16° to 18°C; never above 70°F/21°C). Use a standard indoor potting soil; allow the top half of the soil to dry out between waterings. Average house humidity suits this plant fine. Except during warm months, when *Oxalis* is dormant, apply a complete fertilizer regularly (see page 21). *Oxalis* rarely suffers from any serious pests or diseases.

Favorites

Oxalis acetosella, better known as wood sorrel or shamrock, has leaves divided into four rounded leaflets. It's often sold around St. Patrick's Day.

Oxalis bowiei produces pink or rose flowers in summer and performs well in a hanging basket.

Oxalis hirta starts growing in an upright manner; in time, branching stems gradually fall over under the weight of leaves and flowers (pink flowers bloom in late autumn or in winter). Good in a hanging basket.

Oxalis purpurea puts forth large leaves; rosy red, 1-inch flowers bloom from November through March.

Palms & palmlike plants

Dramatic and exotic palm silhouettes bring stately elegance to almost any interior setting. Two additional palmlike plants are *Cordyline* (page 49) and *Dracaena* (pages 51–52).

In general, palms are subtropical or tropical in origin. Most send up single, unbranched trunks of considerable height; some grow in clusters, though, and others are dwarf or stemless (lacking a true trunk). Palms' leaves, also called fronds, are usually divided into many leaflets. In fan palms, leaflets "fan" out from the leaf base like the ribs of a fan; in other types, leaves look like feathers, with many parallel leaflets growing outward from a long central stem.

General growing requirements

Most palms aren't too fussy about their requirements.

Soil. Palms grow vigorously in standard indoor potting soil. Some growers like to make the soil denser and richer for larger plants by adding a little good-quality garden loam (approximately one-quarter of the total mixture) to the soil.

Water. During the warm spring and summer months, when most palms are actively growing, they need regular watering—enough to keep their soil consistently moist (like a squeezed-out sponge), but not soggy. During the cool winter months, allow the top inch or so of the soil to dry out between waterings; palm roots rot quickly if kept damp and cool for too long.

Temperature and humidity. Palms relish the relatively warm temperatures of most homes. A cozy range of 65° to 75°F/18° to 24°C suits them ideally, though most can survive much lower temperatures.

Appreciative of higher humidity than is typical of most households, palms benefit from a humidity tray (see page 20) or frequent misting or showering.

Light. While quite adaptable to varying light conditions, palms prefer something similar to their native environment. Most specimens small enough to grow indoors are young plants; in the wild, they'd be growing under a high canopy of mature trees. This canopy screens out the most intense sunlight, so the plants below receive only dappled or filtered light. If you can provide similar light in your home, as through a window partially screened by a leafy tree or a sheer curtain, almost any palm will bask there contentedly. (A few palms can survive a dark corner.)

Fertilizer. Except in late autumn and winter, apply a complete fertilizer regularly (see page 21).

Pests. To keep leaves clean and free of insects, give your palm regular showers (see page 27). Though most palms show more resistance to pests than other plants do, red spider mites and scale may cause problems; see pages 29–31 for methods of control.

Chrysalidocarpus lutescens (areca palm)

Favorite palms and their special needs

The following nine kinds of palm make elegant additions to interiors.

Archontophoenix *(ahr-kahn-to-FEE-niks)*. These stately straight-trunked Australians, known in their native land as bangalow or piccabeen palms, may tower up to 50 feet or more if grown outdoors. Indoors, of course, they grow much lower, but they do spread out as far as 10 to 15 feet. On mature specimens, feathery leaves may reach 6 to 8 feet or more in length. All year, let the soil dry out between waterings.

Archontophoenix alexandrae, commonly called the alexandra palm, fits the above description, but its trunk enlarges toward the base.

Archontophoenix cunninghamiana, the king palm, does not have an enlarged trunk. Mature plants bear clustered amethyst flowers.

Beaucarnea *(bo-KAHR-nee-uh)*. Though this plant looks like a palm, it's really an odd-looking succulent shrub or tree, with several equally odd common names: ponytail, bottle palm, and elephant-foot tree. The last name refers to the appearance of the stem—it's greatly swollen at the base. In younger specimens, it looks like a big onion sitting on the soil; in very old trees, the ''onion'' may have grown to a woody mass several feet across, resembling an elephant's foot.

This conversation piece grows happily indoors, but will eventually exceed house plant size—its only limit is the height of your ceiling. Its trunk starts out single, but later on sprouts a few branches. At the top of the plant and at the ends of branches, ¾-inch-wide leaves cluster in dense tufts, arching and drooping to more than 3 feet in length.

This plant flourishes in the warm, dry atmosphere found in most homes. Let the soil dry out completely between waterings.

Beaucarnea recurvata fits the above description.

Caryota *(kah-ree-AH-tuh)*. Nicknamed fishtail palm, this strikingly elegant palm has won ever-increasing favor with indoor gardeners. The leaves are finely divided into leaflets that are

Howea forsterana
(paradise palm)

Chamaedorea costaricana

Caryota ochlandra
(Canton fishtail palm)

Cycas revoluta
(sago palm)

Rhapis excelsa
(lady palm)

Chamaedorea elegans
(parlor palm)

Rhapis excelsa variegata
(variegated lady palm)

flattened and split at the tips, like fish tails.

Since *Caryota* grows in full sun in its native southeast Asia, as a house plant it requires bright filtered (as through a sheer curtain) or reflected light. Though rather slow-paced, palms of this group will, after many years, outgrow most indoor locations.

Caryota mitis, or clustered fishtail palm, grows slowly, eventually attaining 20 to 25 feet. Basal offshoots eventually form a clustered trunk; foliage is light green. This plant isn't easy to grow; it requires ideal condi-

tions and is not recommended for beginners.

Caryota ochlandra, commonly called the Canton fishtail palm, eventually reaches a height of 25 feet. Foliage is medium dark green. This is probably the easiest to grow of the *Caryotas.*

Caryota urens, commonly called the fishtail wine palm, has dark green leaves and grows 15 to 20 feet tall.

Chamaedorea *(kam-ee-do-REE-uh)*. These feathery-leafed palms are among the easiest palms to grow indoors. Generally slow-growing, they

have either single trunks or several trunks in a cluster. All need ample water and good drainage.

Chamaedorea costaricana grows relatively quickly, if watered and fertilized regularly, into bamboolike clumps of 8 to 10-foot trunks. Its lacy, feathery leaves extend 3 to 4 feet in length.

Chamaedorea elegans (widely sold as *Neanthe bella*) goes by the familiar name of parlor palm. This *Chamaedorea* is the most foolproof indoor choice; it tolerates crowded roots and low light. A single-stemmed palm, it's a favorite for close planting in

Livistona chinensis (Chinese fountain palm)

Archontophoenix cunninghamiana (king palm)

clumps of three or more. Eventually these will reach a height of 3 to 4 feet. Repot *C. elegans* every 2 or 3 years, using a slightly larger container and fresh indoor potting soil; be careful, because roots are brittle.

Chrysalidocarpus *(kri-suh-luh-do-KAHR-pus).* Widely sold as *Areca lutescens,* this beautiful palm almost always appears at the nursery in clumps of trunks (which grow to 4 to 5 feet) producing a feathery profusion of yellow-stemmed green leaves. *Chrysalidocarpus* likes bright filtered (as through a sheer curtain) or reflected light and fairly warm (65° to 75°F/ 18° to 24°C) temperatures. During spring and summer, keep its soil evenly moist (like a squeezed-out sponge), but not soggy; never let the pot stand in a water-filled saucer for any length of time. During the cooler autumn and winter months, allow the top inch of the soil to dry out between waterings. Red spider mites may cause *Chrysalidocarpus* problems, so keep a close watch for them; see page 30.

Chrysalidocarpus lutescens, the most commonly available form, has the above characteristics.

Cycas *(SY-kus).* Also called sago palms, these take their time to grow. In youth (2 to 3 years old), they look something like ferns, airy and lacy. Only with age do they look more like palms. (In fact, these very primitive cone-bearing plants aren't true palms at all.) After a decade or so, plants can reach a height of 10 feet or more. From the top of a single, heavily textured, dark brown trunk, their featherlike leaves form a rosette pattern. Split like a comb into many flat, glossy, dark green leaflets, leaves eventually reach a length of 2 to 3 feet on mature plants. Never allow the pot to stand in a water-filled saucer.

Beaucarnea recurvata (bottle palm)

Cycas revoluta is the only commonly available form.

Howea *(HOW-ee-uh).* Classic parlor palms of yesteryear, these natives of Lord Howe Island in the South Pacific are often sold today as kentia palm. Their large, feathery leaves arch gracefully; with age, old leaves drop off, revealing a smooth green trunk ringed with leaf scars. *Howea* is tolerant of low light. As a safeguard against red spider mites, keep fronds clean and free of dust.

Howea belmoreana, commonly called sentry palm, has a smaller and more compact shape than the more common *H. forsterana.* Arching fronds reach 6 to 7 feet. This rugged palm can tolerate some watering neglect, drafts, and dust.

Howea forsterana, commonly called paradise palm, is larger than *H. belmoreana;* its arching fronds may grow to 9 feet long, with drooping leaflets.

Livistona *(liv-uh-STO-nuh).* This slow-growing palm, native from China down to Australia, looks best in a spacious room where its dramatic beauty won't overwhelm. Roundish, shiny, bright green leaves, 3 to 5 feet across, droop at the outer edges.

Livistona chinensis, the Chinese fountain palm, is the most commonly available type for growing indoors. It fits the description given above.

Rhapis *(RAY-pis).* Rapidly gaining in popularity, members of this group grow in bamboolike clumps with shiny, usually deep green foliage. Trunks are covered with a net of dark, fibrous leaf sheaths. These slow-growing palms make choice indoor plants, lending a look both refined and tropical to a room.

Rhapis excelsa, commonly called lady palm, grows slowly to about 12 feet. Variegated forms display yellow and green-striped leaves. It's a sturdy plant that will tolerate low light, dust, and an uneven watering schedule.

Rhapis humilis, often called rattan palm or slender lady palm, sends up tall, bamboolike stems to 18 feet; these create a lush yet graceful tropical look. Its leaves are larger and longer than *R. excelsa's*—but like *R. excelsa,* the rattan palm is especially tolerant of dim light.

Pandanus

(pan-DAY-nus)

Screw pine

This living conversation piece, a native of the South Pacific, often reaches a height of 5 to 8 feet. It's easy to grow, tolerant of less than perfect conditions, and most unusual.

As *Pandanus* matures, a woody trunk develops; a thatch of dark green leaves, growing in a spiral, sprouts at the top. Sometimes banded with white or silver, the spearlike leaves, 3 inches wide and 3 feet long, have sharp, prickly edges.

With age, the plant's trunk sprouts thick, stiltlike aerial roots that apparently help to prop it up. They extend outward and downward to the soil.

Growing requirements

This plant appreciates a standard indoor potting soil, bright, filtered light (protect from hot, direct sunlight), and moderate to high humidity, especially during the warm summer months. *Pandanus* grows best in the 60° to 75°F temperature range (16° to 24°C); never let the temperature drop below 55°F/13°C. Water well in summer: drench the soil, then let it dry out before watering again. Except in winter, apply a complete fertilizer regularly (see page 21).

During the winter months, give *Pandanus* a rest by cutting back on water and withholding fertilizer. Mist daily during the summer months.

Use care when handling the leaves; the edges are sharp enough to cut.

Aphids, mealybugs, red spider mites, scale, and thrips may attack *Pandanus;* see pages 29–31 for methods of control.

Favorites

Pandanus veitchii, the most widely available form, fits the description given previously. A more compact version, *P.v.* 'Compacta', is a little harder to find than the larger plant.

Pandanus veitchii (screw pine)

Pelargonium

(pel-ahr-GO-nee-um)

Geranium

Nothing looks quite so cheerful and homey as a potted *Pelargonium*—better known as geranium—growing on a sunny kitchen windowsill.

Of the literally hundreds of types of *Pelargonium*, most grow happily indoors with very little care. Too much fussy attention can actually harm *Pelargonium;* all it really needs is plenty of sunshine.

The wide-ranging *Pelargonium* group includes a great diversity of flower and leaf forms; some are grown more for their deliciously scented leaves than for flowers.

Growing requirements

Pelargonium likes a standard indoor potting soil, as much direct sun as possible (4 or more hours a day is best), and a dry (not humid) atmosphere. Let the soil dry out slightly between waterings. On a regular basis, apply a complete fertilizer that's low

Pelargonium hortum 'Cherie'
(garden geranium)

in nitrogen (see page 21). Too much nitrogen promotes growth of lush foliage at the expense of flower quantity and quality.

Because *Pelargonium* thrives in the arid atmosphere of most homes, it's obviously best not to mist. Overwatering is a common mistake with this plant, and it spells trouble fast—too much water causes rot.

Most forms need pinching when young to develop a pleasingly bushy shape. You can prune overgrown plants severely: they'll resprout promptly. You'll have to remove dead leaves and flowers frequently—but this grooming keeps *Pelargonium* healthy and looking its best. Keep it somewhat potbound for best bloom.

Pelargonium occasionally suffers from aphids, mealybugs, red spider mites, and whiteflies; it's also subject to the diseases stem rot and powdery mildew. See pages 29–31 for methods of pest and disease control.

Favorites

This is a large group of plants:

Pelargonium domesticum, better known as Lady Washington geranium, Martha Washington geranium, or regal geranium, is a small shrub (up to 3 feet tall) with crinkly, toothededged leaves. Large, showy flowers, 2 or more inches across, bloom in spring and summer in loose, rounded clusters. Available types of *P. domesticum* have blossoms in white or shades of pink, red, lavender, and purple—almost always brilliantly blotched and marked in darker colors.

Pelargonium hortorum, commonly called garden or common geranium, is also a shrub growing to about 3 feet. Its round or kidney-shaped leaves are velvety to the touch, their edges indistinctly lobed and scalloped; in most types, a zone of deeper color tinges leaves just inside their edges. Besides varieties with plain green leaves, this species includes "color-leafed" or "fancy-leafed" varieties displaying variously patterned zones, borders, or splashes of brown, gold, red, white, or green on each leaf. Single or double, flowers of *P. hortorum* are smaller than those of *P. domesticum.* But from spring through autumn they bloom with many more individual flowers to a cluster, usually in solid colors—white, pink, rose, red, orange, or violet.

Pelargonium peltatum, popular for hanging baskets and window boxes, is commonly called ivy geranium, since it grows like a vine. Its stems, covered with glossy bright green leaves, will trail 2 to 3 feet. *P. peltatum*'s white, pink, rose, red, or lavender flowers resemble those of *P. hortorum.*

Scented. Types of *Pelargonium* grown especially for their highly scented leaves include lemon-scented *P. crispum;* rose-scented *P. graveolens;* limescented *P. nervosum;* apple-scented *P. odoratissimum;* and peppermintscented *P. tomentosum.*

Peperomia

(pep-uh-RO-mee-uh)

Radiator plant

Popular for use in dish gardens and terrariums, *Peperomia* includes many commonly available types. Its lowgrowing, compact foliage offers much diversity of leaf shape and color. Foliage is its prime attraction, but *Peperomia* usually produces tiny flowers as well, in dense, small, slender spikes.

Growing requirements

Peperomia needs protection from direct sun; it appreciates a window with northern exposure, or any window with filtered light (as through a sheer curtain). It prefers temperatures in the 60° to 65°F/16° to 18°C range, but will also grow happily at warmer temperatures (65° to 75°F/18° to 24°C).

Plants need misting occasionally in spring and summer, but not during the cooler winter months. Use a standard indoor potting soil and keep it moist (like a squeezed-out sponge), but not soggy. During winter, allow the top inch of the soil to dry out between waterings. Except in autumn and winter, apply a liquid fertilizer diluted to half strength once a month.

Mealybugs, red spider mites, and whiteflies occasionally pester *Peperomia* (see pages 29–31).

Favorites

Peperomia argyreia, commonly called the watermelon peperomia, grows in a compact shape, forming a rosette of round 3 to 5-inch-long, graystriped leaves on long red stems. This plant can reach a height of 10 to 12 inches.

Peperomia caperata 'Emerald Ripple' puts forth heart-shaped leaves. Rich green and deeply veined, they grow thickly on short reddish stalks. Tight clusters of tiny greenish white flowers are spike-shaped. Plants rarely grow beyond 3 to 4 inches tall. *P.c.* 'Little Fantasy' is a miniature variety that resembles *P.c.* 'Emerald Ripple'.

Peperomia fraseri has small, pointed leaves with reddish undersides. Its fragrant flowers are very long and thin (almost like pipecleaners), packed densely around flower stalks up to 2 feet tall.

Peperomia metallica has erect dark red stems carrying narrow, waxy leaves with a metallic, coppery luster. Silver-green bands run down the centers of leaves.

Peperomia obtusifolia, an old favorite, has thick, upright or trailing stems, to 6 inches long. Fleshy dark green leaves are round, about 4 inches across. *P.o.* 'Minima' is a miniature form with oval leaves, dark green above and paler beneath. Variegated types are also available.

Peperomia rotundifolia has tiny round leaves, only ¼ inch across. Dark green above, they're often reddish underneath. Stems are trailing.

Peperomia scandens 'Variegata', a climbing or trailing plant, puts forth pointed 2-inch-long leaves, variegated yellow and light green.

Peperomia caperata 'Emerald Ripple'

Peperomia argyreia (watermelon peperomi

Peperomia obtusifolia

Peperomia scandens 'Variegata'

Peperomia frase

Philodendron
(fil-o-DEN-drun)

The evergreen vines and shrubs that make up the large *Philodendron* group are perennially popular. They're easy to care for, and people love their attractive, glossy leaves.

Arborescent types of *Philodendron* grow to giant size—6 to 8 feet tall (or even taller) and just as wide. Their large leaves grow from a sturdy, self-supporting trunk. This type summers outdoors happily in a sheltered spot.

Vining *Philodendrons* must stay inside. There are many kinds, with a variety of leaf shapes and sizes. Members of this category fall into two groups: vining and self-heading. The vining type doesn't really climb the way ivy does; you'll have to lean it against (or tie it to) a support. You can use almost anything as a support, but certain water-absorbent columns are a good choice because they help to keep the plant moist. Such columns include sections of tree fern stems, moss-covered poles (wire and sphagnum "totem poles"), and slabs of redwood bark.

"Self-heading" types of *Philodendron* branch out at the growing tips without pinching or pruning. This *Philodendron* develops into a short, broad plant with sets of leaves radiating out from a very short main stem.

Growing requirements

Philodendrons need only basic care. All types want standard indoor potting soil with good drainage, and average to warm house temperatures (65° to 75°F/18° to 24°C). Keep the soil continuously moist (like a squeezed-out sponge), but not soggy. *Philodendron* thrives in bright reflected or filtered light (as through a sheer curtain); keep out of direct sun.

Provide a little extra humidity by daily misting or by placing the pot on a humidity tray (page 20). Throughout the year, apply a liquid fertilizer diluted to half strength monthly.

Philodendrons occasionally attract mealybugs and aphids. If conditions are too warm and humid, fungus disease may take hold. For methods of control, see pages 29–31.

(Continued on next page)

Philodendron domesticum 'Red Princess'

Philodendron wendlandii

Philodendron selloum

Philodendron scandens oxycardium

Aerial roots form on some types of *Philodendron;* if you don't like their looks, push them into the soil (when they get long enough) or cut them off. Flowers resembling calla lilies may appear on mature plants grown in optimum conditions. Flower bracts are usually green, white, or reddish.

Favorites

Several arborescent and vining *Philodendrons* are described below.

Philodendron bipennifolium, commonly called the fiddleleaf philodendron, is a vining type that grows fairly fast. Its oddly lobed, rich green, 10-inch leaves resemble violins. Though it's an excellent house plant, its foliage becomes sparse after about 3 years of vigorous growth; plant several fiddleleaf philodendrons in one pot for a lush effect.

Philodendron domesticum (usually sold as *P. hastatum*), a vining type with fairly fast, open growth, puts forth foot-long, arrow-shaped leaves. This species is subject to leaf spot if kept too warm and moist (see page 30 for remedy). However, a number of named varieties and hybrids with better resistance to leaf spot have become available. These tend to be a more compact and upright shape, and some show reddish color in new foliage and leaf stalks. 'Emerald Queen' is a choice deep green form; 'Royal Queen' offers deep red color; 'Red Princess' displays dark red stalks.

Philodendron 'Evansii', an arborescent type, grows enormous leaves shaped like an elephant's ears; they're scalloped and ruffled, but not deeply cut. A mature plant's leaves may reach 4 to 5 feet long.

Philodendron 'Florida', a vining type, has slightly crinkled leaves with pronounced veins and reddish undersides, split into five broad, sharp-pointed lobes. *P.* 'Florida Compacta' is slower growing, more compact.

Philodendron 'Mandaianum', a vining type, puts forth arrow-shaped leaves, 12 to 14 inches long. Borne on maroon stalks, they're dark green above, maroon underneath.

Philodendron pedatum is a vining type with dark green 8-inch leaves. These are deeply slashed into broad, sharp-pointed lobes of unequal size. *P. pedatum* retains lower, older leaves well (these tend to drop off other types of *Philodendron*).

Philodendron pertusum is the name under which the splitleaf phil-

odendron (*Monstera,* page 65) is often sold.

Philodendron scandens oxycardium, a vining type, is perhaps the most common and popular philodendron. Its heart-shaped leaves are deep green—5 inches long or smaller on young plants, but up to a foot long on mature plants. Thin stems travel up a support (see page 75 for more information), or trail.

Philodendron selloum, an arborescent type, grows large, deeply cut leaves to 3 feet long. The variety 'Lundii' has a more compact shape.

Philodendron wendlandii is a self-heading type with tough, compact foliage. Broad, foot-long lance-shaped leaves of deep green reach out from short broad stalks, in clusters of a dozen or more.

Pilea

(PY-lee-uh)

Aluminum plant, Artillery plant, Baby's tears, Creeping Charlie, Creeping Jenny, Pan-American friendship plant, Panamiga

Encompassing a large group of foliage house plants, *Pilea* offers an unusually wide range of leaf size, shape, color, and texture. (It has flowers, too, but they're inconspicuous.) It grows either upright or trailing, depending on the type. Generally easy to grow.

Growing requirements

Pilea is content with a standard indoor potting soil. Grow it in a location that catches bright, filtered light (as through a sheer curtain).

Take care not to overwater your *Pilea*; give it a liberal drink when you do water (stop when water runs through the drainage hole), but allow soil to dry out almost completely before watering again.

Except in autumn and winter, apply a complete fertilizer regularly (see page 21). *Pilea* accepts average household temperatures, but prefers slightly warmer conditions—in the 70° to 75°F/21° to 23°C range. Keep humidity high with frequent misting or by setting the pot on a humidity tray (see page 20).

Pilea suffers when potbound; move the plant to a larger pot (see page 26) when you see roots growing out of the drain hole. To produce a bushy, well-shaped specimen, occasionally pinch off growing tips. Generally pest-free, *Pilea* sometimes suffers attacks from mealybugs, scale, or gray mold. See pages 29–31.

Favorites

Pilea cadierei, commonly known as aluminum plant, grows quickly (to 1 to 1½ feet tall) on succulent stems. The fleshy, tooth-edged leaves grow 3 to 4 inches long; they're vivid green to bluish green with conspicuous silvery mottling. Flowers are very tiny.

Pilea depressa, commonly known as baby's tears or creeping Jenny, spreads in a creeping or trailing manner, setting down roots wherever stems touch the soil. Small, pale green leaves are ¼ inch wide at the bases, broader toward the tips. *P. depressa* is often used in terrariums or as a ground cover in large dish gardens.

Pilea involucrata, often called the Pan-American friendship plant, panamiga, or panamigo, grows 6 to 8 inches tall, branching freely. Leaves form roundish ovals, as long as 2 inches with heavily veined or puckered seersucker-like surfaces. Leaf color is brownish green above, purplish beneath.

Pilea microphylla spreads a fine thicket of branches and twigs 6 to 18 inches high; the plant looks almost like a fern. Tiny, thickly set leaves are bright green. *P. microphylla*'s common name—artillery plant—refers to its forceful manner of discharging pollen.

Pilea nummulariifolia, commonly called creeping Charlie, resembles *P. depressa,* but its leaves are more precisely rounded and more evenly scalloped along the edges. This is a good plant for a small hanging basket. (Note: A number of other plants go by the same common name.)

Pilea 'Silver Tree' has dark olive green leaves with silver center stripes.

Pilea cadierei (aluminum plant)

Pisonia

(pi-so-NEE-uh)

Birdcatcher tree, Map plant

In its native New Zealand, *Pisonia* grows as tall as 12 to 20 feet. Fortunately, it behaves more reasonably in indoor situations, rarely exceeding 3 to 4 feet in height.

The most common indoor variety, a variegated plant (*Pisonia umbellifera* 'Variegata'), produces 4 to 6-inch-long oval leaves, boldly patterned with pale green, medium green, and creamy white. These markings are so distinct that the leaf surfaces resemble maps—hence the common name, map plant.

Pisonia rarely flowers indoors, and the flowers are inconspicuous; but the sticky fruit that forms later led to an-other of the plant's common names—the birdcatcher tree.

Growing requirements

Pisonia likes warm temperatures (70° to 75°F/21° to 24°C) and bright filtered or reflected light. Don't place *Pisonia* in direct sunlight, and keep it away from wind or warm drafts. *Pisonia* is content with a standard indoor potting soil. When you water, do a thorough job (stop when water runs out of the drain hole), but allow the top inch of the soil to dry out between waterings. During the winter months, allow soil to dry out almost completely between waterings. Except in autumn and winter, apply a complete fertilizer regularly (see page 21). *Pisonia* appreciates extra humidity; mist it daily, or place the pot on a humidity tray (see page 20).

In general, highly variegated leaves contain less chlorophyll than leaves that are solid green. Because of this relative deficiency, such leaves may be unable to produce enough food for the plant in low-light conditions. If your *Pisonia* is highly variegated, be sure to grow it in a location receiving bright reflected or filtered light; this will help it to make the maximum use of the chlorophyll it does have.

To produce multibranched, bushy plants, be sure to pinch out the growing tips while plants are young.

Generally pest-free, *Pisonia* is occasionally attacked by aphids and scale. See pages 29–31 for methods of control.

Favorites

Pisonia umbellifera is only rarely available; it fits the previous description, but its leaves are uniformly green.

Pisonia umbellifera 'Variegata' (map plant)

Much more common is the variety *P.u.* 'Variegata', which offers distinctly variegated leaves (described earlier).

Plectranthus

(plek-TRAN-thus)

Candle plant, Royal Charlie, Swedish ivy

Pleasingly easy to grow, *Plectranthus* is usually displayed trailing its foliage from a hanging basket. But this popular plant, a cousin of *Coleus,* also makes an attractive ground cover in large-scale indoor gardens. Its thickish pale to medium green leaves have scalloped edges and prominent veins. Stems and branches of *Plectranthus* are often purplish.

When grown in a hanging basket, *Plectranthus* will dangle to a length of 2 feet or more; grown as a ground cover, it reaches a height of about 1 foot. Cuttings root very easily, either in water or in damp soil.

Small white or bluish flowers are borne on spikes. The blossoms aren't especially attractive; some people nip them off before they fully form or shear off the spikes after flowering.

Growing requirements

Plectranthus adapts to a wide range of light, from dimly lit situations to bright, filtered light (as through a sheer curtain); keep it out of direct sunlight, though. Temperatures in the 60° to 70°F/16° to 21°C range suit *Plectranthus* fine. The plant appreciates extra humidity; give it a daily misting or place the pot on a humidity tray (see page 20). Throughout the year, apply a complete fertilizer regularly (see page 21). Unlike many other plants, *Plectranthus* requires fertilizer even in winter.

Provide *Plectranthus* with a standard indoor potting soil and water the plant regularly, keeping the soil moist (like a squeezed-out sponge), but not soggy.

Most forms of *Plectranthus* are naturally lanky and require regular pinching of their growing tips to produce bushy plants. On older plants, long, hanging stems may become leafless near the base. If this problem leads to an unsightly plant, simply prune off the top third (or more) of the sparsely foliaged stems; new leaves should quickly sprout.

A severe pruning such as this gives you a good opportunity to start new *Plectranthus* plants from all the left-over prunings or cuttings. You can root the cuttings (see page 27)—root them in a new pot, or just stick them back into the soil of the old pot to create an even bushier, fuller specimen. You'll be able to tell when the cuttings have taken hold by the appearance of new leaves.

Plectranthus oertendahlii (royal Charlie)

Mealybugs and whiteflies may bother *Plectranthus* occasionally; see pages 29–31 for methods of control.

Favorites

Plectranthus australis, commonly called Swedish ivy, produces shiny dark green leaves, 1½ inches long. Sometimes leaves are variegated with white. *P. australis* has a more upright growth habit than the other types.

Plectranthus coleoides 'Marginatus' starts out growing upright, then trails as branches grow longer. Green leaves are 2 to 2½ inches long, marked with gray green and edged with creamy white.

Plectranthus nummularius is a trailing type, with solid green rounded leaves from 2 to 2½ inches across.

Plectranthus oertendahlii, commonly called royal Charlie or candle plant, has small (1 inch) brownish green leaves with silvery veins and scalloped purplish margins; leaves have purplish undersides.

Polyscias fruticosa 'Elegans' (Ming aralia)

Polyscias

(po-LIS-ee-us)

Balfour aralia, Ming aralia, Parsley panax

A member of the *Aralia* family, *Polyscias* comes from tropical Asia and Polynesia. (True *Aralias* are Chinese natives.) An unusual house plant with an Oriental elegance, *Polyscias* looks good when grown in a deep bonsai container. *Polyscias* isn't easy to grow—it's somewhat finicky about its needs.

When well grown, this plant is extremely attractive, almost like a piece of sculpture.

Growing requirements

Plant *Polyscias* in a standard indoor potting soil. When you water, give your plant a good drink (stop when water runs out of the drain hole), but allow the top inch of the soil to dry out between waterings. Place the plant where it will receive bright filtered or reflected light; keep it out of direct sunlight. *Polyscias* prefers temperatures on the warm side (65° to 75°F/18° to 24°C) and detests drafts. Keep humidity high with frequent mistings or by placing the pot on a humidity tray (see page 20). Except in winter, apply a complete fertilizer regularly (see page 21 for more information).

Once you find a place where *Polyscias* grows happily, don't change its location; this is a very temperamental plant. One thing it doesn't object to, though, is being potbound; repot (see page 26) only when you see lots of roots coming out of the drain hole. *Polyscias* occasionally suffers attack by aphids, mealybugs, red spider mites, scale, and thrips; see pages 29–31 for methods of control.

Favorites

Polyscias balfouriana, commonly called Balfour aralia, has solid green 2-inch-wide leaves, round and slightly scalloped. Plants grow as high as 3 feet. *P.b.* 'Marginata' is very similar, except that its leaves have white margins. This *Polyscias* tolerates either sun or shade.

Polyscias fruticosa, commonly called the Ming aralia or parsley panax, produces distinctly cut and curled, parsley-fine foliage on a woody stem. *P.f.* 'Elegans' is a compact form.

Polyscias guilfoylei 'Victoriae' has leathery leaves, thin and curled, with white, toothed edges.

Rhoeo spathacea 'Vittata' (Moses-in-the-cradle)

Rhoeo

(REE-o)

Boat lily, Moses-in-the-cradle, Moses-in-the-boat, Three-men-in-a-boat

Looking like a small palm tree, easy-to-grow *Rhoeo* is a favorite with children. Its sword-shaped, rather erect leaves are dark green with deep purple undersides; there's also an attractive variegated form, as noted below under "Favorites." Some gardeners prefer to plant three or more *Rhoeos* in a single pot to produce a bushier appearance. Small, white, three-petaled flowers crowd into purplish boat-shaped bracts, giving the plant its "boat" nicknames.

Growing requirements

Rhoeo does fine in a standard indoor potting soil, with temperatures in the 60° to 75°F/16° to 24°C range. It likes a location with bright reflected or filtered light (keep it out of direct sunlight). To keep the humidity high, mist the plant frequently or set the pot on a humidity tray (see page 20). During spring and summer, keep the soil moist (like a squeezed-out sponge), but not soggy; during the cooler autumn and winter months, cut water way back, allowing the soil to dry out almost completely between waterings. Except in autumn and winter, apply a complete fertilizer regularly (see page 21).

Generally pest-free, *Rhoeo* is sometimes bothered by mealybugs and red spider mites; see pages 29–31 for methods of control.

Favorites

Rhoeo spathacea, the most commonly available form, has the characteristics described previously. *R.s.* 'Vittata' is similar in growing requirements and general appearance, but its leaves are striped red and chartreuse.

Saintpaulia
(saynt-PAW-lee-uh)
African violet

In 1892, Baron von Saint Paul, a German colonial official working in Tanzania, came across some plants that caught his attention. He dug up a few and sent them to his father in Germany; before long, they bloomed, producing such beautiful flowers that the older Saint Paul brought them to the attention of the director of Germany's Royal Botanic Garden.

This director named the plants *Saintpaulia,* in honor of the men who had discovered and grown them. Several years later, it came to light that the Baron had actually sent his father two different species of *Saintpaulia.* These were distinguished as *Saintpaulia confusa*—because of the original confusion—and *Saintpaulia ionantha* (*ionantha* means "with violetlike flowers").

Today's African violet derives from years of intensive hybridization, most of it involving only the two species.

The hybridization continues to this day; there's an almost infinite variety of leaf texture, flower color, and flower form. Some blossoms resemble buttercups, others resemble stars. Flowers may have fringed or ruffled petals, or may be single, semidouble, or fully double.

Available varieties have flowers of snowy white and in all shades of pink, crimson red, wine, and purplish red, along with every variation and intensity of the original blue and purple colors. And flowers aren't available only in solid colors; you can also find blooms delicately edged with red, blue, white, or green, or splashed with irregular dots and streaks of color. Still other flowers have dark centers that fade out to the petal edges, or their upper petals may be darker than the lower ones.

Growing requirements

Light. Generally, African violets need abundant filtered light throughout the year, except in summer when full sun may shine too intensely. Any window that offers some light (not densely blocked by trees or buildings) is a good location for these plants. Best of all is direct sunlight diffused somewhat by tree branches. Light filtered through opaque or textured glass is also good.

If your African violet sits in a south-facing window, keep a thin curtain between the glass and the plant during late spring and summer. Rotate the violet 360 degrees every month so that all leaves will bathe equally in sunlight—give the pot a quarter turn each week, always moving the plant in the same direction.

Temperature. African violets will probably feel comfortable in your home atmosphere if you do. A daytime temperature on the warm side—72° to 75°F/22° to 24°C—is ideal; night temperatures should hover near 65°F/18°C.

Humidity. African violets prefer relatively high humidity levels. Increase humidity around your plant by placing the pot on a humidity tray (see page 20). (Some hobbyists use an electric humidifier.)

Soil. An African violet won't put up with just any ordinary potting soil. It's easiest to use commercial potting soil formulated especially for African violets (and their gesneriad relatives), but you can make your own soil: mix 1 part leaf mold, 1 part loam, and 1 part builder's sand (not beach sand). (For other formulas, see the *Sunset* book *How to Grow African Violets.)*

Water. Never allow African violets' soil to become soggy; it should be evenly moist (like a squeezed-out sponge). Generally, an African violet in a 5 to 6-inch pot needs to be watered about

Saintpaulia ionantha varieties (miniature African violets)

African violet hybrid variety list:

WHITE	PINK	RED/CORAL	BLUE/PURPLE	ORCHID/LAVENDER
Butterfly White	Ann Slocumb	Astro Star	After Dark	Cherry Sundae
Forever White	Astro Pink	Bonus Babe	Blue Chips	Edith V. Peterson
Granger's Arctic Mist	Becky	Christie Love	Blue Jean	Floral Fantasy
Kathleen	Fanfare	Coral Caper	Blue Power	Lavender Fluff
Miriam Steel	Gotcha	Coral Cascade	Blue Reverie	Mrs. Greg
Pure Innocence	Gypsy Pink	Granger's Red Flair	Blue Warrior	Orchid Melody
Silver Dollar	Jean Marie	Helene	Concord Purple	Touch of Grace
Star Shine	Margaret Rose	Hi-lander	Exhibition	Wisteria
White Swan	Mary C	Inca Maid	Granger's Blue Fashionaire	
	Miriam Steel, Pink Sport	Mary D	Lovely Lady	
	Pink Philly	Red Star	Lullaby	
	Pixie Trail	Tina	Plum Perfect	
	Ramblin' Rose		Richter's Step Up	
	Ruth Carey		The King	
	Triple Threat		William Bruce	

Saintpaulia ionantha (African violet)

Saintpaulia ionantha varieties
(African violets)

Saintpaulia ionantha varieties (African violets)

3 times a week; smaller pots will need water more often. When the soil surface begins to feel dry to the touch, it's time to water again. Avoid dampening leaves or the crown of the plant—this will cause leaf spot. (A specially designed wick-irrigated pot is ideal for African violets.) Always use water at room temperature or slightly warmer; plants may respond to cold water by developing leaf spot or refusing to develop new buds. Don't let drained water stand in saucers for more than 2 hours after watering.

Fertilizer. Except in winter, apply a slightly acid fertilizer (see page 21) every 2 to 4 weeks. Always apply fertilizer to moist soil; never apply it to sick or newly planted plants.

Problems. Far from suffering from potbound conditions, African violets actually bloom more beautifully when their roots are somewhat constricted by a small pot. Plants occasionally suffer from aphids, cyclamen mites, thrips, scale, and gray mold. See pages 29–31 for methods of control.

Favorites

Besides concentrating on improved flower color and form, hybridizers have been working to create different growth habits. Available today are African violet hybrids in four growth habit categories: standard-size plants (1 foot or more across), semi-miniature plants (6 to 8-inch plants with standard, full-size flowers), true miniatures (6 to 8-inch plants with small flowers), and a trailing form. In addition to these frequently seen types, there are species (nonhybridized) African violets (the kind that Baron Saint Paul sent his father), grown primarily by specialists.

So many hybrid, named varieties of African violet exist that we can't possibly give them all the detailed descriptions they deserve. The list on page 79 names most of the popular, widely available varieties (according to flower color)—but countless more choices are waiting for you at your local nursery or garden center. Use our list only as a starting point and general guide.

If the nonhybridized "species" African violets stir your interest, consult the *Sunset* book *How to Grow African Violets,* where you'll find descriptions of 18 of the most popular species now recognized.

Saxifraga

(saks-IF-ruh-guh)

Mother-of-thousands, Strawberry begonia, Strawberry geranium

Like a strawberry plant, *Saxifraga*, native to China and Japan, produces creeping runners that bear new plantlets on their ends. Its common name, mother-of-thousands, reflects the fact that a mature *Saxifraga*'s runners produce dozens of "baby" plants. Though the "mother" itself rarely grows taller than 9 inches, its runners sometimes wander as far as 2 feet. Runners will trail attractively.

Saxifraga has roundish, fuzzy, white-veined leaves, almost 4 inches across. In late summer, the stems produce 2-foot-tall flower spikes; the white blossoms, borne in loose, open clusters, are 1 inch across.

Growing requirements

Saxifraga requires a standard indoor potting soil, bright reflected or filtered light (as through a sheer curtain), and cool temperatures (50° to 60°F/ 10° to 16°C). Water regularly during spring and summer, keeping soil moist (like a squeezed-out sponge), but not soggy. In early autumn, after flowering, cut back on water—let the soil dry out almost completely between waterings. Except in autumn and winter, apply a complete fertilizer regularly (see page 21). *Saxifraga* appreciates daily misting; or increase humidity by placing the pot on a humidity tray (see page 20).

Saxifraga is occasionally attacked by mealybugs, scale, and whiteflies; see pages 29–31 for methods of control.

Favorites

Saxifraga stolonifera, the most commonly available form, fits the description given at left. *S.s.* 'Tricolor' offers green leaves generously bordered in white, with pink undersides. This plant isn't as rugged as *S. stolonifera;* it requires higher temperatures (70° to 75°F/21° to 24°C) and more light— several hours of direct sunlight daily, preferably in the morning.

Saxifraga stolonifera (strawberry begonia)

Schefflera

SHEF-luh-ruh

Octopus tree, Queensland umbrella tree, Umbrella tree

Usually seen as an attractive and lofty indoor tree, *Schefflera* towers from 6 to 12 feet in height (outdoors, it grows as tall as 20 feet). There are smaller forms, but these are less popular. The common name, umbrella tree, refers to the way the plant carries its giant shiny leaves. Borne in horizontal tiers, the long-stalked leaves are split into 7 to 16 leaflets, each up to a foot long; these radiate outward, resembling ribs of an umbrella. Though *Schefflera* may flower outdoors, it rarely does so indoors.

Growing requirements

Schefflera has an accommodating temperament; it prefers bright reflected or filtered light (as through a sheer curtain), but will also adapt to lower light levels. It can't take direct sunlight, though. Grow the plant in a standard indoor potting soil; during spring and summer, keep the soil moist (like a squeezed-out sponge), but not soggy. Allow the top 2 inches of the soil to dry out between waterings during autumn and winter.

Except in autumn and winter, apply a complete fertilizer regularly (see page 21). *Schefflera* thrives in average to warm indoor temperatures (65° to 75°F/18° to 24°C), but does prefer a higher than usual level of humidity. To achieve this, mist the plant daily or set the pot on a humidity tray (see page 20).

Schefflera is usually pest-free, but may suffer occasional attack by aphids, red spider mites, and mealybugs. See pages 29–31 for methods of control.

Favorites

Schefflera actinophylla, the most common indoor form, fits the description at left. This plant is often sold as *Brassaia actinophylla*.

Schefflera arboricola resembles *S. actinophylla*, but has much smaller leaves.

Schefflera actinophylla (umbrella tree)

Senecio

(se-NEE-shee-o)

Cape ivy, German ivy, Kenya ivy, Natal ivy, Parlor ivy, Water ivy, Wax vine

Senecio comprises a large and very diverse group of plants, many of which

Senecio mikanioides (German ivy)

bear absolutely no resemblance to one another. The two most common house plant choices, *Senecio macroglossus* 'Variegatum' and *S. mikanioides,* do look similar, though; both resemble ivy. These easy-to-grow types of *Senecio* are good in hanging baskets.

Growing requirements

Senecio needs standard indoor potting soil. From spring through autumn, keep the soil moist (like a squeezed-out sponge), but not soggy. During winter, water much less frequently—only enough to keep the soil from drying out completely.

Give your plant a location that catches bright reflected light; *Senecio* tolerates as much as 2 to 3 hours of direct sunlight daily. Temperatures in the 60° to 75°F/16° to 24°C range suit *Senecio* fine during the spring-through-autumn growing season; but during its winter rest period, the plant likes it a little cooler (50° to 55°F/10° to 13°C). Though *Senecio* survives average house humidity, it prefers higher than usual levels—so mist your plant frequently or place the pot on a humidity tray (page 20). Except in winter, apply a complete fertilizer regularly (page 21).

Generally pest-free, *Senecio* sometimes attracts aphids. See page 29 for methods of control.

Favorites

Senecio hybridus, commonly called cineraria, is a popular gift plant; it's not really a year-round house plant, though—see page 98.

Senecio macroglossus, a twining or trailing vine, grows succulent stems with thick waxy or rubbery leaves, 2 to 3 inches across. Shaped like ivy leaves, they're divided into three, five, or seven shallow lobes. Common names for this plant are Cape ivy, Kenya ivy, Natal ivy, and wax vine. *S. macroglossus* occasionally produces tiny yellow daisylike flowers. *S.m.* 'Variegatum' has leaves brightly splashed with creamy white.

Senecio mikanioides, like *S. macroglossus,* grows in a vining manner. Leaves are roundish, with five or seven sharply pointed lobes, ½ to 3 inches long. Flowers—small, yellow, and daisylike—appear in winter. Its common names are German ivy, parlor ivy, and water ivy. Pinch growing tips frequently to promote a bush shape.

Senecio rowleyanus, commonly called string of beads, is a succulent. For plant description and more information, see page 90.

Senecio stapeliiformis is an unusual-looking upright-growing succulent. For plant description and more information, see page 90.

Sinningia

(si-NIN-jee-uh)

Brazilian edelweiss, Gloxinia

Included in the *Sinningia* group are three distinctly different types of plants. First and most famous is the spectacular florist's favorite, *Sinningia speciosa,* better known as gloxinia. Second are the other species of standard-size *Sinningia* (their beauty less showy, but still stunning). The third type

Sinningia speciosa (gloxinia)

comprises a large group of miniature hybrids and species grown mostly by specialists.

All types grow from tubers. Most have fuzzy dark green leaves; leaf size and shape vary, though. Showy tubular flowers appear in white as well as in every shade of blue, purple, pink, and red. Plants go dormant—die down completely—for a period each year, usually during the winter months.

Growing requirements

Often available in May, blooming plants are popular around Mother's Day. You can usually get tubers from December through March—order them from a catalog or visit a grower specializing in gesneriads. Plant each tuber about 1 inch deep in a standard indoor potting soil. Water moderately until the roots are established; then increase water as the plant begins to put out leaves. During the growing and flowering season, keep the soil moist (like a squeezed-out sponge), but not soggy. Apply tepid water around the base of the plant, or use a wick-irrigated pot; don't water on leaves.

Sinningia does best in bright reflected or filtered light (as through a sheer curtain); keep it out of direct sunlight. Cool room temperatures (around 60°F/16°C) best suit this plant. It also appreciates extra humidity, easily created by placing the pot on a humidity tray (see page 20). Apply a high phosphorus fertilizer (available at nurseries and garden centers) once a month, from the end of the plant's flowering period until the foliage has died down. Do not apply fertilizer at other times of the year.

After the plant has flowered, gradually taper off watering and store the tuber-filled pot in a very cool (around 50°F/10°C) dark place. Mist the soil every 2 to 3 weeks, giving just enough water to keep the tuber from shriveling; after misting, the top inch of the soil should be just barely damp. Keep the tuber in these conditions until January or February, then repot it in a slightly larger pot. Move it to a brighter location; resume normal care.

Aphids, gray mold, and red spider mites occasionally present problems; see pages 29–31 for methods of control.

Favorites

Sinningia cardinalis grows broad, fuzzy, heart-shaped leaves that form a compactly shaped plant. Its brilliant red 2-inch-long flowers bloom in summer.

Sinningia leucotricha is also known as Brazilian edelweiss. Its silvery leaves, covered with white hairs, create an eye-catching background for its salmon pink flowers.

Sinningia regina looks much like gloxinia *(S. speciosa)*. But its silver-veined leaves with red undersides distinguish it from its florist-shop relative. Flowers—2-inch-long violet trumpets with pale, speckled throats—bob their heads singly on stems rising about 6 inches above the leaves.

Sinningia speciosa (the florist's gloxinia) has 6-inch or longer oblong leaves—dark green, toothed, and fuzzy. Its flowers are spectacular—large, velvety, bell-shaped, with ruffled edges. Colors include blue, purple, violet, pink, red, and white. Some flowers show dark dots or blotches; others show contrasting bands at petal rims.

Smithiantha
(smith-ee-AN-thuh)

Temple bells

Native to the mountains of Mexico and Guatemala, *Smithiantha* bears flowers that resemble bells (hence the plant's common name). These blossoms appear in quite a wide range of solid and combined colors (primarily yellow, orange, and pink); they're borne hanging down like bells, in flower spikes at the ends of stems that may be up to 2 feet tall. Usually heart-shaped, the leaves have a velvety texture. The plant grows from a scaly rhizome.

This plant, like its relative the African violet, is somewhat finicky in its requirements.

Growing requirements

Give *Smithiantha* bright filtered (as through a sheer curtain) or reflected light; don't place it in direct sun. This plant prefers temperatures in the 65° to 75°F/18° to 24°C range and high humidity—it's best to place the pot on a humidity tray (see page 20). *Smithiantha* likes a standard indoor potting soil; keep it moist (like a squeezed-out sponge), but not soggy. Allow the top ½ inch of the soil to dry out between waterings. Except in winter, apply a liquid fertilizer diluted to half strength (see page 21) every 2 weeks.

After flowering, *Smithiantha* goes into a natural dormant period; during warm months, all its top growth withers and dies. Stop watering after the plant has flowered. As soon as the foliage dies back, remove the rhizome from the pot and place it in a mesh bag or in sawdust. Store in a dark, cool (about 50°F/10°C) location for 3 months; then repot in a slightly larger pot and resume regular care in a bright, warm location.

Smithiantha sometimes suffers from aphids, red spider mites, and thrips; see pages 29–31 for methods of control.

Favorites

Smithiantha cinnabarina is a striking plant: velvety hairs coating its green leaves make foliage look solid red or reddish brown. Flowers are brick red.

Cornell Temple Bell hybrids comprise a series of robust, bushy, and showy plants, growing 1½ to 2 feet tall. Named hybrids come in a variety of colors—mostly shades of yellow, orange, red, and magenta. Named hybrids include 'Abbey', 'Capistrano', 'Carmel', 'Cathedral', 'Matins', 'San Gabriel', 'Santa Barbara', 'Santa Clara', and 'Vespers'.

Miniature Temple Bell hybrids are much smaller (only 6 to 8 inches tall) than the Cornell hybrids. Two popular named varieties are 'Little Tudor' and 'Little Wonder'.

Smithiantha hybrid (temple bells)

Soleirolia
(so-luh-RO-lee-uh)

Angel's tears, Baby's tears, Helxine

Covering the soil with a lush, bright green carpet, *Soleirolia* is a favorite for terrariums and dish gardens. It's also ideal as a "base" for large-scale indoor gardens, or as a cool-looking ground cover under ferns and other shade-loving greenery.

Unique in the house plant world for its growth habit, *Soleirolia* hugs the ground more closely and mounds in a more compact shape than any other indoor species. Fast-growing, creeping, and mosslike, this little native of Sardinia and Corsica produces extremely tiny leaves, only ¹⁄₁₆ to ⅛ inch across. In bright light, the plant rarely grows taller than 3 inches; with less light, it may become slightly taller. *Soleirolia* produces tiny, inconspicuous (almost invisible) flowers, hidden among its leaves.

Soleirolia is easily propagated from small chunks taken from the mother plant. It grows rapidly. Any time of the year, cut *Soleirolia* back by one-half to promote a lusher look (and to make the plant grow even faster).

Growing requirements

Soleirolia prefers filtered light (as through a sheer curtain) or light shade; keep it out of direct sun. Plant it in standard indoor potting soil. Keep the soil moist (like a squeezed-out sponge), but not soggy. When water collects in the saucer beneath your plant's pot, pour it off promptly; don't let the pot stand in water.

This plant appreciates cool to average temperatures (in the 60° to 70°F/16° to 21°C range), but tolerates warmer conditions well. Provide extra humidity with daily misting. Once a month during spring only, apply a very weak dilution (one-quarter strength or less) of liquid fertilizer (see page 21); anything stronger will burn this plant's tender leaves.

Despite its delicate appearance, *Soleirolia* is a rugged plant, blissfully free of trouble from pests and diseases.

Favorites

Soleirolia soleirolii, the most common form, fits the above description. (A golden green variety also exists, but it's only rarely available.)

Soleirolia soleirolii (baby's tears)

Spathiphyllum 'Clevelandii' (peace lily)

Spathiphyllum
(spath-i-FIL-um)

Peace lily, White flag

Lush, tropical-looking *Spathiphyllum* is one of the few flowering plants that grows and blooms reliably indoors. Its large, dark green oval leaves taper to a point; they stand erect or arch slightly on slender leaf stalks that rise directly from the soil. White flowers resembling calla lilies bloom on slender stems; flowers are most profuse in spring and summer.

Growing requirements

It's best to re-create tropical conditions for *Spathiphyllum:* high humidity, temperatures in the 60° to 70°F range (16° to 21°C), and filtered light (as through a sheer curtain). It prefers a porous potting soil—loose and fibrous. Except in late autumn and winter, apply a liquid fertilizer diluted to half or one-fourth strength weekly (see page 21). Keep away from hot, sunny locations, and keep the soil moist (like a squeezed-out sponge), but not soggy. In winter months, allow the top inch of the soil to dry out between waterings.

Spathiphyllum is generally pest-free, but it's occasionally attacked by mealybugs, red spider mites, and whiteflies (see pages 29–31).

Favorites

Spathiphyllum 'Clevelandii' is about 2 feet tall; *S.* 'Mauna Loa', about 3 feet tall; otherwise, they're similar.

Streptocarpus
(strep-to-KAHR-pus)

Cape primrose

Streptocarpus includes many widely differing species.

The most popular types are hybrids which produce a rosette of strap-shaped leaves up to a foot long; the leaves are somewhat crinkly, usually with a fleshy or velvety texture. Flower stalks—from 6 to 12 inches tall, depending on the type—grow from the center of the leaf rosette. Some hybrids produce one flower per stalk; others have clusters of flowers on each.

The flowers are typically trumpet shaped: like long tubes with spreading mouths. They're usually beautifully striped or ruffled, in pastel to dark shades of blue, violet, lavender, and red; some have yellow throats. Most types have a fairly long blooming season, spanning several months (usually in autumn and winter); others have shorter (2-week) blooming periods intermittently throughout the year.

Growing requirements

In general, treat *Streptocarpus* like an African violet (pages 79–80), but give it more light and cooler temperatures. The plant will grow happily in an African-violet-type soil mix; keep the soil moist (like a squeezed-out sponge), but not soggy. Allow the top ½ inch of the soil to dry out between waterings. *Streptocarpus* likes temperatures in the 70° to 75°F/21° to 24°C range—slightly cooler than the ideal range for African violets. (Never let the temperature drop below 55°F/13°C, since temperatures this low will send *Streptocarpus* into a dormant state.) Be sure to keep your plant out of hot or cold drafts.

Streptocarpus needs plenty of filtered (as through a sheer curtain) or reflected light; protect it from direct sunlight. This plant also appreciates extra humidity, best achieved by placing the pot on a humidity tray (see page 20). Don't mist *Streptocarpus,* since misting can cause leaf spot. Every 2 weeks, apply a high-phosphorus liquid fertilizer (see page 21) diluted to half strength. If your plant has a dormant period in winter (top growth withers), reduce water (give just enough to keep the soil barely moist) and withhold fertilizer until early spring.

Streptocarpus is subject to attack by red spider mites, mealybugs, thrips, whiteflies, and mildew; see pages 29–31 for methods of control.

Favorites

Streptocarpus 'Constant Nymph' bears delicate-looking flowers that rise high above the compact foliage. Colors are usually in the pastel range, with darker veining on lower petals and yellow in the throat.

Streptocarpus 'John Innes' Hybrids resemble 'Constant Nymph' except that flowers are generally in darker shades of pink, blue, and purple.

Streptocarpus Large Flowered Hybrids, sometimes referred to as Giant Hybrids, grow clumps of long, narrow leaves; from their centers grow foot-tall stems carrying long-tubed, 1½ to 2-inch-wide flowers in white, blue, pink, and red, often blotched with contrasting color. If the plants are grown from seed, they'll usually bloom about a year after sprouting.

Streptocarpus saxorum grows in a spreading mound. Long-stemmed flowers, lavender blue and white, bloom intermittently through much of the year.

Streptocarpus 'Wiesmoor' Hybrids offer fringed and crested flowers, up to 4 or 5 inches wide, on 2-foot stems. These hybrids are usually grown from seed. Colors range from white through shades of blue and red.

Streptocarpus 'Constant Nymph' (Cape primrose)

Succulents

Typical succulents are the camels of the plant world: they store water in fleshy leaves, stems, or roots, creating a reserve supply for survival in droughts.

Fleshiness alone doesn't define a succulent, though—the group is an amazingly diverse one, and any general definition of "succulent" has exceptions. Certain groups commonly known as succulents include such nonfleshy desert specimens as *Yuccas,* with thin sword-shaped leaves. And some fleshy plants, like epiphytic orchids, are not succulents. Adding to the confusion, cactuses—true succulents—have a category of their own.

General growing requirements

Though a few succulents require such specialized environments that they'd challenge the most experienced gardener, most grow more successfully in the home than many other house plants, cheerfully tolerating modest neglect and other vagaries of surviving indoors. But don't be tempted to really neglect these generally low-maintenance plants. Given too little attention, succulents look shabby; though they may live through long periods without watering, they'll drop their leaves, shrivel, and lose color.

Succulents have the same temperature and humidity requirements as cactuses, and are subject to the same pests and diseases; see page 40.

Soil and containers. Succulents grow successfully in either plastic or clay pots. But if you use plastic pots (which allow no evaporation), be extra careful to avoid overwatering. Do this by using a fast-draining soil mix and watering only after the soil surface has dried. If you use clay pots, overwatering is less likely to cause problems.

Buy a standard indoor potting soil or make your own. Commercial soil-based mixes should contain about half organic matter (peat moss or leaf mold), half sand or perlite—use the same proportions in homemade potting soil. For richer soil, increase the proportion of organic matter.

Agave attenuata

Repotting. Once a year, check your succulents to see if they need repotting—if roots are coming out of the pot's drain hole, or if offsets are crowding the parent plant, it's time for a move to a larger container. Some succulents may need to be repotted each year, but in the case of larger, slow-growing plants, the same pot will often serve for 2 or even 3 years. It's best to repot just before the period of vigorous growth (usually in spring).

A plant in a clay pot may have attached itself firmly. To loosen its grip, upend the pot and gently tap its rim on a wooden surface. Sometimes, a gentle push with your finger or a pencil through tne drainage hole helps to loosen the root ball. Plants in plastic pots usually drop right out, requiring at most a gentle squeeze.

Water. Drought-tolerant succulents won't wilt as readily as other house plants. But don't expect the impossible; confined to a pot, taken out of its natural environment, a succulent can die for lack of water as easily as the tenderest of fine-foliaged plants. A more likely problem, though—particularly during periods of slow growth—occurs when too much water causes stems to rot at the soil level.

The safest regime is to imitate conditions in the succulents' natural environment. In the wild, these plants' growth season coincides with periods of abundant moisture—so water most when your plant is growing fast, usually in spring and summer. During natural rest periods (usually in winter), water only enough to prevent the soil from drying out completely.

(Continued on next page)

Light. Succulents yearn for as much direct sunlight as possible (exceptions are *Haworthia* and *Gasteria*). Give your succulent the brightest window in the house, usually one that faces south or west. Especially during spring and early summer, take care to rotate the plant—a quarter turn each week, always in the same direction—to keep it from growing in only one direction and becoming lopsided. Many experienced growers keep succulents outdoors in warm weather.

Fertilizer. Let your succulent's growth pattern guide your fertilizing schedule. During periods of active growth (usually spring and summer), apply a liquid fertilizer (see page 21), diluted to half strength, every 2 weeks. Some people also use dry or slow-release fertilizers; to be safe, cut the amount suggested on the package in half. During autumn and winter, withhold fertilizer.

Favorite succulents and their special needs

Succulents adapt to the dryness and warmth of most home interiors better than do many house plants. A few exceptions are noted.

Aeonium (*ee-O-nee-um*) is among the most decorative succulents. Lower leaves continually drop away leaving the plant with rosettes of leaves atop succulent stems. Brightly colored flowers—yellow, red, white, or pink—are borne on short stalks; they usually appear in spring, though a few types of *Aeonium* choose to bloom in the dead of winter or in early summer.

Aeonium arboreum. Stems branching from this 3-foot-tall plant form 6 to 8-inch-wide rosettes of light green, fleshy leaves. Yellow flowers appear in long clusters. *A.a.* 'Atropurpureum' has dark purple rosettes; those of *A.a.* 'Zwartkop' are nearly black.

Aeonium decorum. A bushy, rounded plant, this *Aeonium* grows to a height of about 10 inches. Rosettes are about 2 inches wide; leaves have a reddish tint and red edges. Flowers are pink.

Aeonium haworthii. Free-branching yet shrubby, this succulent grows as high as 2 feet. Blue green rosettes, 2 to 3 inches wide, are edged in red.

Aeonium 'Pseudotabuliforme' forms smooth, flat, pale green rosettes as wide as 10 inches. It spreads quickly by producing offsets (new plants).

Aeonium simsii (A. caespitosum), bright green and very leafy, grows low (to 6 inches tall), dense, and spreading. Flowers are yellow.

Aeonium urbicum has huge "dinner plate" rosettes spanning 8 to 10 inches. Its loosely arranged, pale green leaves are long and narrow.

Agave (*uh-GAH-vee*), commonly called century plant, puts forth generous clumps of fleshy, strap-shaped leaves. Though big, its clusters of small, tubular flowers don't supply the bright color typical of succulents. After flowering, which may not occur for years, the foliage clump dies, but it usually leaves suckers or offshoots to make new plants. Drought-resistant *Agave* may shrivel without water, but will plump up again when watered.

Agave americana. Century plant. Blue green leaves, armed with hooked spines along their edges and a wicked spine at the tip, extend 6 feet long.

Agave attenuata. Soft green or gray green leaves are 2½ feet long, fleshy, somewhat translucent, and spineless. This *Agave* gets to be very large, and can live in the house only when young. Greenish yellow flowers bloom densely on arching spikes up to 12 to 14 feet long. *A. attenuata* does best with rich soil and ample water.

Agave deserti. This small, clumping *Agave*'s yellow flowers are especially attractive.

Agave victoriae-reginae. Forming clumps only a foot or so in width, this is a small *Agave*. Dark green leaves, 6 inches long and 2 inches wide, are stiff and thickly marked with narrow white lines. This plant grows slowly, and can remain in a pot for up to 20 years. At about this age, it flowers for the first time, producing greenish blooms on tall stalks. After they fade, the plant dies.

Agave vilmoriniana, or octopus agave, has pale green or chartreuse rosettes spanning 3 feet. Its fleshy, 3 to 4-inch-wide leaves, heavily ridged above, have a single long spine at the tip. The leaves are arched and twisted.

Aloe (*AL-o*). Comprising a diverse and showy group of South African succu-

lents, *Aloe* offers a wide size range, from 6-inch miniatures to lofty trees. Most make outstanding indoor plants.

Aloe arborescens, commonly called tree aloe, grows to 18 feet tall (or taller). Its branching stems carry big clumps of gray green, spiny-edged leaves. Flowers appear from mid to late winter in long, spiky clusters; they're bright vermilion to clear yellow. This plant tolerates low light and infrequent watering.

Aloe aristata. This dwarf *Aloe*, ideal for a window sill, grows to about 8 to 12 inches high and wide. Rosettes are densely packed, with 4-inch-long, ¾-inch-wide leaves ending in whiplike threads. In winter, orange red flowers bloom in 1 to 1½-foot-tall clusters.

Aloe bainesii is a slow-growing tree with a heavy, forking trunk and branches, grown mainly for its stately, sculptured-looking form. It produces rosettes of 2 to 3-foot leaves and spikes of rose pink flowers on 1½ to 2-foot stalks.

Aloe barbadensis (A. vera). Barbados aloe, medicinal aloe, unguentine cactus. Clustering rosettes of narrow, fleshy, stiffly upright leaves grow 1 to 2 feet long; yellow flowers grow in a dense spike atop a 3-foot stalk. Analgesic pulp from this aloe is used to treat burns, bites, inflammations, and a host of other ills. Easy to grow and attractive; it needs regular watering.

Aloe brevifolia produces low clumps of blunt, thick leaves, gray green and spiny edged, each about 3 inches long. Clusters of red flowers, nearly 2 feet tall, appear intermittently all year.

Aloe distans. Jeweled aloe. Running, rooting, branching stems sprout clumps of fleshy, blue green, 6-inch-long leaves with scattered whitish spots and white teeth along edges. Forked flower stems, 1½ to 2 feet long, carry clusters of red flowers.

Aloe ferox. The thick, 15-foot trunk of this *Aloe* carries rosettes of very spiny, dull green, 2½-foot-long leaves. Glowing scarlet flower clusters look like giant candelabra.

Aloe humilis. Leaves have jagged, toothed edges; growing in tight clumps, they're about 4 inches long, ¾ inch wide. Red flowers appear on stalks 10 to 16 inches tall.

Aloe marlothii. When small, this *Aloe* performs beautifully in pots or

even dish gardens. Eventually, though, it becomes a 6 to 18-foot-tall tree, with spiny 2½-foot-long leaves and red flowers that resemble large candelabra.

Aloe nobilis. This *Aloe* has small, dark green leaves edged with small hooked teeth. It grows in rosettes to a foot across and about as tall. In June, clustered orange red flowers appear on 2-foot stalks; blooms last for about 6 weeks.

Aloe saponaria. This short-stemmed *Aloe* forms broad clumps. Wide, thick, green leaves are 8 inches long and spattered with white spots. Flowers, orange red to shrimp pink, bloom over a period of several months.

Aloe striata, or coral aloe, has broad, spineless, gray green leaves edged with pinkish red. Leaves grow to almost 2 feet long and form 2-foot-wide rosettes. Beginning late in winter, brilliant coral pink to orange flowers blossom in branched clusters.

Aloe variegata. Partridge-breast or tiger aloe. This plant's fleshy, triangular leaves, about 5 inches long, are dark green, strikingly banded and edged with white. Plants are about a foot tall. Loose clusters of flowers, pink to dull red, bloom intermittently all year.

Ceropegia woodii (*see-ro-PEE-jee-uh WOOD-ee-eye*). Rosary vine or string of hearts. This little vine with thin, hanging or trailing stems comes from South Africa. Growing in pairs, its heart-shaped leaves are thick and succulent, ⅔ inch long. Little tubers form on the stems and can be planted. Flowers are small, dull pink or purplish; they're not showy, but have an interesting appearance. *C. woodii* needs filtered light and regular watering.

Crassula (*KRA-soo-luh*). These South African shrubs are drought tolerant; many are classic indoor plants. They can thrive in the same pot for years, requiring little more than the basics—a good bright location all year long, and ample fertilizer and water during the growing season.

Crassula arborescens. Shrubby and heavy-branched, *C. arborescens* resembles the more common jade plant (*C. argentea*), but it's smaller and grows more slowly. Its leaves also differ from *C. argentea*'s—they're gray green, dotted and edged with red. Star-

Crassula argentea
(jade plant)

Ceropegia woodii
(rosary vine)

Senecio rowleyanus
(string of beads)

Aeonium arboreum
'Zwartkop'

Aloe barbadensis
(*A. vera*)
(medicinal aloe)

Crassula
'Springtime'

Gasteria nigricans
'Marmorata'

Gasworthia
'Royal Highness'

Sedum furfuraceum
(stonecrop)

*Pedilanthus
tithymaloides*
'Nana Compacta'
(devil's backbone)

Haworthia retusa

shaped flowers, white or pink, usually appear only on old plants.

Crassula argentea (C. portulacea). Jade plant. This excellent house plant usually stays small in containers indoors. Its thick, fleshy, oblong leaves are 1 to 2 inches long. Clusters of pink, star-shaped flowers bloom profusely from November through April.

Crassula falcata. Full-grown plants are 4 feet high and just as wide. Fleshy, sickle-shaped, gray green leaves are arranged vertically along stems, in opposite rows. Dense, branched clusters of scarlet flowers appear in summer.

Crassula lycopodioides. Branching, foot-tall stems stand erect; closely packed with tiny green leaves in four vertical rows, they look like braided watch chains. Greenish flowers are very small. This easy-to-grow *Crassula* is ideal for dish gardens.

Crassula 'Morgan's Pink', a miniature type, has densely packed, fleshy leaves growing in tight clusters to 4 inches tall. In spring, pink flowers appear in bushlike clusters nearly as big as the plant.

Crassula multicava. This dark green, fast-growing, spreading plant is a good choice for a hanging basket.

Sedum morganianum 'Burrito'

In late winter and spring, light pink flowers, resembling mosquitoes, bloom in loose clusters.

Crassula schmidtii, a spreading plant growing to 4 inches tall, forms mats with long, slender, rich green leaves. Winter or spring brings dense clusters of small dark rose or purplish flowers.

Crassula 'Springtime' has fleshy green leaves which form a compact, neat plant. Blooming plants, with pinkish flower clusters held slightly above leaves, are very showy.

Crassula tetragona. This upright, treelike plant, 1 to 2 feet high, is sometimes used in miniature gardens to suggest a pine tree. It has narrow, inch-long leaves and white flowers.

Echeveria *(ek-uh-VER-ee-uh)*. Forming stemless rosettes, all *Echeverias* produce fleshy green or gray leaves, often marked with deeper colors. Bell-shaped, nodding flowers, usually pink, red, or yellow, are borne in long, slender, sometimes branched clusters. Plants tolerate underwatering.

Echeveria agavoides (Urbinia agavoides). Rosettes, 6 to 8 inches across, consist of bright green, sharp-pointed leaves—stiff, smooth, and fleshy, they're sometimes marked with deep reddish brown at the tips and edges. Small red or yellow flowers bloom on a stalk up to 1½ feet tall.

Echeveria crenulata, a striking plant, has pale green or white-powdered leaves growing in loose rosettes on short, thick stems. Leaves are about a foot long and 6 inches wide; their wavy edges are purplish red. Flower stalks stand as high as 3 feet, but produce just a few yellow or red flowers.

Echeveria derenbergii grows in small, tight rosettes that spread to form mats. Its grayish white leaves, 1½ inches long, have red edges, and sharp tips. Reddish yellow flowers form one-sided clusters to 2½ inches long.

Echeveria elegans. Hen and chicks. This plant's tight, grayish white rosettes expand to 4 inches across and spread freely by producing offsets (new plants). Flowers, blooming in clusters to 8 inches long, are pink lined with yellow.

Echeveria gibbiflora. This striking succulent grows to 3 feet tall, its broad-leafed rosettes reaching 2½ feet wide. Slender flowering stems grow from among the gray green leaves and may stand as tall as 5 feet, but the flowers aren't especially showy. A number of varieties are available; one common variety, *E.g.* 'Metallica', offers purplish lilac to bronzy leaves.

Echeveria imbricata. Hen and chicks. This is probably the most common "hen and chicks." Its saucer-shaped, gray green rosettes, about 4 to 6 inches across, produce loose clusters of small bell-shaped orange red flowers. It produces offsets (new plants) freely.

Echeveria 'Paul Bunyan' grows in a 6 to 8-inch-tall rosette. Each gray green, wavy-edged leaf is tinged with pink.

Echeveria pulvinata. Small, loose rosettes of very thick leaves are covered with down—silvery in young plants, turning red or brownish in older ones. In early spring, bright red flowers appear.

Echeveria secunda, another form of "hen and chicks," has gray green or blue green rosettes growing to 4 inches across. It produces offsets (new plants) freely. *E.s. glauca (E. glauca)* produces rosettes of blue green leaves tinged with purplish red at the edges.

Echeveria 'Set-oliver'. This plant's rosettes are similar to *E. setosa*'s, but looser. Profuse, red and yellow flowers are very showy.

Echeveria setosa has dense, dark green rosettes up to 4 inches wide, covered thickly with stiff white hairs. Its red flowers have yellow tips.

Echeveria hybrids. In addition to the *Echeverias* listed above, a number of named hybrids are available. Most have large, loose rosettes of big leaves on single or branched stems. In some types, leaves are waved, wrinkled, or heavily shaded with red, bronze, or purple. All are easy-care plants.

Euphorbia *(yoo-FOR-bee-uh)*. Spurge. This large and diverse group of succulents counts the colorful poinsettia (see page 98) as its best-known member—an unlikely relative of the prickly crown of thorns (see above right). Most *Euphorbias* have an acrid, milky white sap; sometimes poisonous, it can irritate skin and cause pain if it contacts eyes or open cuts. *Euphorbia*'s "flowers" are actually modified leaves called bracts; the real flowers hide within the bracts.

Because of their strong, uniquely defined shapes, many *Euphorbias* serve the same decorative function as sculpture. They're striking in form, attractive in texture and color, slow growing enough to stay in scale with their surroundings, and reasonably tolerant of dry indoor air.

Euphorbia lactea 'Cristata'. Elkhorn. This very odd-looking specimen owes its common name to its crested, contorted branches.

Euphorbia milii (E. splendens), called crown of thorns, is a unique, intriguing house plant. Its shrubby stems, armed with long, sharp thorns, reach 3 to 4 feet. Thin, pale green leaves are roundish, 1½ to 2 inches long, usually appearing only near branch ends. The plant bears clustered pairs of bright red bracts nearly all year. *E. milii* is available in many varieties, offering varying form, size and color of bracts.

Euphorbia obesa. Baseball plant. Growing to a height of about 8 inches, *E. obesa* is a solid, fleshy, gray green plant shaped like a sphere or short cylinder. Its brownish stripings and brown dots call to mind the stitching on a baseball. Tiny flowers, borne atop the plant, are insignificant. Good drainage, bright light, warmth, and protection from sudden temperature changes are essential for *E. obesa*'s good health. Guard against overwatering; in winter, keep soil dry.

Euphorbia pulcherrima. Poinsettia. See "Indoor-Outdoor & Gift Plants," page 99.

Euphorbia tirucalli. Milkbush, pencilbush, pencil tree. A tree or large shrub, this plant can reach ceiling height. Its single or multiple trunks support a tangle of succulent, pencil-thin branches, pale green and quite naked of leaves. Though *E. tirucalli* blooms, its flowers are insignificant. Still, the plant puts on a striking show of silhouette. It thrives as a house plant in even the driest atmosphere, but needs all the light you can give it.

Gasteria *(gas-TER-ee-uh)*. Dutch wings, lawyer's tongue, ox tongue. Because it thrives in the warm, dry air of most living rooms, *Gasteria* makes an ideal house plant. It also needs less light than most succulents do, adapting successfully to low-light situations.

An aloelike succulent, *Gasteria* produces leaves growing opposite each other in two flattened rows (or occasionally in rosettes). People appreciate this plant both for its mottled and twisted leaves and for the small, attractive flowers that develop along tall flower stalks. Growing 15 to 20 per stalk, flowers are red to orange, sometimes tipped with green. *Gasteria* grows fastest in summer; in winter, it needs a cool rest period.

Gasteria liliputana has small, lance-shaped leaves, 1¼ to 2¼ inches long and ½ inch wide, arranged in a spiral rosette.

Gasteria maculata, the most common *Gasteria,* has blunt-tipped, tongue-shaped, glossy leaves, about 6 inches long and 2 inches wide.

Gasteria nigricans '**Marmorata**'. This *Gasteria*'s small (4 to 6-inch), blunt-tipped leaves are grayish green with white markings. Pendulous, pinkish, tubular flowers bloom on a 1 to 1½-foot-tall stalk.

Gasteria pseudonigricans puts forth glossy, dark green leaves, heavily spotted with white. Leaves are 5 to 6 inches long and about 1½ inches wide; they extend almost horizontally at the base, but arch upward at tips.

Gasteria verrucosa. Rice or wart gasteria. Each of *G. verrucosa*'s 4 to 6-inch-long leaves tapers gradually to a point. Arranged in pairs, the leaves form two distinct rows down a central stalk.

Gasworthia *(gaz-WURTH-ee-uh).* A recent hybrid between *Gasteria* and *Haworthia,* this rugged new arrival on the succulent scene has the growth habit of *Haworthia,* but its stiff, thick, dark green leaves, marked with white, resemble those of *Gasteria.* An easy-to-grow house plant, it does fine in low-light situations. Flowers in pastel colors blossom in March or April on 14-inch stalks.

Haworthia *(ha-WURTH-ee-uh).* Wart plant. This easy-to-grow plant thrives indoors and requires less light than most succulents. It's closely related to *Aloe,* and resembles some of this group's smaller members. Whitish flowers, narrow and tubular, extend about 1 inch in length, ¼ inch in width.

Sansevieria 'Futura'

Euphorbia lactea 'Cristata' (elkhorn)

Aloe aristata

Agave victoriae-reginae

Echeveria 'Paul Bunyan'

Stapelia variegata (starfish flower)

Sempervivum 'Ashes of Roses' (houseleek)

Haworthia attenuata's dark green leaves, heavily marked with raised white dots, are arranged in stemless or short-stemmed rosettes up to 6 inches wide. Dull pink flowers are borne in clusters on 2-foot stalks.

Haworthia fasciata grows in stemless rosettes consisting of many narrow, 3-inch-long, dark green leaves, marked by contrasting crosswise bands of raised white dots. Greenish white flowers bloom in 6-inch clusters. *H. fasciata* produces offsets (new plants) freely, and spreads quickly.

Haworthia retusa has fat, glossy green leaves marked with a hound's-tooth check pattern in grayish green. Fine white teeth edge the sides of leaves. Small, inconspicuous flowers are borne on 2 to 3-inch wiry stalks.

Haworthia setata. Lace haworthia. *H. setata* grows in small, stemless, many-leafed rosettes. The dark green leaves, 1¼ inches long and half as wide, are marked with whitish translucent areas and edged with long, bristly, white "teeth" that give the plant a lacy look.

Kalanchoe *(ka-lun-KO-ee).* Grown principally as house plants, members of this group owe their popularity to their attractive foliage or long-lasting blooms. Bell-shaped flowers are fairly large, erect or drooping, and brightly colored in a few types.

Kalanchoe beharensis (Kitchingia mandrakensis). Felt plant. Stems, typically unbranched, reach 4 to 5 feet. Leaves appear at stem tips, usually in 6 to 8 pairs. Each leaf, 4 to 8 inches or more in length and half as wide, wears a thick, feltlike coating of white to brown hairs. Flowers aren't showy.

Kalanchoe blossfeldiana. See photo on page 94 and "Indoor-Outdoor & Gift Plants," page 98.

Kalanchoe daigremontiana. Maternity plant. Upright and single-stemmed, this plant grows 1½ to 3 feet tall. Gray green, fleshy leaves, spotted with red, are 6 to 8 inches long, 1¼ inches or more across. Leaf edges are notched; young plants sprout in these notches, producing short roots even while on the plant. Small, grayish purple flowers are borne in clusters.

Kalanchoe uniflora is a trailing plant with thick, fleshy, inch-long leaves, each one scalloped several times near the rounded tip. Inch-long flowers are pinkish or purplish red.

Lithops *(LI-thops).* Stoneface, stone plant. See page 109.

Pedilanthus tithymaloides *(pe-duh-LAN-thus ti-thee-muh-LOI-deez).* Devil's backbone. Though this succulent's slow-growing, zigzag stems may reach 2 to 3 feet tall, you'll usually see them at about 1½ feet. Erect and fleshy, the cylindrical stems contain milky juice. Leaves sprout from the stem in two rows, looking like ribs attached to a backbone. Small flowers, encased in showy red bracts, form dense clusters atop the stems.

All types of *Pedilanthus* need warmth, good light, standard indoor potting soil, and regular watering.

P.t. 'Variegatus', the most common type, produces 4-inch-long oval leaves, pale green variegated with white and pink. *P.t.* 'Nana Compacta' has dark

green leaves crowded onto short, erect stems.

Sansevieria *(san-suh-VER-ee-uh).* Bowstring hemp, devil's tongue, snake plant. *Sansevieria* is native to both Africa and India. Its thick, patterned leaves grow in a cluster; 1 to 4 feet tall and 2 inches wide, they radiate up and out from the plant's base. Leaf shapes vary from short, blunt triangles to long, pointed swords. Clusters of greenish white flowers appear only rarely. Use a standard indoor potting soil; give average house temperature and humidity.

Sansevieria 'Futura', a dwarf variety, forms a rosette of sword-shaped leaves, dark green banded with lighter green. Good in dish gardens.

Sansevieria trifasciata. Often sold as *S. zeylanica*, this plant has dark green leaves banded with gray green. Measuring 2 to 4 feet long and 2 or more inches wide, the leaves stand rigidly upright or spread slightly at the top. *S.t.* 'Hahnii', a dwarf variety, grows in rosettes of broad, triangular, 6-inch-long leaves, dark green with silvery banding. Like *S.* 'Futura', it's a good choice for small pots or dish gardens. *S.t.* 'Laurentii' resembles *S. trifasciata*, but its leaf edges are broadly striped with creamy yellow.

Sedum *(SEE-dum).* Stonecrop. Coming from many parts of the world, *Sedum* varies in care requirements. Some types are tiny and trailing, others grow upright. Leaves are always fleshy, but vary widely in size, shape, and color. Plant in equal parts standard potting soil and coarse sand.

Sedum brevifolium. This tiny, slow-growing plant has tightly packed, fleshy leaves, grayish white flushed with red. Flowers are pinkish or white. *S. brevifolium* needs good drainage.

Sedum dasyphyllum grows to 2 inches high, with blue gray leaves and hairy white flowers.

Sedum dendroideum is a branching, spreading plant that can reach a height of about 2 feet. Rounded, fleshy leaves, to 2 inches long, are yellow green, often tinged with bronze. Deep yellow flowers appear in spring and early summer.

Sedum furfuraceum's very small, fat, oblong leaves grow close together on its stems. This plant tends to creep

along, never reaching heights of more than a couple of inches. Tiny pink or white flowers bloom in early spring.

Sedum morganianum. Burro tail, donkey tail. This *Sedum*'s stems trail, reaching 3 to 4 feet in 6 to 8 years. Pale gray green leaves, thick and fleshy, overlap along stems to give a braided effect. Flowers appear only rarely. If well cared for, this is an attractive plant; grow it in a hanging pot or wall pot. It needs fast-draining, rich soil. Water freely and apply liquid fertilizer two or three times during summer. *S.m.* 'Burrito' is a compact, thicker version.

Sedum rubrotinctum (S. guatemalense). Pork and beans. Sprawling, leaning stems, 6 to 8 inches long, carry ¾-inch leaves that look like jelly beans. Leaves are green with reddish brown tips; on plants grown in the sun, they're often entirely bronze red. Easily detached from stems, they root readily. Flowers are reddish yellow.

Sedum stahlii, called coral beads, is native to Mexico. It's twiggy, trailing, 4 to 8 inches tall; tiny (¼ to ½-inch-wide), beanlike leaves are dark green, usually tinted brown. Yellow flowers appear in summer or autumn.

Sempervivum *(sem-pur-VYE-vum).* Houseleek. This plant forms tightly packed rosettes of leaves. Little offsets (new plants) cluster around the parent rosette. In summer, star-shaped flowers, white, yellowish, pink, red, or greenish, bloom in clusters. After setting seed, blooming rosettes die, but offsets continue to grow.

Sempervivum arachnoideum. Cobweb houseleek. This native of Europe grows in tiny, gray green rosettes, ¾ inch across. Fine hairs link the densely packed leaves, giving the plant a cobweb-covered look. Bright red flowers appear on 4-inch stems.

Sempervivum 'Ashes of Roses' produces a tightly packed clump of many small, green to bronze rosettes. This creeping plant has a fine-textured appearance. Inconspicuous flowers bloom on limp 2-inch stalks.

Sempervivum tectorum. Hen and chickens. Gray green rosettes, 4 to 6 inches across, spread quickly by producing offsets (new plants). Tipped red brown, leaves have bristly points. Red or red orange flowers grow in clusters on 2-foot stems.

Senecio *(sub-NEE-shee-o).* This is a large group of very diverse plants. The succulent types are often sold as *Kleinia,* an earlier name. See also *Senecio* on page 82 and *Senecio hybridus* (cineraria) on page 98.

Senecio rowleyanus. String of beads. Succulent, trailing or hanging stems grow 6 to 8 feet long, carrying spherical green leaves about ½ inch across. Small white flowers have a carnationlike scent. This *Senecio* grows happily in both bright and low light.

Senecio stapeliiformis has ¾-inch-thick stems that look like candles. The stems grow to a height of 6 to 8 inches; lined up along them in vertical rows are tiny green leaves that eventually harden into blunt spines. Red flowers appear in spring or summer. It's best to grow *S. stapeliiformis* in a broad, shallow pot that will accommodate its creeping rhizomes. This plant can take some direct sun; it needs very little water and excellent drainage.

Stapelia *(sta-PEEL-yuh).* Carrion flower, starfish flower. Growing in clumps of four-sided, spineless stems, *Stapelia* resembles a cactus. Yellow flowers with reddish brown markings bloom in summer; they're large, fleshy, and shaped like five-pointed stars. Each usually has an elaborate fleshy disk in the center. Some types of *Stapelia* have unpleasant-smelling flowers. This plant needs a cool, dry rest period in winter, sun and moderate water in summer.

Stapelia gigantea is a novelty, with 9-inch stems and flowers 10 to 16 inches across. Blossoms are brownish purple marked with yellow.

Stapelia variegata, the most common type of *Stapelia,* has yellow flowers—3 inches across, heavily spotted and barred with dark purplish brown—borne on 6-inch stems. Flowers don't have a strong scent.

Yucca *(YUK-uh).* Although they're not really succulents, *Yuccas* are usually included in this group because of their appearance. All forms have tough, green, sword-shaped leaves and clusters of white flowers.

Yucca gloriosa, sometimes called Spanish dagger, is a multitrunked plant that can reach 10 feet in height. This *Yucca*'s leaves are softer than those of most types. Clusters of white flowers appear in midsummer.

Syngonium

(sin-GO-nee-um)

Arrowhead plant, Arrowhead vine, Goosefoot plant

Like its relative, *Philodendron,* this house plant is popular and easy to grow, though it grows somewhat slowly. *Syngonium* puts forth long-stalked leaves of dull green or green variegated with white or yellow. It has flowers, too, but you'll hardly notice them. Useful in terrariums and dish gardens, *Syngonium* also trails effectively; or you can train it against a support as you'd train a vining philodendron. Grown in this way, it can reach a length of 10 to 15 feet.

If you want a bushier, less vining *Syngonium,* just pinch off the plant's growing tips. Turning the pot (a quarter turn each week, always in the same direction) will also help to produce a bushy, well-rounded look—*Syngonium* is notorious for heading off toward the sunlight, growing into a lopsided shape in no time at all.

Syngonium's most intriguing characteristic is its changing leaf shape: as the plant matures, leaf shape changes dramatically. In some types, the leaves start out arrow shaped, then evolve to a three-lobed trident and finally to a five-lobed star. The number of lobes doesn't always stop at five—it can keep right on increasing, and some types wind up with eleven-lobed leaves. Many-lobed leaves and the original arrow-shaped leaves appear on the same *Syngonium.*

Growing requirements

Plant *Syngonium* in a standard indoor potting soil. From spring through autumn, keep the soil moist (like a squeezed-out sponge), but not soggy; during winter, allow the top inch of the soil to dry out between waterings. Variegated forms need slightly more light than do solid green forms, but all should be kept out of direct sun. Bright filtered (as through a sheer curtain) or reflected light is best for these plants.

Except in winter, apply a complete fertilizer regularly (see page 21). *Syn-gonium* appreciates extra humidity, so mist it daily or place the pot on a humidity tray (see page 20). *Syngonium* thrives at temperatures in the 60° to 75°F/16° to 24° C range.

Syngonium is generally pest-free, but watch for occasional attacks from aphids, mealybugs, red spider mites, scale, and thrips; see pages 29–31.

Favorites

Syngonium angustatum 'Albolineatum' has the unusual habit of changing the shape of its variegated green and white leaves as the plant matures. Young leaves start out trident-shaped, but eventually produce five pointed lobes arranged like a lopsided star.

Syngonium podophyllum is the most common kind. Its leaves have three lobes when young, seven or more when mature. The many varieties include *S.p.* 'Trileaf Wonder', with green leaves covered with a whitish powder; *S.p.* "California Silver Wonder', with narrow silvery leaves; and *S.p.* 'Emerald Gem', with crinkled dark green leaves veined with lighter green.

Syngonium podophyllum (arrowhead plant)

Tolmiea

(tol-MEE-uh)

Mother-of-thousands, Pick-a-back plant, Piggyback plant, Youth-on-age

A popular house plant, *Tolmiea* is native to coastal mountain ranges from northern California all the way up to Alaska.

Colored an attractive apple green, the heart-shaped leaves, covered with a delicate fuzz, have toothed edges. New plantlets grow on top of older leaves (at the junction of leaf stalk and blade), giving the plant its nicknames. (Note that *Saxifraga,* page 81, is also called mother-of-thousands.) Fast-growing *Tolmiea* tends to trail with age, adapting well to a hanging basket. A mature plant may reach a foot in height, spreading as far as 16 inches. Its rather inconspicuous reddish brown flowers are borne atop 1 to 2-foot stems.

Since these plants are so popular, you should be able to find them in various stages of maturity. Though large, lush, mature specimens may look appealing, the younger, smaller plants have an easier time adapting to new environments. If you choose a young plant, don't be put off by its relatively small size; its rapid growth rate will probably surprise you.

Growing requirements

Plant *Tolmiea* in a standard indoor potting soil. From spring through autumn, keep the soil moist (like a squeezed-out sponge), but not soggy. Allow the top ½ inch of the soil to dry out between waterings during the winter months. Except in winter, apply a complete fertilizer regularly (see page 21). *Tolmiea* is happy growing in the 60° to 75°F/16° to 24°C temperature range, with average house humidity. Keep this plant out of direct sun; it needs a location with filtered light (as through a sheer curtain), and will also adapt to lower light levels.

Tolmiea suffers occasional attack by mealybugs and whiteflies, and frequent attack by red spider mites. See pages 29–31 for methods of control.

Red spider mites abhor cool temperatures and high humidity—so keep your plant in a relatively cool (60° to 65°F/16° to 18°C) place and set the pot on a humidity tray (see page 20). If your *Tolmiea* does become infested, normal spraying with an insecticide won't solve the problem: since *Tolmiea*'s leaves overlap each other, the mites can hide on leaf undersides and escape annihilation. If you must treat an infested *Tolmiea,* you'll have to immerse the plant, pot and all, in a pail of insecticide (diluted according to the instructions on the label) and keep it there for 3 to 5 minutes. This treatment may seem a bit extreme—but it's the only cure.

Favorites

Tolmiea menziesii, the only commonly available form, fits the description given at left.

Tolmiea menziesii (piggyback plant)

Tradescantia

(trad-es-KAN-shee-uh)

Chain plant, Giant inch plant, Wandering Jew

A fast-growing perennial vine, *Tradescantia* grows wild in Central and South America. Since most types tend to trail, they look graceful in hanging baskets. Leaves of most kinds are small (1 to 2 inches), oblong, and pointed.

Several kinds grow variegated leaves of various hues. Since it's very easy to grow, *Tradescantia* is a good choice for beginning gardeners.

This popular plant is practically indestructible. Even if it does falter, you can easily root pieces of the stems in water; then pot them in fresh soil and start all over again. In large-scale indoor plantings, *Tradescantia* makes an interesting ground cover. However, use it cautiously in mixed plantings—it can crowd out other plants.

Tradescantia belongs to a group of plants—other members are *Callisia, Tripogandra,* and *Zebrina*—which are all commonly sold as wandering Jew. There is considerable confusion between these groups, a problem of more interest to botanists than to home gardeners.

Growing requirements

Tradescantia thrives in a standard indoor potting soil. From spring through autumn, keep the soil moist (like a squeezed-out sponge), but not soggy. During winter, allow the top ½ inch of the soil to dry out between waterings. Except in winter, apply a complete fertilizer regularly (see page 21). Place *Tradescantia* where it will receive bright, filtered (as through a sheer curtain) or reflected light; variegated types need slightly more light than those with solid green leaves. *Tradescantia* is content in the 60° to 75°F/16° to 24°C temperature range; to increase humidity, mist plants daily or place the pot on a humidity tray (see page 20).

Keep plants attractively bushy by frequently pinching off growing tips. Though not too prone to insect attack, *Tradescantia* is occasionally bothered by mealybugs, red spider mites, scale, and whiteflies. See pages 29–31.

If soil is constantly kept too damp, stems will rot at soil level.

Favorites

Tradescantia albiflora, commonly called giant inch plant or wandering Jew, has long stems that trail or sprawl. Its leaves are 2 to 3 inches long; small, rather inconspicuous flowers are white. *T.a.* 'Albovittata' offers leaves that are finely and evenly streaked with white. *T.a.* 'Aurea' (sometimes called 'Gold Leaf') has chartreuse and yellow foliage. *T.a.* 'Laekenensis' (also called 'Rainbow') shows bandings of white and pale lavender.

Tradescantia blossfeldiana has a semi-upright growth habit—its fleshy, furry stems spread and lean without really trailing or hanging. Leaves, up to 4 inches long, are dark shiny green above, purple and furry underneath. Its flowers look showier than those of most trailing or semi-trailing types: clusters of furry purplish buds open into ½-inch pink blossoms with white centers.

Tradescantia navicularis, commonly known as the chain plant, creates a compact shape with short, barely trailing branches packed with fleshy, folded, brownish purple leaves. Miniature plants as well as tiny purplish red flowers form along stems.

Tradescantia sillamontana puts forth short trailing or ascending branches carrying 2 to 2½-inch leaves densely coated with soft white fur. Its tiny flowers are purple.

Tradescantia albiflora
(wandering Jew)

Tradescantia albiflora 'Aurea'
(wandering Jew)

Tripogandra

(try-po-GAN-druh)

Bridal veil, Fernleaf wandering Jew, Tahitian bridal veil

Tripogandra resembles the more common forms of wandering Jew (see page 92) in its growth habit and care requirements, though it's finer in texture, with thinner stems and smaller leaves. Its narrow, 1 to 2-inch-long leaves are dark green above, purplish underneath. Tiny white flowers bloom abundantly, on slender, almost hairlike stalks. Stems can trail to astonishing lengths—to 3 feet or more—making *Tripogandra* an excellent hanging basket plant.

Growing requirements

Grow *Tripogandra* in a standard indoor potting soil. From spring through autumn, keep soil moist (like a squeezed-out sponge), but not soggy; during winter, allow the top ½ inch of the soil to dry out between waterings. Except in winter, apply a complete fertilizer regularly (see page 21). Place *Tripogandra* in a spot that catches bright reflected or filtered (as through a sheer curtain) light. This plant thrives at temperatures in the 60° to 75°F/16° to 24°C range, and likes higher than typical levels of humidity; mist daily or place the pot on a humidity tray (see page 20).

Tripogandra multiflora (bridal veil)

Although bright light encourages flowering, direct sunlight can damage *Tripogandra*'s delicate leaves. Cut any sun-damaged foliage back; healthy new leaves will appear shortly.

Keep plants bushy by frequently pinching off growing tips. Generally pest-free, *Tripogandra* may suffer attack by mealybugs, red spider mites, and whiteflies. See pages 29–31.

Favorites

Tripogandra multiflora, the most commonly available form, fits the description given at left. Its flowers resemble baby's breath.

Zebrina

(zuh-BRY-nuh)

Inch plant, Wandering Jew

Lookalike to the *Tradescantia* group (page 92), with much the same growth pattern, *Zebrina* doesn't offer the same sturdiness. However, because of its similarity to *Tradescantia,* most house plant growers simply know *Zebrina* as yet another variation of wandering Jew.

This plant grows very rapidly, producing 1 to 2-foot-long trailing branches; ideal in a hanging basket.

Forms of *Zebrina* with variegated leaves have proved the most popular: the green and white striped upper surfaces contrast beautifully with the deep reddish purple undersides. In sunlight, the leaf surfaces have an unusual iridescent quality, giving them an almost sparkling effect. Throughout the year, *Zebrina* produces small clusters of rose and white flowers.

Growing requirements

Give *Zebrina* a standard indoor potting soil. From spring through autumn, keep soil moist (like a squeezed-out sponge), but not soggy; during winter, allow the top ½ inch of the soil to dry out between waterings. Except in winter, apply a complete fertilizer regularly (see page 21). Place *Zebrina* in a spot where it can bask in bright reflected or filtered (as through a sheer curtain) light. It grows well at temperatures between 60° and 75°F/ 16° and 24°C, favoring the warmer end of the scale. It also appreciates increased humidity; mist the plant daily or place the pot on a humidity tray (see page 20).

Keep plants bushy by frequently pinching off growing tips. Mealybugs, red spider mites, and whiteflies occasionally bother *Zebrina;* see pages 29–31 for methods of control.

Favorites

Zebrina pendula, the most common form, fits the description given at left. *Z.p.* 'Quadricolor' grows purplish green leaves with longitudinal bands of white, pink, and carmine red. *Z.p.* 'Purpusii' has leaves of dark red or greenish red. Other varieties add white, pink, and cream.

Zebrina pendula (wandering Jew)

INDOOR-OUTDOOR & GIFT PLANTS

Holiday cheer *for an indoor gardener: a beribboned pot of* Kalanchoe blossfeldiana *with flowers in red, pink, yellow or orange.*

Presented on the next few pages are 30 plants that—though people do enjoy them indoors for limited periods—don't strictly qualify as house plants. True house plants adapt smoothly to a year-round indoor environment, since it matches their native conditions fairly closely. But most of the plants on these pages need to spend some period outdoors. In general, you can safely keep these specimens in the house for a couple of weeks at a time—or longer: certain frost-tender types, for example, may fare best if they spend the entire winter indoors.

On these pages, too, we've included some bulbs and rhizomes that don't necessarily need time outdoors. But since they die back each year and go through a dormant period (sometimes spent outside, sometimes in a basement), we don't consider them true year-round house plants.

We've also listed the most popular florist's plants, usually showy with flowers or fruit, sold at holiday time or as gifts. Since these far outlast bouquets of cut flowers, they've become favorites for special occasions. Here you'll find out how to keep these plants healthy after their brief indoor bloom has faded.

If your climate is right, you'll be able to plant your gift chrysanthemum or azalea outdoors, as a permanent addition to your garden, after its flowers have decorated the interior of your house.

She's made her choice *from the floral wonderland around her, including (clockwise from top right)* lilies, amaryllis (Hippeastrum), *fancy-leafed caladium,* azaleas, Chrysanthemums, *more lilies, birds of paradise* (Strelitzia reginae), *and Norfolk pine* (Araucaria heterophylla). *She holds a* Kalanchoe blossfeldiana.

A gallery of choices

Though you can't enjoy them indoors all year, the plants on these pages do make a stunning contribution to a home's interior. Whether massed poinsettias at Christmas or a flaming pink azalea to herald springtime, these plants offer an impressive show for very little investment. After their blooming period ends, some can go into the garden; others return to beauty indoors after a dormant or rest period. To include the most plants, we mention just the types most commonly grown indoors, and give only short care descriptions; for fuller detail, consult pages 16–31 and *Sunset's New Western Garden Book*.

Achimenes
Cupid's bower, Magic flower

Spilling over with colorful spring and summer flowers, *Achimenes* grows from a rhizome planted 1 inch deep in moist peat moss and sand. Transplant 3-inch plants into soil. In autumn, let dry out. Store in cool, dry spot; repot rhizome in fresh soil in spring.

Bulbs (Crocus, Daffodil, Hyacinth, Tulip)

Spring-flowering bulbs—daffodils and other *Narcissus,* tulips, hyacinths, crocus—are favorites for gifts. After flowering, move pots outside. Water to keep foliage green as long as possible; when it starts to die, stop watering and let wither. Plant bulbs outdoors in autumn.

On an April morning, *an inquisitive ceramic rabbit seems spellbound by the purple glory of the crocuses blooming in the center of the table. Brought inside to celebrate spring, they grow in a pot hidden under sphagnum moss inside the white centerpiece bowl.*

Citrus
Lemon, Orange

Members of *Citrus* don't easily grow indoors the year around; summer them outside. *C. mitis* (calamondin orange) does better than most. Plants need at least 4 hours of direct sun daily, high humidity, moderate water, and fertilizer twice a month during growing season.

Agapanthus africanus
Lily-of-the-Nile

Starting in spring, clusters of blue or white flowers appear at tips of tall spikes. Grow *Agapanthus* in a sunny window; give lots of water during growing season. Keep potbound for good bloom, but divide when necessary. Should spend summer outdoors.

Araucaria heterophylla
Norfolk Island pine

Its branches in graceful tiers, this slow-growing conifer makes a popular living Christmas tree. Can stay in pot for years, but should summer outdoors (out of hot sun). Likes cool temperatures, good light. Needs good air circulation, ample water, good drainage.

Bambusa
Bamboo

Bamboo will tolerate several weeks indoors at a time, 3 or 4 times a year. Indoors or out, place in similar conditions—cool temperatures, bright light. To restrain growth, keep soil fairly dry. Fertilize regularly; repot every 2 or 3 years.

Caladium bicolor
Angel's wings, Heart of Jesus

Caladium offers vividly colored leaves. Mist often when in leaf; apply liquid fertilizer weekly. Start to withhold water when leaves begin to wither; after leaves die down, lift tubers from soil, shake off, let dry out. Store in cool, dry place; repot in spring.

Capsicum annuum
Ornamental pepper

Usually sold in pots in autumn, *Capsicum* also grows well from seed. White flowers in spring are followed by small, bright red peppers in autumn. Likes at least 4 hours of sun daily, cool temperatures, ample watering. An annual, *Capsicum* usually dies after fruiting.

Chrysanthemum
Mum

Ever-popular potted mums bloom at the florist's all year. After enjoying flowers indoors, cut off faded blooms, leaving stems 6 to 8 inches long. Remove from pot; gently separate plants. Plant outdoors any time, in sunny location, for bloom the following year.

Colocasia esculenta
Elephant's ears, Taro

Exotic-looking *Colocasia* grows mammoth heart-shaped leaves. Plant tubers in rich, moist soil; they need warm temperatures, filtered light. Keep soil constantly moist; fertilize monthly during growing season. In summer, put outdoors in sheltered, shaded location.

Cyclamen persicum
Florist's cyclamen

An elegant gift plant, *Cyclamen* offers flowers resembling shooting stars. To prolong indoor bloom, provide cool temperatures, bright light (no direct sun), constantly moist soil. After blooms fade, let foliage die back; then plant tubers outdoors in shade.

Cyperus
Papyrus, Umbrella plant

Grown for striking umbrella-shaped leaf clusters, *Cyperus* likes bright light, cool temperatures, high humidity. Needs constant moisture; soak soil by submerging pot in water occasionally. Fertilize regularly in spring, summer. Summer outdoors in sheltered spot.

Euphorbia pulcherrima
Poinsettia

Large bracts are red, more rarely pink, white, green. Grow in sunny window; keep temperature constant, soil moist. After blooming, cut stems back to 2 leaf buds, reduce water, keep cool. Set outside in sunny spot when frost danger is past. May not bloom again indoors.

Fatsia japonica
Japanese aralia

Fatsia displays fanlike leaves; to promote best foliage, remove buds of small whitish flowers. Young plant does best indoors; prune or pinch to keep compact. Likes bright light, cool temperatures (not over 70°F/21°C), ample moisture. Keep outdoors in summer.

Fuchsia hybrida
Lady's eardrop

Some *Fuchsias* grow upright, some trail. Lovely flowers in varying colors, sizes, shapes. Bring indoors for about 3 months at a time, to enjoy bloom or protect from frost. Likes filtered light, cool temperatures, regular fertilizing, high humidity, constantly moist soil.

Hydrangea
Garden hydrangea

Indoors, give bright indirect light, cool temperatures, ample water; apply liquid fertilizer monthly. After flowers fade, plant outside in semishade, in rich, porous soil. For blue flowers, apply aluminum sulfate to soil; for red blooms, superphosphate or lime.

Justicia brandegeana
Shrimp plant

Unusual floral spikes resemble shrimps: coppery bronze bracts enclose small white-spotted purple flowers. While indoors, plant needs bright light, some direct sun, minimal water. Fertilize regularly from late winter through early autumn. Put outdoors in summer.

Kalanchoe blossfeldiana
Kalanchoe

Clusters of cheery red, yellow, salmon pink, or orange flowers are held above foliage. Plants like direct sun, warmth, good drainage; water only when soil dries out. After blooming, cut off flower stems and stop watering until new growth starts. Put outdoors in summer.

Rosa chinensis
Miniature rose

Miniature roses produce petite blooms in a rainbow of color choices. Indoors, they need bright light with some direct sun, moderate humidity, and soil that's moist but not soggy. Keep rather cool. After first blossoms fade, plant outdoors in sunny location.

Senecio hybridus
Cineraria

Cineraria's brilliant, bouquet-like blooms range from white through magenta and purple to sensational shades of blue. Indoors, plant needs bright filtered light, cool temperatures, moist soil. After flowers fade, plant outdoors in protected, shady spot.

Sinningia speciosa
Florist's gloxinia

When flowers fade, withhold water until leaves turn yellow and soil dries out. For next 1½ to 3 months (dormant period), store at 60°F/16°C and give just enough water to keep soil barely moist. When new growth appears, move plant to a warm, light spot.

Gardenia jasminoides
Gardenia

Famous for richly perfumed flowers, glossy dark green leaves. Needs warm days, cool nights, bright light, regular fertilizing, more water than most house plants. Give equal parts standard potting soil and peat moss or ground bark; keep soil moist. Put outdoors in summer.

Hibiscus rosa-sinensis
Chinese hibiscus

Compact varieties are best for containers. Large single or double flowers bloom in white, pink, red, yellow, orange, apricot. Bring indoors when frost threatens. Will bloom inside at constant 60° to 70°F/16° to 21°C. Needs sun, good drainage, regular fertilizing, ample water.

Hippeastrum
Amaryllis

Pot in rich sandy soil, leaving upper half of bulb exposed; keep barely moist until leaves appear. Grow in warm, light place; fertilize every 2 weeks until flowers form. Allow foliage to grow, then to wither; then stop watering. Repot in late autumn or early winter.

Lilium
Lily

Keep lilies in a cool spot in the house. When flowers fade, plant outside in deep, porous, fast-draining soil. Provide ample moisture all year, cool shade at roots, and full or filtered sun at top of plant. Once established, will bloom again in midsummer.

Musa
Banana tree

Dwarf forms (2 to 5 feet) are best for indoors. Broad, shiny, exotic-looking leaves are eye-catching. Likes sun, regular fertilizing, warmth, high humidity. Give ample water, soil mix of equal parts potting soil and peat moss. Put outdoors in summer, but protect from wind.

Rhododendron
Azalea

Indoors, give cool temperatures, bright indirect light, moist soil; apply acid fertilizer regularly throughout growing season. When flowers fade, plant outdoors in sheltered spot with semishade or dappled sun; add plenty of peat moss to soil.

Solanum pseudocapsicum
Jerusalem cherry

White flowers precede *Solanum*'s wintertime red fruit, which resembles tiny tomatoes (not edible). Pinch or prune often to control shape. Likes bright light (some direct sun), regular watering and fertilizing, average house temperatures. Usually dies after fruiting.

Stephanotis floribunda
Madagascar jasmine

To ensure spring blooming, give winter rest by letting top half of soil dry out between waterings; fragrant blooms appear 6 weeks after growth resumes. In growing season, give bright, indirect light, ample water; fertilize regularly. Outdoors, blooms all summer long.

Strelitzia reginae
Bird of paradise

Exotic flowers—orange, blue, and white—bloom intermittently all year atop long, stiff stems. Indoors or out (where it likes to spend summers), plant needs sun (light shade in hot areas), average to warm temperatures, frequent heavy fertilizing, regular watering.

WHICH PLANT SUITS YOU BEST?

People vary in their approach to picking out house plants, just as they do in shopping for anything else. The impulsive type falls in love at first sight and snatches up, on the spot, the prettiest, greenest plant in the store. Where the plant will go in the house, whether it can thrive there, or how to take care of the thing at all—these questions don't enter the impulsive shopper's mind until later.

Another type of gardener-to-be chooses plants exclusively from a decorator's point of view. "What that chest needs is something lavishly leafy," decides this shopper, then rushes off to find a plant with just the right color, shape, size, and texture of foliage. So far, so good—but what about the plant's needs and how well they can be met?

Obviously, to make the happiest house plant choice, you must take into account both house *and* plant. With your help, your home environment has to accommodate the plant's growing needs; otherwise, it won't look good—or even live—for long. It's just as important that the plant suit your taste and decorating needs: what use is a 3-inch cactus when you need a billowy indoor tree?

We hope that this book has already helped you to balance these factors in one or more satisfying decisions. We've organized the following section to help simplify decision making still further. Listing plants by category, it starts out with those that have variegated or colorful foliage. Next come easy-to-grow plants, plants that prosper in low-light situations, plants that drape or trail, climbing plants, indoor trees and other big plants, dramatic plants, plants that bloom indoors, plant oddities, and plants grown from kitchen scraps. Taken together, these categories cover just about every special house plant need, whether care-oriented or decorative.

We've briefly described each plant's appearance and growth pattern, accompanying each description with an illustration to help you identify the plant easily. Many are listed both by botanical name and by common name (beware of the latter, used inconsistently throughout the country). For most, you'll find more thorough coverage in our catalog (pages 23–93); in these cases, we refer you to the pertinent page. Look for specific varieties at nurseries, florist shops, and garden centers.

Variegated or colorful foliage plants

We say plants have "variegated" foliage when a pattern of stripes, veins, splotches, or spots—usually of white, yellow, or pale green—contrasts with the basic green of the leaves.

Colorful plants have leaves variously patterned with one or more colors—usually bright.

Like flowering plants, house plants that flaunt eye-catching foliage create brilliant accents in your interior landscape. They also lend variety to plant groupings and dish gardens. But purchase these plants sparingly until you've tried them out at home; too much of their showy foliage easily overwhelms a room.

Calathea
Peacock plant
Often sold as *Maranta,* its close relative, this plant puts forth foliage beautifully "painted" in shades of green, white, and pink. See page 44.

Codiaeum
Croton
This vividly colorful indoor plant has glossy leaves patterned in green, red, yellow, purple, bronze, pink, or almost any combination of these. See page 47.

Coleus
Painted nettle
This popular plant has intricately patterned leaves in brilliant combinations of green, chartreuse, yellow, salmon, red, orange, magenta, and brown. See page 48.

Dieffenbachia
Dumb cane
An old favorite, this large plant has pointed leaves; colors vary from dark green to shades of chartreuse, variegated with flecks, dots, or stripes of white or pale cream. See page 50.

Fittonia
Nerve plant
A low-growing, creeping plant, *Fittonia* has oval green leaves with red or bright pink veins. Intricate and precise vein pattern inspires its common name. See page 60.

Hypoestes
Polka dot plant
This medium-size plant's oval green leaves are splashed with cheerful pink polka dots. To keep plant bushy, pinch off growing tips. See page 63.

Iresine
Bloodleaf plant
The oval leaves of this plant are so vibrantly colored they seem almost iridescent. Colors vary from fiery crimson to magenta to yellow. See page 63.

Maranta
Prayer plant
Large green leaves on this low, bushy plant show paired brown spots along the midrib; spots turn dark green with age. At night, leaves fold. See page 64.

Pisonia
Map plant
Pisonia grows 4 to 6 feet tall; each of its ivory-edged leaves, variegated in shades of green, shows an intriguing maplike pattern. See page 77.

Plants that are easy to grow

If you're new to the house plant game, the plants pictured on this page can help make your first indoor gardening experience a positive one. These plants adapt easily to the environment found inside most homes (as do many of the plants on the facing page). Even with less-than-perfect light situations, low levels of humidity, and inconsistent amounts of water and fertilizer, these specimens will probably survive; with better treatment, they'll thrive.

Most indoor gardeners learn from the mistakes made on their first house plants. But if your initial efforts involve these forgiving plants, the errors need not be fatal ones (see pages 28–31 for help if you do have problems). And once you've gained your indoor gardening confidence, you can move on to more demanding plants.

Begonia
Most types
Some begonias are grown for their foliage, others for their flowers. Among the easiest to grow are the flowering, cane-type begonias. See pages 35–37.

Bromeliads
Most types
Their unusual shapes, colors, and flowers have made *Bromeliads* favorites with many indoor gardeners. Follow the simple care guidelines on page 38.

Cactuses
Most types
Though a few cactuses are difficult to grow, the majority will thrive with only a modest amount of care; they tolerate neglect. See pages 40–43.

Cissus
Grape ivy
Dark green leaves and trailing form give *Cissus* the look of a miniature grape vine. Generally easy to grow, it's good in a hanging basket. See page 45.

Pelargonium
Geranium
These sturdy, old-fashioned plants have been easy-to-grow favorites for generations. Be sure to give them some direct sun each day. See pages 73–74.

Philodendron
Most types
This large family of much-loved house plants has been popular for years, thanks to its members' leafy good looks, large size, and easy care. See pages 75–76.

Spathiphyllum
Peace lily
One of the few plants that blooms in low-light conditions. Large, oval, dark green leaves arch from stalks arising directly from the soil. See page 84.

Syngonium
Arrowhead plant
This slow-growing, vining plant can be trained to climb; it also looks good in a hanging basket. Arrow-shaped leaves are green or variegated. See page 91.

Tolmiea
Piggyback plant
Heart-shaped, apple green leaves are covered with delicate fuzz; miniature plants appear at leaf joints. Low-growing, somewhat trailing. See page 91.

Plants that need little light

Most homes have at least one spot where a plant could make all the difference between barren and beautiful—but where the light is uncertain or even dim. Though these locations are too sunless for most plants, there are several that will tolerate lower light levels fairly well. (Check the plants listed on the facing page, also—a number of these do fine under low-light conditions.)

Illustrated here are foliage plants of this type, easily cultivated where light is poor. But even these need a modicum of light—though not direct sun—to survive and produce new growth. In other words, a really dark hall or deeply shadowed corner won't do for any plant, unless artificial light is added (see page 18).

Aglaonema
Chinese evergreen

Growing 2 to 3 feet tall, *Agla-onema* has glossy, dark green leaves and greenish white flowers. Tolerates low-light situations very well. Keep soil moist. See page 34.

Aspidistra
Cast-iron plant

Probably the low-light champion, it grows where nothing else will. Dark green, shiny leaves grow to 2 feet or more. Let soil dry out between waterings. See page 35.

Chlorophytum
Spider plant

"Baby" plantlets sprout at ends of long stems; long, curved leaves, like broad grass blades, grow in clumps. Prefers bright light, but tolerates low light. See page 45.

Dieffenbachia
Dumb cane

This large, popular plant with variegated green and white leaves does fine in a sunless northern exposure; just turn the pot occasionally. See page 50.

Dracaena
Cornplant

This dramatic, good-looking plant can grow quite tall. Broad, long leaves arch from a central trunk. Some varieties have striped leaves. Tolerates some neglect. See pages 51–52.

Ferns
Most types

A very large group of feathery, lacy, or otherwise delicate-leafed plants. For most, a north or east-facing window is best. See pages 54–57.

Ficus
Figs

The *Ficus* family includes some of the most popular indoor plants. Most grow to considerable height, tolerating low light. See pages 58–59.

Palms
Most types

The parlor palm of Victorian times survived neglect and dim light; today, selected palms still make dramatic low-light choices. See pages 70–72.

Peperomia
Most types

Often found in terrariums and dish gardens, this small plant grows well in a northern exposure. Pleasing with other diminutive plants. See page 74.

Plants that drape or trail

House plants that grow in a trailing manner often look most attractive up high. Let their foliage spill gracefully from a lofty perch such as a bookcase, or grow them in suspended pots or hanging baskets. You'll find a wide choice of hangers—from thin strips of metal to almost invisible plastic filaments to elaborate weavings.

Since plants in hanging containers dry out faster than those grown nearer the ground, they need more frequent watering. To protect your floor, you can provide a waterproof drip saucer for each hanging plant; or just lift plants down to a sink or tub for watering.

Watch where you place hanging plants, too—be sure you won't bump into them. That innocent-looking pot of ivy can deliver quite a clout on the head.

Aeschynanthus
Basket vine
Its tubular flowers of green, yellow, orange, or red make this vine a particularly showy specimen. Several forms are available, all trailing. See page 33.

Callisia
Striped inch plant
Often sold as wandering Jew, this creeping, eventually trailing plant is perfect in a hanging basket. Cream-striped leaves have purple undersides. See page 44.

Chlorophytum
Spider plant
A favorite hanging plant, with clumps of long, curving leaves. Miniature plants growing at tips of long stems can be potted to start new plants. See page 45.

Plectranthus
Swedish ivy
Tolerant, trailing, and fast-growing, this is a popular plant. Tiny white flowers bloom in candelabra formations among its roundish leaves. See page 77.

Saxifraga stolonifera
Strawberry begonia
New plantlets form on runners; white flowers cluster on tall, upright stems. White-veined, nearly round leaves have pink undersides. See page 81.

Senecio
German ivy, String of beads
The two most widely grown forms of this plant look strikingly different, but both grow happily in a hanging basket. See pages 82 and 90.

Tradescantia
Wandering Jew
These fast-growing vines are popular hanging plants. Some types bloom, perking up a room with tiny flowers; all are easy to grow. See page 92.

Tripogandra
Bridal veil
Lookalike to most of those plants sold as wandering Jew, this one's more svelte, with narrower leaves and stems. Tiny white flowers. See page 93.

Zebrina
Wandering Jew
Another of the many plants sold as wandering Jew. Most varieties display variegated foliage, sometimes tinged with pink or purple. See page 93.

Plants that climb

The truth is that very few indoor plants climb willingly, at least on their own. Most need your help, plus some kind of support, to accomplish such a feat. Once given these things, away they go: upwards, sideways, almost wherever you guide them. (Some can traverse an entire room.) Looking novel and cheery, they also seem to soften any stark-looking architectural structure they scale.

If you're training a plant to a fairly permanent system of wires or string—around a kitchen window, for example—choose the site with care, because moving a well-established plant, long branches and all, could be difficult. Poles and trellises for indoor plants, readily available at nurseries, provide more portable possibilities.

Cissus
Grape ivy
Resembling a miniature grape vine, this leafy plant looks elegant climbing or trailing. Tendrils will wind around a trellis. See page 45.

Clerodendrum
Bleeding heart vine
Trained upright on supports, can grow to 6 feet or more. Clusters of lovely flowers appear in autumn. Give bright light, warmth. See page 46.

Epipremnum aureum
Pothos
Often sold as *Philodendron*. Easy to grow and to train upright. Usually grown on posts, but can also vine around a window. See page 53.

Fatshedera lizei
Tree ivy
This plant resembles large-leafed ivy, but grows upright. Often grown on posts; thick stems can be trained to take a variety of shapes. See page 53.

Hedera helix
Ivy
A popular group of climbing or trailing plants in a wide array of leaf shapes and colors. Vining stems can grow surprisingly long. See page 61.

Hoya
Wax plant
Appreciated for its clusters of often fragrant flowers, *Hoya* needs training and tying to climb. Train upright on a post or around a hoop. See page 62.

Monstera
Splitleaf philodendron
Given good support, this large vining plant with leathery, dark green leaves can be trained to climb vertically. Often grown on posts. See page 65.

Philodendron
Some kinds
Several members of this large and popular house plant group perform well as climbers. Usually grown on water-absorbent columns. See page 75–76.

Syngonium
Arrowhead plant
Variegated, arrow-shaped leaves make this an especially attractive plant. Let it drape and trail, or train its vining growth to a vertical support. See page 91.

Indoor trees & large plants

A big plant makes it presence felt. It works hard for its living in your home—filling in empty spaces, camouflaging flaws, and softening any severity in its surroundings. Beyond performing these purely cosmetic jobs, it simply brings drama to a room. You'll be surprised by the spectacular effect of even one grand-scale specimen, as it infuses its environment with a new sense of space, calm, and leafy splendor.

Big plants often grow slowly and live a long time; more than smaller plants, they tend to become almost as permanent in a home as the furniture. Some owners even give their indoor trees names, treating them as beloved members of the family.

Abutilon
Flowering maple
This good-looking plant's leaves resemble those of a maple tree. It may grow to 6 feet or more in less than 2 years. See page 33.

Coffea arabica
Coffee tree
The coffee tree of commerce. Fragrant white blooms are followed by small fruits, each containing 2 seeds—coffee beans. Reaches 15 feet. See page 47.

Ctenanthe oppenheimiana
Giant bamburanta
Narrow, dark green, silver-banded leaves with purple undersides grow at an angle from downy stalks. Reaches 3 to 5 feet high. See page 50.

Dracaena
Cornplant
These palmlike plants can reach tree size. Some display broad, curved, ribbony leaves; others have very stiff, swordlike leaves. See pages 51–52.

Ficus
Figs
Members of *Ficus* include a wide variety of shrubs, vines, and trees. Some types of *Ficus* will reach ceiling height indoors. See pages 58–59.

Monstera
Splitleaf philodendron
Though *Monstera* and *Philodendron* look like identical twins, they belong to different groups. *Monstera* grows amazingly fast. See page 65.

Palms
Most types
Classic indoor plants with an elegant appearance, most palms are relatively easy to grow—and most grow to impressive heights. See pages 70–72.

Philodendron
Most types
Requiring more space than most house plants, philodendrons grow fast. Older ones will drop lower leaves, leaving a bare stem. See pages 75–76.

Schefflera actinophylla
Umbrella tree
This tropical-looking plant's long-stalked leaves radiate outward like umbrella ribs. Indoors, it grows rapidly to 6 to 12 feet tall. See page 81.

Plants with dramatic form

Like distinctive sculpture, some plants—such as the ones shown on this page—can be singled out in any crowd; they stand alone by virtue of their arresting shapes. Size makes no difference ... a trim 12-inch cactus can look just as striking as a bold 6-foot one. To enhance their every detail, display them against plain backgrounds.

One of these plants is just the thing to bring noteworthy line and design into a room—attractively, yet inexpensively. But since they do make a particularly stunning impact, especially when generously proportioned, use them with care in room decor. Just one large, dramatic specimen can turn an expanse of empty space into a focal point for the room. Smaller plants, on the other hand, accentuate and draw the eye to smaller areas.

Cactuses
Most types
Almost all cactuses have eye-catching, dramatic form; large specimens are especially impressive in a contemporary interior. See pages 40–43.

Cordyline
Hawaiian ti
Large and palmlike, with long, often variegated, bladelike leaves, this plant evokes a tropical mood. Allow plenty of room. See page 49.

Dizygotheca
False aralia
Long, lacy, bronze-hued leaves make *Dizygotheca* especially stunning. An upright-growing plant, it lends an Oriental feeling to a room. See page 51.

Ferns
Some types
You won't see drama in the form of every fern. But some of them—particularly tree types and staghorn ferns—are impressive. See pages 54–57.

Monstera
Splitleaf philodendron
Large in leaf and limb, this tamed jungle plant has big split leaves. Quite a conversation piece, especially when mature. See page 65.

Palms
Most types
Favored for generations as dramatic, yet refined, house plants. Among their other virtues are longevity and ease of care. See pages 70–72.

Pandanus
Screw pine
A contemporary-looking plant: spearlike leaves, dark green or variegated, are spirally arranged. Aerial roots grow around plant's base. See page 73.

Polyscias
Ming aralia
With its dense, delicate foliage, this woody-stemmed plant has an Oriental look. It's slow growing and rather finicky. See page 78.

Succulents
Most types
Many gardeners collect succulents, prizing them for their unusual forms. Large ones can become very big indeed. See pages 85–90.

Plants that bloom indoors

When a plant flowers inside the house, it means (among other things) that someone has given it tender loving care. To promote indoor blooms, a gardener must strictly attend to a house plant's needs. Ideal temperature, light, and humidity, and just the right amounts of water and fertilizer—all these are critical. Providing such diligent attention will earn you a rare reward: a living bouquet of flowers. Illustrated below are a few flowering favorites—there are many more.

But if all the fuss and bother daunts you, it's much simpler to buy a gift or holiday plant, already in flower. These blooms will last for at least several weeks indoors; see pages 94–99 for details on care.

Begonia
Most types
Many old favorites and new hybrid forms of this ever-popular blooming house plant are available—and most are easy to grow. See pages 35–37.

Bromeliads
Most types
Searching for strange and exotic foliage and flowers? Take a look at some of the *Bromeliads* pictured on page 39. They won't disappoint you.

Clerodendrum
Bleeding heart vine
A real show-stopper, this large indoor-outdoor vine produces clusters of white, lanternlike calyxes which open to show red petals. See page 46.

Clivia
Kaffir lily
One of the more stunning indoor flowering plants, it has funnel-shaped flowers that bloom in large, brilliant orange clusters. See page 46.

Orchids
Most types
Almost everyone names orchids as prime examples of floral beauty—some even say they're the most beautiful of all flowers. See pages 66–69.

Pelargonium
Geranium
Old-fashioned favorites, these still top many people's lists when they choose indoor blooming plants. A wide range is available. See pages 73–74.

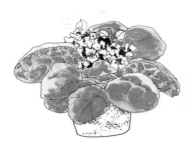

Saintpaulia
African violets
Here, undoubtedly, is the most popular of all indoor blooming plants. African violets give a rich floral reward for moderate effort. See pages 79–80.

Sinningia
Gloxinia
Relatives of African violets, these have similar requirements. Several different forms exist, all producing beautiful, exotic flowers. See page 82.

Spathiphyllum
Peace lily
Dark green leaves form an attractive fountain shape; white flowers resemble calla lilies. Sometimes blooms in low-light conditions. See page 84.

Weird & wonderful plants

Plants, like people, are often endearing not so much for beauty as for character. Such is the case with the following botanical oddities, which have delighted imaginative gardeners for years. They're especially fun for a child, who may learn, from one of these intriguing plants, to enjoy more conventional ones. Two of these plants—the Venus fly trap and the sensitive plant—have characteristics we usually associate with animals.

Eccentric, curious, strange, surprising, unconventional, even weird—no matter how you describe the plants shown below, they're sure to be conversation pieces. So show off your specimen where it can start the conversational ball rolling by prompting the question, "What's THAT?"

Plants from the kitchen

Did you know that you could grow a small house plant from fruit and vegetable scraps that, ordinarily, you'd just toss out? For many indoor gardeners, young and old, there's a special appeal to starting a plant this simple way.

Besides gaining the usual satisfactions of gardening, you'll be able to witness, first-hand, the way a new plant sprouts. Children, of course, find this fascinating to observe day by day. And many of their elders also appreciate getting a lovely, leafy house plant from what would otherwise go to waste. Shown below are a few favorite plants from the kitchen. These plants, except the pineapple (a bromeliad; see pages 38–39) prefer outdoor to indoor conditions over the long run.

Dionaea muscipula
Venus fly trap
This kids' favorite devours insects; gets by without them, too. Likes high humidity, cool temperatures (60°F/16°C), lots of water. Try in a terrarium.

Lithops
Stoneface
This succulent looks like a stone with a fissure down the middle; from the fissure, yellow or white flowers emerge. Likes sun, warmth.

Ananas
Pineapple
You can grow this common bromeliad from the top of a grocery store fruit. Remove flesh, let top dry for a week out of sun, then plant.

Avocado
Stick wooden picks in center of avocado pit, then suspend it in a glass of water (bottom of pit should barely touch water). Sprouts within weeks. Plant in potting soil.

Mimosa pudica
Sensitive plant
Touch it, and its feathery leaves fold, then quickly open again. A child's delight. Likes some direct sun, warm temperatures, high humidity, moderate water.

Ornithogalum caudatum
Pregnant onion
Strap-shaped leaves grow atop a smooth-skinned bulb; beneath its papery outer layer, baby bulblets form and swell, eventually fall. Likes direct sun.

Citrus
Lemon, grapefruit, orange
Many are successful growing these plants from seed. Let seeds from grocery store citrus fruits dry for 1 to 2 weeks; then plant ½ inch deep. See page 96.

Sweet potato
Favorite of children. Stick wooden picks in tubers; suspend, upright, in glass of water (water should cover tuber halfway). Plant in pot after roots and leaves appear.

Index to General Subject Matter

Index of Botanical & Common Names